Mapping My Way Home

MAPPING MY WAY HOME

Activism, Nostalgia, and the Downfall of Apartheid South Africa

by STEPHANIE J. URDANG

MONTHLY REVIEW PRESS
New York

Library of Congress Cataloging-in-Publication Data
available from the publisher

ISBN paper: 978-1-58367-667-7
ISBN cloth: 978-1-58367-668-4

Typeset in Minion Pro and Bliss

MONTHLY REVIEW PRESS, NEW YORK
monthlyreview.org

5 4 3 2 1

Contents

Acknowledgments

THIS MEMOIR WAS CONCEIVED and reconceived over many years. During that time I have benefited from the support of friends. I can't express my gratitude enough for the input of Gloria Jacobs and Jane Rosenman, whose superior editing skills were critical to the reshaping of *Mapping My Way Home*. Special thanks, too, to Jennifer Davis, Alcinda Honwana, Gail Hovey, Karen Judd, and Teresa Smart, who read the manuscript at different stages and whose insights and comments were invaluable. I am also grateful to the many others who encouraged and supported me through the long process of bringing this memoir to fruition, among whom are my women's group of forty-five years—Suzette Abbott, Jennifer Davis, Janet Hoope,r and Gail Hovey—as well as Michelle Fine, Pippa Green, Hanaa Hamdi, Hermione Harris, Richard Knight, Judith Marshall, Ann McClintock, Margaret Marshall, Barbara Reisman, and Janis Zadel.

And most especially, there are my stalwart cheerleaders, husband John Woodburn and daughter Kendra Urdang, who lived with this book through good times and bad, with my moods to match. Their support means the world to me.

Martha Cameron, through her scrupulous editing, spotted a number of inaccuracies that saved me embarrassment. On that note, I am the only one responsible for all remaining errors and inaccuracies. Thanks as well go to Martin Paddio and Michael Yates at Monthly Review Press for their enthusiasm for the project. It was a pleasure to work with all three.

There are those who I need to thank posthumously. A number of my friends and family who were part of my story, even if not included in my book, died while I was writing it. Some, like my parents and my sister Leonie, feature in my memoir, as do Becky Reiss and Lina Magaia. Others, even though an important part of my story, were not included. Among the latter are Danish anthropologist Jette Bukh, with whom I stayed in Guinea-Bissau after independence and who became a close friend; David Emanuel, fellow southern African, whose wisdom and support saw me through my cancer and Kendra's birth; and Anthony Lewis, whose friendship, humor, and generosity meant a lot to me. Particular memories are for Eve and Tony Hall. The fleeting idea for a memoir became grounded through discussions with Tony at Matumi, their home outside of Nelspruit, after they returned to South Africa. His enthusiasm for my book was infectious. I first met Eve and Tony in Nairobi in 1973 on my travels in Africa. Introduced through a mutual friend, I arrived at their house for tea one Saturday afternoon and stayed for six weeks. They had gone into exile in the early 1960s with their three young sons, after Eve had served a six-month sentence for promoting the banned ANC with a leaflet and poster campaign, and Tony, a journalist, was no longer allowed to practice his craft. I slipped into their lives and we remained close friends until their untimely deaths: Eve from breast cancer in 2007 at age seventy; Tony at age seventy-one from a heart attack a few months later, in 2008. All are sorely missed.

Friends provided beautiful writing retreats. I returned often to idyllic Matumi, my computer on a small table in front of "my" bedroom, a view of the stunning valley below; Margaret Marshall and Anthony Lewis's house overlooking a pond on Martha's Vineyard was a yearly treat; Pippa Green's house in Cape Town gave me a magnificent view of Table Mountain as I worked; Hermione Harris's house in London was home from home after my parents died. In addition, I had the opportunity to spend time at the indescribably wonderful Blue Mountain Center for writers, artists, and activists on a lake in the Adirondacks.

My grateful thanks to Alice Brown, director of the Ford Foundation regional office in southern Africa, which provided a grant for research and travel to South Africa and Mozambique in 2011.

Note: A few of the names of people who appear in this book have been changed.

Mother Mountain

Table Mountain shimmers in the heat this late summer's day in March 1991. Even from the distance of the Cape Town airport, the magnificence of the flat-topped mountain takes hold of me. Its image, a constant symbol of my city and of the country I left behind in 1967, continued to occupy a corner of my being through-out the decades of my absence, sometimes in hibernation, sometimes vigorously alive as I succumbed to bouts of yearning and nostalgia.

By twenty-three, I could no longer tolerate apartheid's tyranny. Neither could my parents, who emigrated that same year. While their destination was London, mine was New York. My decision to return to South Africa for a visit took hold when, a year earlier, I celebrated my now widowed mother's eightieth birthday. On February 11, 1990, my family sat glued to the small TV in the living room of her cozy semidetached house in north London, awaiting Nelson Mandela's release after twenty-seven years in prison. Outside the windows the weather was listless and bleak, a typical winter's day where perpetu-ally gray skies appear to hover just above one's head. In South Africa it was summer, the colors bright, the African sky high and blue.

There was a limit to how much a camera could show crowds wait-ing. To build tension for the viewers, reporters prattled on with endless commentary on what might be expected from the release of the world's most prominent and revered political prisoner, while cam-eras scanned the scene. Pundits and commentators speculated and analyzed and then re-speculated and re-analyzed. Artists' sketches projected what he might look like. It had been illegal to publish any photos of him while he was in prison.

Kendra, my four-year-old daughter, couldn't fathom why we were staring at a TV screen for so many hours. We played games with her, her grandmother read her book after book, but the time dragged on along with her boredom. Then the moment arrived and Mandela walked into view. Dignified, thin, tall, graceful: nothing like the artists' sketches. I could hardly see him through the blur of my tears. The bond with my past stretched taut as I delved into a hidden space where I am still the child of Africa, of South Africa, of Cape Town.

I looked at John, my husband, who had never been to Africa— John, forever the good listener, who had heard my tales of growing up South African and tolerated my passion for my country beyond endurance, had tears running down his face as freely as mine, while my mother quietly wept. At that moment, I vowed to take him to my South Africa, and soon.

Kendra looked at one parent, then the other, puzzled. I explained again, a simpler task now that I could point to Mandela before us on the screen, that this was a truly great man that bad people had put in prison many, many years ago, long before she was born.

"We're crying because we're happy that he is free," I explained.

"Will they put the bad people in jail now, Mummy?" she asked. Oh, that it were so simple.

AND SO HERE WE ARE at the airport, waiting in limbo between landing and being met by our friend Pippa. She and her husband, Alan, had returned to South Africa two years earlier after studying at Columbia University. Pippa Green was working as a journalist and Alan was teaching at the University of Cape Town. We had become close during their time in New York, Kendra having adopted Pippa, full of affection and fun, as a special aunt.

John surveys the surroundings with a somewhat bemused expression, watching scenes still cast in apartheid play out around him: black service workers swish brooms back and forth in wide swaths, garbage bags are pulled from bins and tied up, bowed heads are focused on the tasks at hand, ignoring the affluent travelers who in turn are oblivious to their presence. Typical flat white South African accents that he had often heard me and my South African friends mimic, fill the hall, obscuring the Afrikaans he does not understand and the sounds of Xhosa with its distinctive clicks that he has only heard when listening to the songs of Miriam Makeba.

While we wait, I replay the returning-home scenario I have envisioned. We will drive from the airport along the highway that goes straight as an arrow toward the heart of Table Mountain. The mountain will grow steadily larger as all the familiar folds and crevices and crannies, the browns and grays and dull greens of rainless summer months, come sharply into focus. Once the road merges with De Waal Drive, which hugs the mountain like a low-slung belt heading toward the city center, its slopes will tower over us and Table Bay, the docks of my childhood, will stretch out below. And as its grandeur overwhelms us both, John will at last understand why the mountain—and this city and my country—continue to exert such a hold over me.

I am aware that returning home is far more complex than this scenario. Leaving had not been a simple matter of boarding a plane for a new life. For me apartheid had been a riptide under a deceptively languid surface. I had to swim with firm strokes to get away from it. By returning at this moment, I would be drawn into the tumultuous upheavals after the fall of a brutal regime and the heady anticipation of a future as yet unknown. Mandela is free but South Africa is yet to be. At this moment, though, I want to reconnect with my personal memories, to fill a gaping hole rough-hewn by the longing I carried with me through all the years I was effectively exiled from my country. I want this drive to move me from my yearning for Cape Town to being in Cape Town—to feel the prickling of my skin as it happens. I want to hold this moment and ride the emotions that will tell me: *I am home.*

One problem: Only I am familiar with the script I have crafted. As we drive toward the mountain, my travel mates obliviously pursue their own paths. Kendra, sitting on my lap in the backseat of the small jeep, scrunched up against one of our suitcases, wriggles with excitement. Eager to see Pippa's son—her "godbrother," now two and a half—and generally strung out with anticipation that this five-year-old is incapable of containing, she provides a counterpoint of exhilaration-fueled chatter.

Pippa and John for their part, lose no time in delving into questions that volley back and forth between them in the front seats. They want to know everything at once but must make do with snippets, pointers for later long-into-the-night conversations.

Pippa has disturbing news. Our mutual friend, Pat, lost her brother the previous weekend to a carjacking in Johannesburg. In his thirties, Michael had owned a successful sporting goods store. He was making a delivery in an affluent suburb when two armed men accosted him and demanded the keys to his car. They drove off, but not before one of them shot him in his stomach, leaving him for dead at the side of the road. "A couple who saw it happen stopped to help," Pippa relates, her voice straining. "Michael died cradled in the young woman's arms." This style of crime has become common; we had already heard many similar stories. But this one is of Pat's brother, not some random incident reported in the news, and it hits us personally.

John's shoulders tighten. He is the most streetwise person I know—in New York City, that is—where survival smarts have often guided him out of potentially dangerous situations. Here he has no point of reference. In a voice as tense as his shoulders, he asks: "What about Cape Town? Is it as violent as Johannesburg?"

No, I confidently answer in my head. The Cape Town remembered from my (white) childhood was as safe as houses. My teenage friends and I listened as Joburg boys, down for their summer holidays, regaled us with bravado-laced stories about life in the most populated, biggest, baddest South African city with its security guards and burglar alarms. Deeply tanned, they sported a particular swagger, spending their money more freely than their Cape Town counterparts, driving flashy cars, and dating gorgeous "bikini girls" for which Cape Town was renowned. My friends and I felt not a little smug that the need for such security was unnecessary in Cape Town.

When I was a child and young adult the city center and suburbs were a haven for the whites who lived there. No high fences. No locked gates. No burglar alarms. From the age of eight I fearlessly explored my neighborhood on my bike. I was about twelve when I rode with my friends the ten miles to the Muizenberg beach. It meant pedaling along Prince George Drive, past segregated townships and through the windswept sandy flats that could scarcely support a few spindly trees. As a university student I drove my car wherever I chose, paying little heed to my father, who insisted that I never drive alone at night. One time, as I was heading home along a desolate road, the car began to veer off course. Damn, a flat tire. I got out and opened the trunk to remove the jack and spare. Out of the dark, a man approached. Oh Shit! My father's rape fears that I had derided snuck into my head. In South Africa those fears always cast the rapist as African or coloured, the race of the man approaching me. I froze. He came toward me, smiled a gap-toothed smile, and quietly, without fuss, took the jack from my hands and proceeded to change my tire, placing the flat in the trunk. With no more than a brief *Dankie, meisie*—Thank you, little madam—when he accepted my tip, he walked on and disappeared back into the dark.

I OPEN MY MOUTH TO assure John that Cape Town is perfectly safe. But Pippa gets in first: "Cape Town is fast becoming one of the most violent cities in South Africa." She proceeds to emphasize her point. A doctor friend of hers, working in the emergency room at Groote Schuur, Cape Town's large teaching hospital where Christiaan Barnard pioneered the first heart transplant, says he is treating more and more victims of violent crimes each week. He is particularly unnerved by the way people are being shot gratuitously when they've already handed over their goods; intruders in masks rob houses and then shoot the homeowners, still tied up, as they depart with the loot.

This accelerating criminal violence is surpassed only by the political violence between supporters of the African National Congress, the party of Nelson Mandela, and the Zulu Inkatha Freedom Party, which has collaborated with apartheid security forces to destroy the ANC. Just this past weekend, Pippa informs us, Inkatha attacked ANC mourners at a funeral, killing twenty-three people.

Reality seeps in as I take in Pippa's tales of South Africa's violence told in the matter-of-fact tones of someone acclimatized to them. The stories swirling around inside the jeep derail my fanciful scenario. I stare out of the window at the row upon row of *pondoks* stretching back from the road: shacks constructed from metal scraps and wood and plastic sheeting that dire poverty has sprung onto the unforgiving landscape. We pass the long-established African townships of Langa and Nyanga crowded on the sandy, inhospitable Cape Flats, with their small, identical brick houses, cheek by jowl. Under apartheid, they housed a cheap labor pool, where only those who had permission to work in the area stamped into their passbooks were allowed to live. Harsh edges of dissonance between my memories and reality scrape up against the inside of my skin so that it crawls in discomfort. I look again at the mountain and see it from the perspective of those who grew up in these townships. Far, elusive. A symbol of a place where whites live shrouded in privilege. I wonder how much this inequality and discrimination will persist. Apartheid may be over, but its legacy continues as a new South Africa tries to pry itself loose from its stranglehold.

South Africa. My South Africa! How could I have imagined for one instant that I could return to its beauty and not to its pain? It is the contradiction I had been raised with: beauty so magnificent it is almost unimaginable; brutality, oppression, and tyranny so loathsome it is almost impossible to conceive.

Yes, indeed, I am home.

Part One

1 — "Such a Show of Power!"

The assembly bell rings unexpectedly after lunch at the beginning of my final year of high school on March 30, 1960. Our class teacher's slender, athletic body is taut as she enters the classroom. Her normally easy smile is replaced by a grim expression.

"Hurry! Hurry!" Miss Jones urges, using her hands to shoo us out as if we are errant chickens. "We need to get to the auditorium. *Now-now!*"

My friends and I shoot baffled looks at each other as we clatter down the stairs and enter the hall. What can possibly be going on? The principal, Noel Taylor, stops our chatter with a commanding look from the podium as we drop cross-legged on the wooden floor.

"There is a dangerous situation in the city," he says, pausing for effect as he casts his eyes over us. I stare up at this man, his graying hair parted precisely down the middle, not one strand out of place. And then at the vice principal at his side, rocking slightly back and forth on his heels. He seems even more tired and drawn than usual as he studies his clasped hands.

"Thousands of natives are marching to the city," Taylor continues, using the somewhat derogatory word for blacks favored by white South Africans. "We need to be sure you are safe."

Anxiety ripples through the student body, white to the last. The only blacks present are the custodial staff standing at the back of the hall. I feel my stomach contract in fear, a fear reflected on the faces of my schoolmates.

"You must remain here in the auditorium until an adult can come to take you home." Taylor's voice is severe and authoritative. The school is in lockdown. If Africans are marching from farther-out townships, would they not pass through Athlone, an area designated for coloureds—people of mixed race? My father is a lawyer, one of the few whites working in a black area, and his office is in Athlone. I am near panic, terrified for his safety. South Africa was already on edge. Nine days earlier, on March 21, African protestors in Sharpeville, a segregated township forty-five miles from Johannesburg, had participated in the countrywide protest against the pass laws, laws that apply only to the African majority. The police had shot point-blank into the crowd of demonstrators, killing sixty-nine people outright, including eight women and ten children. I had seen photos in the newspaper: bodies of men and women strewn across an open area, contorted into awkward positions, most facing down, shot in the back as they tried to flee. And then, a few days ago, in nearby Langa, five protestors were shot, including a baby tied to his mother's back, and twenty-nine were wounded. Now this march. Would it too become violent?

A friend's parent drives me home and I rush through the door, hoping to find my father. Only my worried mother is there. She had called the office, but his administrator knew only that "Mr. Urdang went out." All we could do is wait. Most days we could set our clocks by the slam of my father's car door. He'd arrived home at precisely six-thirty and walk heavy-footed across the cement backyard, his worn tan-leather briefcase hanging at his side, wanting only to wash his hands and sit down and eat. We—my mother, my older sister Leonie, and I—knew the rule: dinner had to be ready when he pulled back his chair at the head of the table. Only when the first mouthfuls of food began to have an effect would he ask about our day, and sometimes tell us stories about his. This evening, though, the slam is earlier than usual. My father's step is quick and light. His broad smile takes me aback.

"I've just seen the beginning of the end of apartheid!" he exclaims as he walks through the door. His voice is still enthusiastic when he continues over dinner. "As soon as I heard about the march I drove to a spot overlooking De Waal Drive. What a sight!" he says, looking from Leonie to me. There is awe in his voice. "Thousands upon thousands of Africans walked in a silent, orderly manner." He is wolfing down his food in his elation. I can hardly eat as I take in what he is saying. "They were dignified and determined. Such a show of power!" The fear that gripped me earlier has dissolved with his upbeat attitude. I am once again on solid ground. Safe.

"The government can't deny what has just happened. Passes *have* to go."

From a young age, I knew that passes were evil. My parents would often talk about them, going off on a general rant against apartheid. "Just so that the capitalists can ensure a cheap source of labor!" my father would declare. Every African from the age of sixteen had to carry a passbook, about the size of a passport. They were the key to the bearer's life: where he could work, where she could be at that moment, where they could live. When my mother employed an African maid her pass had to be signed regularly by my mother to confirm that she was "legal." She lived in a room in the backyard. Her children lived in the Transkei. She could visit them once a year.

ONLY LATER WOULD WE LEARN MORE. The protestors had slowly, deliberately woven their way for over eight miles along the main artery from their townships on the Cape Flats toward their destination: the architecturally grand white-pillared parliament building in the center of the city, where its members, elected by South Africa's small white population, were in session. The march was led by Philip Kgosana, a former student at the University of Cape Town, now in his early twenties, one of the few Africans to be granted permission to attend the virtually all-white university. His scholarship did not cover living expenses, however, so, virtually destitute, he moved to Langa's substandard single-sex barracks built for male workers. There he received a different education, listening to their stories steeped in suffering. He became a political activist and left university to work for the Pan Africanist Congress. The PAC had recently broken away from the multiracial African National Congress—the party of Nelson Mandela—because they considered the ANC too accommodating of the whites.

When he saw the extent of the military and police presence around Parliament, he changed direction and headed for the police headquarters at Caledon Square. With thirty-thousand protestors jammed into the square and the surrounding streets, the commanding officer refused the minister of justice's demand to open fire. He negotiated with Kgosana, agreeing to set up a face-to-face meeting between him and the minister of justice later that afternoon, as long as the protestors returned to the townships. Fearing the bloodbath that would result if the police used violence, Kgosana agreed. Led by a police van, with army helicopters whirring overhead, the protestors walked back in an orderly fashion to the townships. When Kgosana returned to Caledon Square at the agreed time, he was arrested. After spending nine months in detention without trial, Kgosana was let out on bail. He fled the country, joining the thousands of activists who fled into exile.

THE MARCH ON CAPE TOWN sent a tremor of fear down the spine of government leaders and every member of the all-white South African Parliament. It was one thing for defiant Africans to protest in their overcrowded, segregated townships such as Sharpeville. It was quite another for over thirty thousand to head to the seat of government in the center of the white city. Late that same afternoon, the government declared a state of emergency. The severe clampdown on the press meant that even to this day, many non-Capetonian friends express surprise when I mention this massive demonstration. Within a week, Parliament passed the Unlawful Organizations Act, under which the ANC headed by Nelson Mandela and the PAC headed by Robert Sobukwe were banned, followed by the mass arrests of leaders, strikers, and protestors. An arsenal of draconian laws designed to crush dissent was passed over the coming weeks. South Africa was turning into a police state. With South Africa once again considered "stable" by international capital, the U.S. and Britain rescinded the threat made soon after the Sharpeville massacre, to withdraw their investments.

Oppressive laws were not new. Many were passed soon after the National Party took over power in 1948. The Suppression of Communism Act was aimed at political organizing among nonwhites, effectively driving anti-apartheid opposition underground. The Population Registration Act classified South Africans into racial categories: Bantu (African, approximately 80 percent of the population), White (approximately 10 percent), and Coloured (7 percent); a fourth category, Asian, was later added for people of South Asian origin (3 percent). The Group Areas Act carved up the country according to racial category, ensuring that the white minority would hold 80 percent of the land, including all the cities and the best of the farmland. Years of forced removal followed: homes were bulldozed, possessions destroyed, and communities demolished. Three and a half million blacks, mostly African, but coloured and Asian as well, suffered this fate. This act also changed my father's law practice. He rapidly gained expertise in the complex and often incomprehensible law, interpreting it for his clients and helping them maneuver their way through it. As a white he had to apply for special permission to work in his own office, subject to renewal every five years. Until it no longer was.

He set up his practice in Athlone after graduating from law school. He was the youngest of six brothers and the only one to attend university. A young radical at the time, he was connected with the Unity Movement, a largely coloured, Trotskyist anti-apartheid movement. "I could have opened my office in the center of the city when I qualified," he told me. "But I didn't want to spend my days handling the divorces and wills of privileged white clients." In Athlone, he could train black lawyers and provide legal services to people who confronted real problems.

My father never turned away clients because they couldn't afford his fee. Tucked away at the end of the garden at the back of the house where we lived until I was eight, was a chicken run where gifts from grateful clients happily clucked and scratched and occasionally deigned to lay an egg. We could not bring ourselves to slaughter them, so they would be given away when they got too old to be of use. Or so I was led to believe.

2 — "It Makes No Sense"

One or two afternoons a week I hang out at my father's storefront office after school. As I walk into the busy interior, the first thing I notice is the musty smell of dust that has settled into files and deeds and law books and Hansards; that has filtered in from the unpaved road outside to settle in the cracks and crevices of the rough wood floor. I take delight in lifting the broad, hinged wooden flap, smooth from wear, that opens upward to allow people to pass into the cluttered central area where Khadija, my father's secretary, sits, clacking away on her typewriter. On one side is my father's office. On the other, the offices of the coloured law clerks and administrator, barely large enough for their desks and a chair or two for clients. It feels cozy and familiar. As cozy and familiar as hanging out in our kitchen at home.

It is the early 1950s and I am about eight years old, fascinated by the world spinning around me from my vantage point on the sidewalk. I am neatly dressed in my school uniform, a light green dress with a small round collar, short puff sleeves and belted waist, bright white socks and black lace-ups. My thick curly black hair is parted down the middle, tightly pulled into two large bunches secured in place with an elastic band and bright ribbons, or loose and springy, held back by an Alice band. I smile politely at clients entering the office and then return to my observations of the street. Women—young, middle-aged, elderly—pass at a pace suited to their age and economic standing, some bent over from the weight of their lives, others smartly dressed and striding out. Men of dubious occupation congregate on the corner or hang out in front of the bottle store across the street where they are permitted to buy wine but not hard liquor, a privilege that Africans cannot legally enjoy. They sway on their feet, tattered shirts hanging over tattered trousers. I have been adopted by these men. Khadija calls them *skelms*—scoundrels—and tells me to quit smiling at every no-good *skollie* who walks past. But I tell her they are my friends and I like it when they call out to me: "Hey skattie, hoe gaan'it?" And I reply politely, "Goed, dankie!" Then they laugh and tell me I am their pretty little *gogga* while I ponder that "bug" is a term of endearment.

Honking cars rattle by, backfiring. Dogs bark. People call to each other from opposite sides of the street. The sound of children playing street games fills the afternoon air. So does the yelling, laughing, bantering, conversing in an Afrikaans dialect that I can't quite understand but don't have to. Body language and tone tell me all. The streets crackle with activity and noise. I know, although I am too young to analyze the reasons why, that this area belongs to its residents. Here they can express themselves freely, understand each other and their culture, and know what it means to carve out home in their own community. It is a different world from the one I live in, with its large houses and green lawns and flower gardens, where neighbors nod friendly hellos when they happen upon each other but little else. And where blacks—whether coloured or African—are there to serve their white *baas* and madam and to be subservient.

I am perhaps ten when I begin to question the dissonance between the two Cape Towns I know. Cracks form and light enters. I stare out the window of my father's car as we take the twenty-minute drive home. The Athlone houses are small and cramped; most have no space for gardens or children to play. The paint is worn, the cars are old, and the kids playing outside are wearing clothes that if they were mine, my mother would have said, "These are getting too worn out" or "You are growing like a beanstalk, they're too small," and she would have packed them into a shopping bag and handed it to our maid. We cross the railroad track into Rondebosch. What I see regularly and have accepted as normal begins to trouble me. Here the streets are quiet, broad, paved. The houses always look freshly painted, with neatly cropped hedges, colorful gardens, and rolling lawns all kept up by men and women who come from areas like Athlone or the African townships outside of Cape Town, or even from the Bantustans (the "homelands" in which Africans were forced to live, to keep them out of urban areas) farther away. Cars are parked in locked garages. Everyone living here is white.

I glance sideways at my father's profile, testing his mood. This is the time I have him to myself, but it's not always easy. He has strong views and his authoritarian tone renders me mute. I need to sense approval before I initiate a conversation. Sometimes a silence envelopes the car and he seems to forget that I am there. Other times, if it has been a good day, the mood is more relaxed and I feel free to ask questions. This day is a good day.

"Why, Daddy?" I ask as we near home, "Why the difference?" He looks at me and raises his eyebrows. He suddenly hits the brake as a dog darts across the street, and he thrusts his left hand across my chest so that I won't be thrown forward. My chest hurts a bit. I try to ignore it. He is silent for a moment.

"It's because the government thinks blacks are inferior. This is a very racist country." His voice sounds annoyed, but this time I know it's not because of me. "All privileges are reserved for the whites." Although we are in the minority, he tells me, laws ensure that we live well.

I don't really understand. "What do you mean?"

He tells me that to maintain our good life, blacks, particularly Africans, are relegated all the inferior jobs and are paid very badly. "The children of my clients go to schools that are cramped and overcrowded." I think of my own school, Oakhurst, with its airy class-rooms and playing fields.

"It's even worse for african kids, though," he says. "They don't have to go to school, and their education is different from yours."

I am still puzzled. "But why?"

"The government thinks they don't need the same education as you, because they will end up working in the mines and factories. They won't become doctors or lawyers like you."

My mind battles and fumbles to absorb this. It is as if the color of the air has changed. A film that I didn't know existed dissolves to allow sharper focus. All I can think is that it's so unfair. It makes no sense. He repeats what he has often told me, that I need to understand that my sister and I are very fortunate. "Never ever forget how privileged you are," he says as he turns into our driveway.

When we walk through the wooden door in the high wall surrounding the cement backyard, I slow down. I contemplate Maria's room. We pronounce Ma-*reye*-ya. She is a slight, wiry, coloured woman, older than my mother, who works for us. She adores me. When she asked my father to draw up her will, leaving all her savings to me, he refused, saying that if she insists he can't act as her lawyer. They settled on £50. The rest was left to her nephew, whom she called a no-good *skellum*. She would die of a stroke about four years later. Now as I follow my father from the car through the backyard and into the house my new knowledge hones in on another troubling reality I had not thought about before. Maria's room, off the yard outside the kitchen where the washing is hung on long lines and the garbage pails are set out, is half the size of mine. It's against the law for her to live in the main house. There is only enough room for a single bed, a small dresser, a narrow wardrobe, and a small rug. She keeps her few possessions in boxes under her bed. It smells of cold cement. Her bathroom has a separate entrance and she must go out into the yard to get to it. In contrast, the rooms of our house, which she keeps spotless, are airy and spacious and glisten with polish and elbow grease. In later years, I would see this as a moment that pierced my protective, privileged skin and led me to think more deeply about inequality and oppression, and ultimately led to my activism. A wake-up moment.

Despite the dissolving film, my young self continues to take much for granted. As I leave childhood behind and enter adolescence, friends and parties and boys become the center of my life. But a chill has settled into my bones, to remain mostly contained until I am seventeen and at university, where I am gripped anew by what my father has told me years before. The word "privilege" latches onto at me like a leech and sucks dry my love for this country.

3 — "You Have to Learn to Think for Yourself"

My parents met at the Lenin Club. They were in their twenties, my mother, Rose, three years younger than my father, Joe. He was one of the founders of the club, whose members supported the ideology of Lenin and Trotsky and opposed the rise of Stalinism in the Soviet Union and what they saw as the hard-line position of the South African Communist Party.

Their parents—my grandparents—were among the many Jews who fled eastern Europe when the pogroms were at their height at the end of the nineteenth century. Most sought refuge in the United States, but by 1914, there were forty thousand East European Jews in South Africa, the overwhelming majority from Lithuania and Latvia.

I know little about my paternal grandparents. My grandfather was Lithuanian, a shoemaker. He met my grandmother when he went to seek work in Riga, the capital of neighboring Latvia. My grandmother was more educated than he was. Two of his five brothers were born before they immigrated to South Africa. One died in World War I.

I know more about my maternal grandfather, Moses Schur, and his second wife, Leah Stutzen, who was the one grandparent still living when I was born. She was an ornery presence throughout my childhood, a woman fond of her grandchildren as long as she didn't interact with them too much.

What were my grandmother's first reactions when she saw Table Mountain from the ship as it neared the docks? She must have felt heavy-hearted. She had left behind her true love, a rabbinical student whom her younger brother had forbidden her to marry. At twenty-four she was not going to easily find a man acceptable to both her and her family. Moses Schur, a rich widower, must have seemed like a better-than-nothing alternative, despite being thirty years older than her. She would join her adored older sister who already lived in Cape Town and who arranged the marriage in the first place. She never talked about her betrothed back home, nor why the family had prevented the marriage. I suspect he was one of the radical students who organized a strike at the Yeshiva in her town around the time they were engaged. What she made clear to her daughters was that she had no love for this old man, who had five sons around her age and treated her poorly.

Moses Schur arrived in South Africa in 1880, penniless but determined. Starting off as a *smous*—an itinerant peddler—with no more than a donkey and a back pack, he eventually acquired considerable wealth from the small empire of shops and hotels he built that served the needs of rural Afrikaners in the far reaches of Cape Province. While he was alive they lived well. Photos show her in splendid finery, large and buxom next to an old grizzled man who appears to be half her size. She stares out at the camera, expressionless. When Moses died, he left her with three children—Sam, aged nine; Sophie, aged seven; and Rose, aged five—as well as a small stipend, and a spacious house on the slopes of Table Mountain. His considerable wealth somehow disappeared. According to my father, the executor of the will swindled Leah, the ignorant young woman from the old country, as well as her children, and her stepchildren out of their inheritance. To make ends meet, Leah turned her home into a kosher boarding house for the daughters of Jews who lived in the rural areas and attended school in Cape Town.

"Tell me about your childhood," I would ask my mother, eager for real-life stories. But besides the games she played, only bitter memories would surface. Some of the parents never paid their bills, and my grandmother could never insist. Rose and Sophie—but not their brother, Sam—never had their own bedroom; there was always the need to house one more boarder. At school, they were taunted mercilessly for being the daughters of the poor, disliked landlady. The taunts still stung: with hurt in her eyes, my mother could still name the worst offenders. I once asked my aunt Sophie, who enjoyed writing and had an occasional piece published in local newspapers, to write about her childhood. She shook her head: "I once tried, but I had such nightmares that I stopped."

Once her children were in their late teens, Leah offered rooms to young Jewish men—university students, many of them political radicals. They introduced Rose to the Lenin Club and a new world opened up, one in which discussion and debate centered around the evils of apartheid, the struggles of the working class, socialism, and the way to bring about transformation and secure rights for the majority of South Africans. She was immediately drawn to my father, this charming handsome man, who loved an argument, who laughed easily and told silly jokes. They married in 1937. Leonie was born in 1939, and I was born four and a half years later, in 1943.

My parents were atheists, and rejected the strict religious orthodoxy of my grandparents. Nonetheless, from my earliest memory I knew that we were Jewish. What that actually meant was tested on my first day of kindergarten at Oakhurst Primary School. Twenty new girls sat cross-legged in a circle on the carpeted floor, sun flooding in from the windows. My new friend, Lulu, and I sat shoulder to shoulder as our teacher, Miss Hanny, explained the how, what, and wherefore of the school day. This included twice-weekly religious instruction classes, which she called RI.

"Will the Jewish girls please raise your hands," she said. Four arms went up, including mine and Lulu's. Ms. Hanny went on to explain that as we were Jewish we were excused from attending RI. I turned to my new friend. "I know why," I pronounced with four-and-a-half-year-old certainty. "It's because Jews don't believe in God." Lulu, with a look of disbelief, scuttled away from me as if I had morphed into something vile, leaving a wide gap between us.

"Not so!" she protested with much five-year-old indignation. "Of *course* we believe in God!"

What could she possibly mean? My father and my mother told me that God did not exist. I also knew we were Jewish. Surely that meant Jews did not believe in God? I mulled over Lulu's reaction for the rest of the short school day. It was the first question I asked my mother when she came to pick me up, ignoring her eager "Did you like school? What did you do?"

"Lulu says Jews believe in God. But that's not true, is it, Mummy?" A smile spread across my mother's face. "Most Jews believe in God," she explained gently. "Granny does, and she goes to synagogue every Saturday morning. So do Daddy's brothers, your uncles. We don't. Aunt Sophie doesn't. But we are still all Jews." She added an intriguing fact: "Many non-Jews also don't believe in God," and she listed off, finger by finger, the nonbelievers among our Gentile friends.

I would become familiar with and internalize my father's refrain: "As long as there is anti-Semitism in the world, we will always claim being Jews." In keeping with this he closed his law office every major Jewish holiday as an I-am-a-Jew statement to the community. So while my friends dressed in fine new clothes and went with their families to shul on the high holy days—Rosh Hashanah, Yom Kippur—my mother packed a picnic lunch and my father drove us to the beach or the mountains or Tokai Forest to spend a day of play and relaxation. At dusk on Yom Kippur we would join my father's oldest brother for the breaking of the fast. I was not yet two when World War II ended. The Holocaust must have been very much on their minds. My parents never ever bought German goods. (Years later, when my husband and I drove out of the Volkswagen dealer with our new station wagon, I was momentarily overcome by a wave of nausea—I had just bought a German car! "Sorry, Dad," I said, lifting my eyes to the heaven I didn't believe in.)

A disproportionate number of whites in the anti-apartheid struggle were Jews; many spent time in jail or fled into exile, where they both longed for and worked toward the day that South Africa would be free from apartheid's yoke. Were they radicalized by their own parents fleeing the pogroms and terrible repression in eastern Europe? By the revolutionary fervor that preceded the Russian Revolution? Or by their unique experience as Jewish immigrants in South Africa, combined with the persecution Jews suffered in Europe during the Second World War?

MY FATHER LOVED TELLING JOKES and funny stories. As a teen, I would find his jokes oh-so-embarrassing. The stories that he brought home from his day, however, often captured the essence of South Africa. One evening it was about Pienaar, an Afrikaner lawyer friend and regular golf partner. "I bumped into Pienaar in the city today," he announced over dinner one evening. "I told him that Louis Maurice had come for dinner last night." Louis Maurice was a talented young coloured sculptor and a family friend. A grin began to spread over his face. "He looked a bit horrified and then asked, almost in a whisper"—by then my father was gasping for breath with his signature infectious laughter—"what *dishes* did you serve his food on, Joe?" He often couldn't make it to the punch line. By now we were all in stitches.

But wait, what about the mottled blue-and-white enamel mug and plate with a chip of paint missing from its blue rim that had their specific spot in our kitchen cupboard? These were for Amos, our twice-weekly gardener, a polite, elderly African man. The domestic worker would prepare his breakfast—two thick slices of white bread with a substantial layer of butter and bright orange apricot jam and a mug of strong, sweet tea with milk—and later his lunch, invariably mealie pap, a traditional corn porridge, with meat-and-vegetable stew. He would eat sitting on the cement steps that led from the kitchen door to the backyard, his floppy gray felt hat low over his forehead. When he finished his meal, he would hand the plate and mug to the maid, who would wash and dry them and return them to their place on the shelf next to the green chinaware that we—and Louis Maurice—ate off. At the time, I didn't think it odd: it was simply part of life as I knew it.

I was more aware later when my mother and aunt, sitting having tea in my mother's kitchen in London, bemoaned the plight of a mutual friend whose "maid" had gone home to the Transkei for a holiday but had not returned or contacted her. My mother said, "I don't under-stand it. She was one of the family," and my aunt responded, "Well, I guess they have different value systems." I exploded. I had already left South Africa and was well aware of the conditions in the homelands. "Did you not think she might be ill? Dead? Arrested? Not allowed back in Cape Town because her pass wasn't in order?" I was on a roll.

"Such a member of the family and your friend didn't know where to contact her? So much for being one of the family!"

These contradictions stood out more the older I got, and the more politically aware. Still, I grew up in a home mostly devoid of the willful blindness of whites to the poverty and cruelty around them. More typical was the deep, consistent racism from people who didn't or wouldn't acknowledge it in themselves. One night over dinner, the wife of an Afrikaner physics professor, not much older than me, told me about their visit to Spain: "I have never, ever seen such terrible, terrible poverty," she said, with anguish in her voice. "I found it unbearably distressing." I listened in disbelief. How could she not regard the poverty in South Africa as "unbearably distressing"? Because in Spain, the poor were white.

Nor was I exempt from such blindness. My twenty-first birthday present from my parents was a trip to Europe. I traveled up the east coast of Africa on a ship that docked in Brindisi. As I looked over the railing at the Italian dockworkers unloading luggage and other goods, working fast, working hard, into my head popped the thought: "Can't they get a better job?" Even though I caught myself, my first, unpremeditated assumption was that only blacks should do such menial work. Later I would read in *Long Walk to Freedom* Nelson Mandela's reaction while traveling clandestinely in Africa before he was arrested: "As I was boarding the plane I saw that the pilot was black. I had never seen a black pilot before, and the instant I did I had to quell my panic. How could a black man fly a plane?" I wasn't the only one indoctrinated into apartheid's mind-set.

I AM IN MY MID-TWENTIES, visiting London. Miniskirts are in and I feel good and confident, something I need right now as I get off the bus and head up the street to my parents' house in north London. I anticipate hovering clouds of tension. Living in New York has helped, but my father's continuing attempts to dominate and judge me, even if less successful than when I was a teenager, can still leave me mute or belligerent.

Ahead of me I hear full-blown merriment. I recognize my father's wheezing laughter and see my mother almost doubled up in mirth.

She has her arm in his and their body language radiates a deep connection. I stop and stare. I don't often come across them unawares.
"They still really love each other!" I think, surprised that I am surprised. "More than that, they really enjoy each other." I feel happy
for them, and memories of my childhood surface. One of my father's
rhymes, from their betrothal days, pops into my head.

> Rosie, oh Rose,
> Put on your *shabbosdikker* clothes.
> There's a young man to see you
> With a yiddisher nose.

I think of the scribbled notes my mother has squirreled away in
messy drawers—poems and limericks written on the fly. This one,
written around the time of a hernia operation:

> Despite the troubles in Hibernia,
> I got myself a double hernia.
> Got myself a load of trouble,
> Viscera burst just like a bubble.

Or:

> Doctor said, "Don't make a fuss,
> I'm gonna put you in a truss."
> Aesthetic sense against it fought,
> But the fight though good did come to naught.

Or the letter he wrote to my mother when she visited my Aunt Sophie
in Oudtshoorn when Leonie was a baby.

> Business is nice and quiet and it suits me perfectly. I am sorry but
> no fur coats for you this year. Perhaps next year if a few bears will
> lose their way and walk into my office. I love you, you rat.—JOE

I am more used to my father's rages, including against my mother,
and tend to remember her as scolding and demanding. I'm at a friend's
house on a play date and she calls: "Come home immediately. Your

room is a mess. You have to tidy it." Or: "You didn't practice today. Come home right away." My protestations are ignored. Her voice is to be obeyed. I am humiliated and pouty, but I return home and play my violin for a precise half hour but don't actually practice, knowing she won't know the difference. Later I will appreciate that her anger at me is the anger she can't level at my father. She had her feisty, determined side, head pushed out, lips tight, whether it was digging a hole to plant a tree when she was seven months pregnant or flaring up in outrage at injustice. The poverty in South Africa was a constant source of anger for her.

As a child, I would look hard at photos of my parents in their youth. My father was a handsome, six-foot-tall man in shorts with thick wavy black hair and skinny legs. Some photos show him with a serious expression, others light-hearted. All show his stereotypical Jewish nose, which he was quick to joke about, laughing as he sang along to his LP recordings of Jimmy Durante, the Schnozz, the American comedian renowned for his large proboscis.

Standing next to him, my mother seemed even shorter than her five feet. She was an attractive woman with a bushy head of black hair and a rounded body. She started going gray, as did I, in her thirties, turning completely white by her midfifties. Although she dressed carefully and enjoyed shopping for what she needed, her wardrobe was not large. Consumer goods were not that important to her, but books were. I would often come home from school to find my mother taking an afternoon rest, a book clasped in her hands. She went for the classics, abhorred best sellers, which she considered trashy, but churned through the mysteries such as those of Agatha Christie and Dorothy Sayers. Nothing too violent. Once I graduated to chapter books, I too became an avid reader. Twice a year my mother would take me to Stuttafords department store to choose a hardcover from the children's book section. "No Enid Blyton!" was her one rule, referring to the popular British author whom I loved but she considered trite. I would spend time savoring the new books, mulling over this or that title until I selected one. Back home I would crack it open, eager to start, intoxicated by the new-paper smell.

While books were my lifeline, classical music was even more so. As I listened to my parents' records, and to my own growing collection, I escaped from my insecurities and the family tension that seeped out of the walls. I would be transported by the waves rolling through Jascha Heifetz's Mendelssohn Violin Concerto or Pablo Casals' Bach Cello Suites.

I COULD SLOUGH OFF MY MOTHER'S demands. Not my father's. Full of charm and laughter one moment, he could be withdrawn or explosive the next. I feared his foul moods and outbursts of temper. Swayed by his authoritarian assertions that I was too young to have thoughts of my own but should learn from his experience, I adopted his thinking as mine. I tempered what I wanted to say or censored my own opinions until I could suss out what his were and adapt accordingly. When he berated me sharply I would often dissolve into tears. The next morning I would wake to a small peace offering on my bedside table, a chocolate bar or candy—his way of telling me he was sorry. Until the next time.

My mother, too, was intimidated by my father's anger, and I would absorb her unhappiness when one of his moods descended on our household like a dark cloud. Leonie was more resilient and could stand up to him better than I, but she found it exhausting and annoying. At age twenty-one she emigrated to London, to get away from apartheid but also to break free of our father's hold.

A turning point came when I was sixteen. It was right after the Sharpeville massacre. I was visiting my Aunt Sophie in Camps Bay, standing in her narrow living room to the right of the piano talking to my cousin, Arnold, who was five years older that I. The salty smell of seaweed and ocean entered the room through the open windows, and from beyond the playing fields I could hear its steady ebb and flow and catch the sparkle from the rippled surf.

"What do you think about all that has been happening?" Arnold asked. I felt a tightening in my chest, something I was used to when asked for my opinion. I froze. I assumed my cousins and my sister could only agree that my father's strong opinions as the family intellect were to be learned from, not challenged.

"I don't really know," I spluttered. "I haven't discussed it with Joe yet." I had recently started calling my father Joe, a first unconscious effort to distance myself. Arnold contemplated me for a long minute. I shifted on my feet, rolling them onto the outer edge and back again while scrunching my toes in discomfort as I waited for him to respond to my statement with approval.

"You know, Stephanie," he said, with some condescension in his voice. "Joe is a very smart and knowledgeable man. But he doesn't know everything. You have to learn to think for yourself. You are certainly bright enough."

The ground suddenly shifted. How could Arnold be so dismissive of Joe's opinions? I was truly shocked. At the same time, his words became the catalyst that enabled me to eventually break away from my father's hold, even though it would take many more years to do so. What I did not give up were the values he passed on to me. He was a man passionately intolerant of racism and anti-Semitism, of injustice and inequality. Most of all, he taught me to hate apartheid, a hatred that would define my life.

4 — By the Stroke of a Pen

I t was 1964, the end of the academic year at the University of Cape Town.

I stood among a crush of students, vying for a spot to find my name on one of the sheets of paper pinned to the walls of the long hall. It wasn't there. I slunk away, mortified, to avoid the inevitable questions from friends about my results. I had already stretched the three-year undergraduate degree into four years. Now I had failed too many courses to be readmitted.

I had spent most of my time at university convinced I was unequal to the academic task. I was painfully mute in lectures and seminars, blocked by an inner voice that told me I wasn't smart enough. I was envious of fellow students who seemed to take academics in their stride. But after the initial disappointment, I realized I felt a sense of relief. No more exams! No more procrastinations as I struggled with the rigors of academia. I had to get on with life. I had to find a job.

I had one salable skill: I was a fast and accurate typist, crisply tapping out letters and words at a steady pace. A year earlier, Joe had insisted that I enroll in a summer typing course. "You never know," he said. "One day your husband might have difficulty in supporting you and you can help out by working in an office." My mother had worked in his. I was appalled at the notion, but I now had to admit that being a proficient typist would help me find a job.

My friend Sally Spilhaus came to my rescue. I met Sally at university. She hadn't finished her degree either, but that was by choice. She felt stifled there and had taken a job with the Defence and Aid Fund.

Now she was moving on, and she recommended me for the job. I began work in February 1965.

DEFENCE AND AID, OR D AND A as it was referred to, received funds from overseas to provide legal aid for political prisoners charged under the anti-terrorism acts. It also provided funds for the families of political prisoners who lost their breadwinners as a result of arrests, long trials, and longer prison sentences. The lawyers D and A retained honed their skills with every trial, and as a result many activists—too many for the government's comfort—were found not guilty, received light sentences, or escaped the death penalty altogether. These lawyers were courageous. Some were imprisoned themselves, usually under the 90-day or 180-day detention regulations, which denied trial or representation. Many were slapped with banning orders under the Suppression of Communism Act, which meant they could no longer practice law.

I began working for D and A eight months after the Rivonia trial, which resulted in the imprisonment of Nelson Mandela and seven others. D and A contributed funds for the defense. In his famous three-hour speech from the dock, "I Am Prepared to Die," Mandela made it clear that, given the violence perpetrated against Africans every day, the ANC had no choice but to abandon nonviolence, which had been its tactic since it was founded in 1912. He concluded with words I would only read after I left South Africa:

> During my lifetime I have dedicated myself to this struggle of the African people. I have fought against white domination, and I have fought against black domination. I have cherished the ideal of a democratic and free society in which all persons will live together in harmony and with equal opportunities. It is an ideal which I hope to live for and to achieve. But if needs be, it is an ideal for which I am prepared to die.

He didn't die. Fearing an outbreak of violence across the country, the defendants were sentenced to life imprisonment, not to death.

D and A board members were committed to the cause and passionate about the rule of law. Alan Paton was a board member. His book *Cry, The Beloved Country* was an international best seller and one of the banned books I devoured after leaving South Africa. When he came to Cape Town for a meeting I was given the task of picking him up at the airport. In preparation, I cleared my small gray Ford Prefect of the papers and accumulated debris, but I had no time to give it a much-needed wash. As I drove Paton to the house where he was staying, he turned to me and said: "Stephanie, you are very courageous." I blushed. For such a man to call me courageous! But before I could respond, he continued: "To drive with such a grimy windscreen takes courage indeed!"

A number of the board members were, like Alan Paton, Liberal Party members, a mainly white party opposed to the ANC's position on armed struggle but whose strong anti-apartheid positions and actions had landed many in jail or on the roster of the banned. People under banning orders were forbidden to meet with more than one person at a time; to be in contact with another banned person; to attend any gathering, political or social, including "gatherings" such as funerals; to publish writings whatever the genre; to enter educational institutions, courts of law, or offices of the media. They had to report regularly to the police and could not travel outside of their magisterial district. By the time the act was repealed, soon after Mandela's release, over sixteen hundred men and women had been caught in its net.

Ann was one such. She was arrested for breaking her banning orders when she climbed Table Mountain to meet a banned friend. She applied to D and A for legal help.

"Our funds must go to those who have no possibility of affording legal fees," one of the more forceful members argued, with nods of approval from one or two others. That she was white was there in code.

"But Ann doesn't have the money," countered another, with nods of approval from the rest. "And that's partly due to the fact that she's banned." A vote was taken. Her application was approved, but not without a last word by the initial naysayer, a rather large, blustery member of the committee.

"Stephanie, please note in the minutes," she said, turning to look at me to make sure I was taking in her directive, "that Ann should be informed that we would appreciate a donation at some point." Then she added, "Maybe she could sell some of her used clothes to her maid and make a donation to us."

I saw my discomfort mirrored on other faces in the room. This board member simply could not imagine that Ann, a white person, was unable to afford a "maid" or new clothes. I "forgot" to note this when typing up the minutes the next day. Yet how many whites took the risks the board member did, preferring to hide behind their big houses, their whiteness, their privilege, and ignore what was happening all around them. She did what her conscience dictated with little protection.

On the morning of March 18, 1966, as I sat behind my desk in the small, high-ceilinged office on St. George's Street, where many lawyers had their chambers, there was a knock on the door. Not the tentative knock of a family member or friend of someone recently arrested. Not the rap of a lawyer coming to discuss a case. This one was thunderous. Before I could call out "Come in!" the unlocked door flew open and a bunch of burly plainclothes security police in dark suits strode into the office. They stood there looking around as if surprised that it was only me. I felt my face drain of color. "Am I being arrested?" I thought. I knew I was too much of a small fry for them to bother, unless they were busy right then arresting every member of the board. Waving a document, one of them informed me with great satisfaction in his voice: "Defence and Aid has been banned." By the stroke of a pen, D and A had joined the ANC as an unlawful organization under the Suppression of Communism Act.

They began to search through the file drawers and then proceeded to move the cabinets toward the door, to be carted off to their Cape Town headquarters. The one in charge said curtly, pointing to two police: "Tell them where you live. They will take you to search your house." He continued to flip through papers on my desk. I was escorted out of the building at a brisk pace and onto the street between the two men, right into the path of my father, who was walking toward us. He looked at me aghast, his face draining of color as mine had earlier.

He gave a slight nod in nonverbal acknowledgment as we passed. "At least he knows that I am being arrested," I thought. If, that is, I am.

There was silence in the black sedan as I was driven the five and a half miles around the mountain to the cottage in Newlands that I shared with my boyfriend, Eric, and another male friend. I had met Eric at university when I was nineteen. He had startling blue eyes and pitch black straight hair that hung to his shoulders. He was a physics student who wrote fairy tales, liked poetry, and matched my love of classical music. His professors predicted a bright future for him. Like my father, he tended to dominate conversations. I did not protest. It was familiar territory. He was my first serious love and I knew that this was the man I would marry.

We began living together when I was twenty-two, first in a flat in Long Street, on the edge of the city, then in this cottage near the university. The expectation that young Jewish women only left home when they married was being challenged by my generation. It did not sit comfortably with my parents, but I was an adult and they couldn't stop me. So not wanting to set up a conflict, and fearing that I would reject them altogether, they agreed. There was an unspoken charade that made it easier for them: we were not actually having sex. We were simply living communally with other friends. We each had our own room to maintain this subterfuge. It could not have been easy for my parents, who were always conscious of what others might think and feared judgment by their community. For me it was part of my rebellion against my father, and I took some pleasure out of it.

Now, standing in the living room were the two bulky men, whose large presence made the room seem even smaller than it was. They were polite—I was white after all—but they felt menacing. I sat on the edge of a chair in the living room as they searched, watching warily. Each book was perused, each drawer opened and rummaged through, each bed peered under. A few books were set aside. I doubted any were banned, but the list of banned books, plays, and even music was long and not easy to keep track of. Books that criticized apartheid were invariably on the list. Newspapers from England, such as the *Sunday Observer*, regularly had sentences blacked out by zealous workers in the censor's office. Not only political books caught the attention of the state censor: those deemed too sexually explicit or morally reprehensible got the axe as well. A dog-eared copy of *Peyton Place* had made the rounds from one high school friend to another, its jacket covered with brown paper. One of my all-time favorite books as a child, *Black Beauty*, was temporarily on the list until someone realized that the title referred to a horse. More recently, it had been a recording of *Who's Afraid of Virginia Woolf?* which we had listened to in Ann's apartment, curtains drawn, shortly before she herself was banned. Halfway through, the security police strode into her apartment, took down the names of the ten or so of us there, and confiscated the LPs.

Finding nothing more of interest, the leader, tucking the few books he found questionable under his arm, pointed to the door. "Laat ons gaan," he said. Let's go. They were gone. I was left standing in the middle of the room, both relieved and horrified. Relieved because I had not been arrested. Horrified at the implications of the banning: what would happen to the accused now awaiting trial? Or the hundreds of families suddenly deprived of funds to buy food for their families? I immediately called the chairman of the board, but he already knew. I later heard that two board members had also been raided. I then called my father to let him know that I was safe. His voice cracked in his effort to hide his relief.

The banning of the D and A was, in the scheme of apartheid things, inevitable. It was a thorn gouging deep into the regime's flesh. But it helped clinch my decision to leave South Africa.

MY WORRIES THAT THE BANNING of D and A would end its work were unwarranted. Only after the fall of apartheid did I learn how the work of D and A continued despite its banning. With just a handful of people in the know, a South African lawyer's prestigious law firm in the UK stepped into the breach to instruct and pay lawyers in South Africa to act on behalf of the accused. Funding continued to be provided by the International Defence and Aid Fund for Southern Africa, based in London. Even the spies that infiltrated the anti-apartheid movements throughout Britain, Europe, and North America could not crack the watertight scheme. As for aid to the dependents, a network of willing Brits, housewives, churchgoers, and regular folk

well under the radar of the South African security police committed themselves to secrecy and "adopted" different families. They sent
them monthly stipends with funds that were transferred into their
bank accounts.

5 — "You Can Make More of a Difference Outside"

We were squeezed around the dinner table at Sally and Michael's cottage in Constantia, eight young white South Africans, now satiated by delicious food and slightly tipsy on good but cheap South African wine.

Dinner parties were our main form of Saturday night entertainment. Most of the decent restaurants were too expensive. The cinemas were strictly whites-only, and most of the interesting films were either banned or heavily censored. As for television, that was banned in 1960, to protect our morals and out of fear that the "Bantu" would rise up if they beheld the lifestyle of the rich and white.

Our conversation inevitably moved from idle chatter to The Question: should we stay or should we leave? That we were even discussing it reflected our privilege. As white middle-class South Africans, we had the means to make the decision, with good prospects of studying or finding jobs overseas. There was ambivalence on both sides: Eric and I were in the leaving camp. Sally and Michael were as well. Most of the others were committed to staying.

"By staying we would be doing nothing more than applying Band-Aids," Eric said in a voice full of certainty. It was a favorite line of his. Why waste our lives, making sacrifices that ultimately would lead nowhere? The world out there was beckoning him. He planned to complete a doctorate in physics and enter the world of research not possible at home. He looked forward to escaping South Africa's confines and grabbing onto a life of intellectual stimulus. Unlike Eric, I had doubts, but being a dutiful wife-to-be, I suppressed them.

"Yes," Sally ventured, her long blond hair swaying down her back as she moved her head in emphasis. "We are beneficiaries whether we like it or not."

"I don't agree." said Frank. He was a professor at the university who would later contribute important research to the nature of poverty—and hence oppression—in South Africa. "You can't abandon ship when change is inevitable, and I mean real, transformational change to black-majority rule." Then picking up on an earlier point that Michael made about not wanting to raise children in this country, he added: "It's not a question of whether South Africa is a place to raise children. It's our country. It will be our children's country, and eventually, they will grow up in a just society and perhaps contribute to ensuring that it remains so."

We were rehashing conversations, often heated, that we had been having for months as we attended an increasing number of farewell parties. We were caught in a hiatus between the government clampdown that followed the Sharpeville massacre and the activism and resistance that would pick up again in the 1970s. At the time, though, an eerie political silence seemed to stretch ahead, unbending and uninterrupted. There was no movement to join—it had gone underground. The African Resistance Movement, which was composed mainly of young white men and women my age, had begun a sabotage campaign against government installations and services, explicitly eschewing violence against people. It would turn out that I knew a number of ARM's members, but I was too far outside this level of activism to be involved. In 1964, about nine months before I joined D and A, many of its members were arrested and tried; others managed to flee the country. Many served long prison sentences.

"But," Michael intervened, "we are white, English-speaking South Africans. The struggle for majority rule is not ours. It's between the Afrikaners and the Africans."

I wasn't sure about this argument. Why should the English, as South African as anyone else, be considered exempt? I believed it definitely *was* my struggle. I just didn't know how to pursue it in the current political climate. But I remained silent. Although I could discuss my ideas with Eric or friends like Sally, I had difficulty asserting myself in groups.

We never convinced each other. Those on the side of leaving left. Those who stayed carried the responsibility for all of us, at the risk of banning, jail, and even assassination.

Many years later, while reminiscing about our youth, Sally and I discovered that we had both harbored the same ambivalence. We couldn't voice it—it would have created chasms that we feared we would be unable to bridge. And to what purpose? Neither of our men suffered any such qualms. We were women after all, stuck in our anticipated roles as women, expected to follow our men. So Sally and I nursed our emotions in our separate spaces, trying to suppress the feeling we were abandoning our country.

LEONIE, NOW ENSCONCED IN LONDON, was an additional pull. In her letters, she described the joy in finding a big wide world outside of Cape Town and tried hard to convince me that this too could be mine. When I wrote to her about my qualms, she replied, "You need to leave South Africa. There is so much to be part of outside the country. The theater, art, culture of all sorts, it's just amazing. And there is a lot of anti-apartheid work, if that's what you want to do. You can probably make more of a difference outside, you know."

Here in South Africa, the whole system had been rigged to keep whites in a safe cocoon, to ensure that we basked in privilege. How was it possible to contribute to change while we passively and docilely agreed to live, work, travel, shop, and participate in leisure activities reserved for whites alone? Perhaps it *was* possible to make more of a contribution overseas. I was not contemplating leaving because I had personally suffered the horrors of apartheid. Far from it. I was leaving because I benefited from apartheid. I was leaving because of the privilege that my father had told me never to forget.

WITH THE BANNING OF D AND A, my main avenue to meaningful involvement was gone and the prospect of emigrating became more palatable. One question remained: where to? Both Eric and I had assumed it would be London, where he would enter a physics doctoral program. The link between Britain and English-speaking white South Africa was strong. Part had been a colony. At school we learned as much British history as South African. We read English authors—Dickens, Austen, Brontë. It already felt familiar—an extension of our culture. We had a ready-made community of close friends waiting for us who had settled or were planning to settle there. Leonie was married and pregnant. My parents were well advanced in their own plans to emigrate. All that was missing from this happy London-based picture was the addition of me and my husband-to-be. Fate had other ideas.

One evening, Eric and I were waiting for the traffic on Long Street to clear so that we could cross the road to our apartment. My parents were coming for dinner, and I was eager to cook the perfect meal but also apprehensive about having them in our space, where we would continue the charade of separate rooms. Friday evening traffic up Long Street moved in a steady, sluggish stream. A gap appeared and I darted across at a trot. As I stepped up onto the opposite sidewalk, I heard a screech of brakes and the telltale thud of a body being hit by a car. I turned to see Eric flying into the air and then landing on the road, one leg sticking out at a distorted angle. The driver exited from his Mini Minor, his face blanched. The next moments were a blur. A whites-only ambulance appeared, its siren blaring. "We're taking him to Woodstock Hospital," the medic told me as he clanked shut the ambulance doors, barricading off Eric's pain-contorted face and moans of agony. As I rushed to my car to drive to the hospital, the siren reverberated through the streets and grew fainter, rapidly putting distance between Eric and me. I was numb, barely able to focus on the road. I tried to conjure up comforting thoughts. It's just a broken leg! Nothing life-threatening. He'll be out in no time, in a white plaster of paris cast, learning to maneuver around with crutches, back at his studies, back at home.

At the hospital I was told to wait. Finally, a white-coated doctor came through the doors to tell me that the fracture was especially tricky, that he would have to operate to set it and put in a pin, and that Eric would remain in hospital, his leg up in traction to promote healing. I caught a glimpse of him on a stretcher through the door, white and still groaning. I made a move to go to him. The door was shut in my face. I was not family.

Eric remained in hospital for six weeks with his leg suspended in traction at a 45-degree angle. His fracture healed, but his leg was wasted. After another six weeks of physical therapy, first on crutches, then with a walking stick, he was finally able to walk as he did before and return to his nine-month postgraduate program in physics, a prerequisite for entering a British university. Before the accident, no one doubted that Eric would get a first-class pass, virtually guaranteeing a full scholarship at a top scientific institution in the UK. But having missed half of the program, he didn't get his first and the full scholarship was off the cards. Instead, Eric turned his attention to the United States, where he was accepted at Stevens Institute of Technology in Hoboken, New Jersey, across the Hudson River from Manhattan. The offer of a stipend and a grant to cover his fees and living expenses settled it.

I had to face the fact that I would be living in a truly foreign land. I turned to books. One in particular, displayed on a table in Stuttafords, caught my eye: *The Feminine Mystique* by Betty Friedan. I was pulled in by the opening words.

> The problem lay buried, unspoken, for many years in the minds of American women. It was a strange stirring, a sense of dissatisfaction, a yearning that women suffered in the middle of the twentieth century in the United States. Each suburban wife struggled with it alone. As she made the beds, shopped for groceries, matched slipcover material, ate peanut butter sandwiches with her children, chauffeured Cub Scouts and Brownies, lay beside her husband at night—she was afraid to ask even of herself the silent question—"Is this all?"

South Africa's white women—Friedan was talking to me as a white woman—did not make the beds. Nor did we eat peanut butter sandwiches. Whether I remained in South Africa or went to the United States, could I avoid the fate described by Friedan? I read the book at a fast clip. When I reached the last pages, I was relieved to read there could be a remedy.

Who knows what women can be when they are finally free to become themselves? . . . Who knows of the possibilities of love when men and women share . . . the responsibilities and passions of the work that creates the human future and the full human knowledge of who they are? It has barely begun, the search of women for themselves. But the time is at hand when the voices of the feminine mystique can no longer drown out the inner voice that is driving women on to become complete.

I closed the book, my heart pounding. Friedan's writing had lit up thoughts hidden in my subconscious mind. Her words unsettled and unmoored me. At the same time, they excited, they inspired. At this point, I did not know much about the United States. I was not thinking race or class. Nor did I recognize the turning point this moment was for me. All I knew was that her writing had carved a space ready to be filled once I got to America.

AT THE END OF MAY 1967, the day before we left Cape Town, Eric and I were married at the magistrate's court. It was rather seedy, not geared for ceremony and celebration, but a place couples scuttled to for a shotgun wedding or a marriage that defied parents and community. Sally and Michael, soon to leave for Montreal, were our witnesses. We celebrated with a champagne lunch at the smartest restaurant in town and then, slightly tipsy, drove to the top of Signal Hill to look out over Cape Town for the last time and take some wedding pictures, the last photos I took in South Africa: me smiling in a green wool-knit dress, my black hair shoulder length and sleek with the help of careful drying so it wouldn't frizz up; my new husband and I with our arms around each other; Sally, leaning over in a goofy position, her long blond hair flowing behind her. I was happy. I was in love. I was about to start a new life.

That night, at a small farewell party, we announced our betrothal. Our hosts opened bottles of champagne from their wine cellar and our friends toasted us, berating us for being so secretive. The next day we set off by train to Johannesburg to board a plane to London and spend time with my parents before the final leg of our journey to the

United States. At the station our friends, some choosing to remain, others planning their escape, waved and waved as the train slowly drew away. Leaning far out the window I waved back, broad smiles on my face, masking a sharp sadness that was stirring in my gut.

As we left Cape Town and the scenery changed to the vast open veld, I felt uneasy despite my happiness. Was I abandoning my country? Should I have remained, toughed it out, contributed in whatever way I could to undoing apartheid? Eric was heading for the future he dreamed of, a place in the world of physics. I was heading for . . . what? I had no idea what lay ahead for me in the United States, only that I was going into self-exile and I would have to create a new home. I would not return until there was democracy.

At that moment I was too quick to assume that I could shed my home like an old skin. I knew what I was heading away from: the mountain, the sea, the earth—a beautiful country distorted by an evil system. But my memories of home—the smells, the tastes, the sounds—would cling to me like an invasive vine, knotting together to produce a yearning that would not dim through the years.

The Karoo, the vast semidesert region of the northern cape that we traversed for hours, presented us with a farewell gift. I expected the scenery I loved: the brown and dry scrubby land where woolly sheep aimlessly grazed among stunted trees; the massive rocks that rose out of the veld; the hard, sandy earth where patchy brown grass took hold; the contorted branchless tree trunks with spiky green fronds that stuck out the top; the flat-topped hills that had defied millennia of erosion, set against distant blue-hued mountains. Instead, the Karoo had been doused with a brief rain storm the day before and bright flowers and wisps of green had broken out of the hard earth overnight. The transformed semidesert was a sea of color, putting on its best face as if to wish me well.

6 — Slowly, Haltingly, I Became Acclimatized

I have been in New York for two weeks and I'm trying to get a handle on how to order from one of the surly guys on the other side of a deli counter on the Upper West Side of Manhattan. Behind an expanse of slanted glass is a mind-boggling array of salads heavy with mayonnaise, slabs of processed ham and turkey, and bricks of bright yellow cheese. Nothing looks very enticing. I think longingly of friendly Milly's, Cape Town's version of the Jewish New York deli, or the Indian grocery store near our cottage where I was made to feel welcome before I even hinted at my order. There would be smiles and politeness and discussions of the weather or some congenial tidbit while I made my purchases. Here in Manhattan at the end of September 1967, I am having to cope with a rush-rush culture. I have tried. I say, "Hello, how are you?" when it comes my turn, anticipating a broad smile or a chatty response. Their irritation makes it clear—I was wasting their time. I'm learning though. When my turn comes, my voice is strong as I call out, "Half a pound of turkey!" And when the package is slapped down on the counter in front of me, I respond without a blink: "A medium container of potato salad!" When the second slap comes, I say, "Thank you," and head for the cashier. I have done it! I have mastered the art of being a customer in a New York deli. Now anything is possible.

MY FIRST WEEKS WENT BY in a blur of strangeness and discord. I had to create a tough skin to withstand the constant grazes and pricks from the external world as I encountered one more bizarre sight, made one more astounding observation. I was on auditory overload: the intense drawls, the overly rolled *r*'s, the strangely pronounced *a*'s—an invasion of American accents that I was unable to differentiate. I had anticipated only mild culture shock. After all, I'd watched American movies and seen the suburban life I was familiar with. I'd read American magazines and found ads for the products I used every day—Colgate toothpaste, Coca-Cola, Lifebuoy soap. I'd grown up reading Nancy Drew mysteries and the adventures of the Bobbsey twins. I'd listened to *Superman* on the radio. This should have been easy.

I was oh so wrong.

Eric and I entered North America through Montreal and spent a few days with Sally and Michael in their new home. Then we drove south to the border in our dark blue Mini Minor station wagon—my parents' wedding present that had accompanied me on an Irish cargo boat across the Atlantic from England—and entered the United States at Plattsburgh. As we drove down the New York Thruway, I gawked at the size of the semis that whizzed by, their drivers honking horns that sounded like foghorns, grinning down at our car, apparently finding its toy size hilarious. We pulled into one of the orange-roofed Howard Johnsons that dotted the highway and ordered breakfast. The coffee was weak, the eggs dry, the white toast paper-thin and tasteless. Nothing like the rich multigrain Cape bread, which was already entering my nostalgia store. I stared in disbelief as people around me tucked into mounds of eggs, bacon, pancakes, toast, and jam. I looked on astonished as diners forked scrambled eggs into their mouths and then added a bite of toast smothered with sweet jam and chewed them together. They might as well have added jam to their eggs while scrambling them. Gross.

It began to dawn on me that I had entered a truly foreign country. It would only become more pronounced in the weeks to follow.

There was the language: shovel for spade, sweater for jersey, candy for sweets, french fries for chips, gas for petrol. There was the pronunciation. One evening I stood before a small cured skin that hung on the wall of the apartment of a new acquaintance. It was silky soft, in hues of brown and white. I couldn't figure out the animal. "What animal skin is this?"

"It's a kaff skin from South America," she told me.

What kind of wild animal was that, I wondered? My associations with the word "kaff" were not easy. "Kaffir"—the K-word akin to America's N-word—was the ultimate in racist slurs. I must have seemed very dim to my host. Looking at me quizzically, she said, "You know, a baby cow." Oh, for God's sake, I thought to myself, as I repeated "cahf" in my head, the *a* drawn out.

Whatever the idiosyncrasies of this country, I had to figure out how to establish my life here in earnest. Eric's student stipend of $250 per month could not support both of us and it was becoming clear that we were overstaying our welcome in the guest bedroom of a friend's cousin's apartment. First I had to find a job. Then we had to find an apartment. And fast. We were rapidly depleting our savings.

Finding a job had been easier than I dared dream. My typing skills provided me once again with a marketable skill. Introduced to the wonders of the *Village Voice* classified section, I scoured ads for secretarial positions that were not corporate or big office. I spotted the one for me: secretary for Two Bridges Neighborhood Council, a community-based organization on the Lower East Side between the Brooklyn and Manhattan bridges. On my way from the subway to the storefront office for an interview I passed tall, unprepossessing public housing complexes, cheek by jowl with tenements and rows of storefronts—Italian bakeries, Chinese restaurants, a clothing store selling African-style dashikis, fish markets, bodegas. It was absolutely nothing like segregated South Africa: an alive, multi-ethnic New York community where African Americans, Chinese, Latino, and working-class whites all lived together. I was hooked. I was offered the job. All I needed was a work permit.

The next day standing in front an official at the immigration office I reported that I had found a job and I wanted to apply for a work permit. "And how do you propose to work if you don't have a green card?" he asked in a patronizing voice.

Green card? I explained that all I wanted was a work permit, not a path to citizenship. And he explained that I could only work if I had a green card. *What?!* How could I be granted a visa but then not be allowed to work? This was irrational and cruel. Panic began to replace jaunty confidence, and I began to get teary. His face softened ever so slightly. He sighed.

"Okay, what job do you have?"

"Secretary for a community organization."

He drew a fat ring binder toward him and flipped through it till he found the page he was looking for. "You're in luck. Secretaries are in short supply in New York at the moment." I looked back at him uncomprehending. "You can apply for a green card as long as your employer can show us that they can't find an American to do the job. Is that clear?"

Clear indeed! As I left the building I passed others waiting in line—Latinos, blacks, Europeans, many not speaking English, some looking defeated—and I had a twinge of guilt. Would he have been so accommodating if I hadn't been who I was? As in South Africa, white privilege ruled the day. I shook off these thoughts as I walked outside and headed back to the Lower East Side to deliver the forms to my new employer. In my exhilarated state I thought: "Well *that* was as easy as pie." American pie.

My salary was $80 a week, one and a half times Eric's stipend. We could begin apartment hunting in earnest. Back to the *Village Voice.* Ever since we arrived in the New York area Eric and I had wanted to live in the fabled center of hip culture, Greenwich Village. We soon discovered that the rents far exceeded the $100 per month we had budgeted. Just as we were giving way to despondency Eric heard about a newly completed middle-income housing project in Hoboken, a few blocks from the Stevens Institute. It wasn't Manhattan but the rent was right. We moved in immediately.

I worked for Two Bridges for two years; there I encountered a level of poverty that I had naively thought I would not find in the United States. At first it wasn't all that obvious. The community activists whose homes I visited had jobs. They were working-class men and women who could support their families without the specter of abject poverty. They could envision a better life for their children and were willing to fight for it within their community. This was the promise of the American dream. Then I began to see deeper into the places where the dream had failed.

At Christmastime Two Bridges received an allocation of toys from one of the city agencies to distribute to the children of needy families. I picked out a number of age-appropriate gifts for the young children of Amelia, a single mother I had befriended. A few days before Christmas I walked to Eldridge Street with its rows of dilapidated tenements, looking for her building. Carrying the bag of wrapped gifts, I climbed the two flights of stairs to her apartment. A dank smell emanated from the stairwell. Each landing was lit by a single bare bulb hanging from the ceiling, accentuating the peeling walls. I knocked on her door and she greeted me with a bright smile of surprise. I stepped into her cramped apartment and immediately felt embarrassed that I had arrived without warning. But when I handed her the presents, she hugged me through her tears. She had no money for presents and she'd been worried sick about her children's disappointment on Christmas morning when there was nothing for them. "I can only thank the Lord for sending you to me," she said. I walked back down the stairs, disturbed that a small, effortless gesture such as mine could mean so much.

Amelia and I had both left the countries of our birth. Eric and I were struggling too, or so we thought. We ate each night. We had money to buy inexpensive Christmas presents. Most of all, we knew this to be a temporary state: once he graduated, he could expect a financially secure future in academia. I could then choose to work or not. For Amelia, poverty defined her life. There was no way out, no choice, no safety net for disaster. Immigration to the United States meant very different things depending on one's race, class, and language. I was taking for granted a future in my adopted country that Amelia could not even contemplate.

SLOWLY, HALTINGLY, I BECAME ACCLIMATIZED. For the first time in my life I did not routinely glance over my shoulder to make sure I wasn't being followed. I no longer needed to head for the bottom of the garden to be out of earshot of bugs—the electronic kind—or monitor what I said on the telephone while listening for telltale clicks.

I wasn't always careful. After D and A was banned and my parents had left South Africa, there was the immediate problem of covering legal fees, so I came up with a great solution—or so I thought. My parents still had money in South Africa. If my father transferred money from his account to the law firm in South Africa that was working on behalf of political activists, he could be reimbursed in London. But how could I explain this scheme to him? Mail sent overseas was regularly opened. So I naively asked an Afrikaner journalist friend who was traveling to London to take my letter and mail it when he got there. It didn't occur to me that, given his strong criticism of the government, he might not be the ideal courier. Perhaps I thought that he was immune because he was an Afrikaner. Had he been searched we would all have landed in jail and my father's money would have been confiscated. Luckily, he read my letter and then burned it—and never spoke to me again.

But now, in New York, I had never known such personal freedom—freedom aided by the nature of the city itself. A city of strangers. A city where strangers found other strangers and so the strange became the familiar.

At the same time my longing for home was still raw. Many a weekend Eric and I drove to Boston, Washington, or Montreal to connect with other South African exiles and émigrés. It was bliss to be able to cook together and recreate our Cape Town dinner parties, drinking California wine (naturally we were boycotting the South African varieties), catching up on our lives, and obsessing about South Africa. Oh, how superior we felt in our little South African enclave. I regaled our friends with stories about the foibles of Americans and the brashness of New York City.

For example, the guy unloading a truck on West 86th Street, who rested his dolly and, shaking his head in mock wonder, blew a five-fingered kiss into the air—*mwah!*—calling out, "*Mama mia!* For you I'd leave my wife, my nine children, *and* my mother-in-law!"

Or the time when I was coming out of the subway at Grand Street and I encountered a man standing at the top of the stairs, his fly open, peeing against the wall. Not wanting to miss the opportunity presented by the arrival of a stream of subway riders, he half-turned his torso and stretched out his free hand, calling out: "Anyone have some spare change?"

Or boarding the F train one morning at West 57th Street together with a posse of policemen in their dark blue uniforms, batons gripped in their hands, hips bulging with guns, walkie-talkies, and other paraphernalia so important to the image of a policeman. They stood looking down at a man stretched out asleep on the bench, his head resting on his hands, his shoes neatly arranged on the floor. I braced myself for an inevitable bullying, a physical shakedown, even handcuffs and a frog march off the train. Instead one of the policemen leaned forward and gently shook the man's shoulder. "Wake up! Wake up!" he said in a strong Brooklyn accent. "Breakfast is being soived." Another policeman held the door open while the napper sleepily put on his shoes and shuffled off the train. Only later did it occur to me that the man was white and so were all the policemen.

Ah, New York, New York. Collecting stories helped me settle into my new life. Yet something was missing from this new life. Leonie's words kept playing in my head: "There is a lot of anti-apartheid work, if that's what you want to do. You can probably make more of a difference outside, you know." I still had to find that "outside."

7 — Anti-Apartheid Activist

I was getting ready to meet Janet McLaughlin at the American Committee on Africa, the stellar, internationally respected anti-apartheid organization. Clothes still boosted my confidence, so I chose carefully from my limited wardrobe: thick black stockings, a short burnt-orange corduroy skirt that I had sewn myself, and a soft black woolen sweater. I made sure my naturally frizzy shoulder-length hair was sleek. I put on my "new" coat, a raccoon fur that I had bought for $35 at a secondhand store on West 8th Street in Greenwich Village. It gave me just the right beat-hippy look I favored and kept me warm as I headed out that frigid winter morning in January 1968 to ACOA's office near the UN.

As I waited for Janet in the front reception area, I looked around. Prestigious address notwithstanding, the place looked just like any anti-apartheid office in South Africa. It had the same feel: mismatched furniture, posters on the walls, a sense of busyness amidst the clutter, books and papers scattered over desks and tables, a typewriter clacking in the background. I found this comforting. Janet was an American, as were all the staff members except one, Jennifer Davis, the part-time researcher, who was a South African exile. She had left with her husband and young children about a year before I did. Not that many exiles were able to come to the United States, unless they were studying or had offers of specific jobs. Britain was bound to South Africa by its colonial past; in the United States, anti-apartheid work was jump-started by a few dedicated Americans—both African American and white—who had been active in the civil rights movement. They came from various political persuasions—pacifism, nonviolent civil disobedience, communism, anticolonialism, the radical black movements of the 1950s and 1960s—but they saw the parallels between racism in the United States and South Africa, parallels that I was only just beginning to grasp.

Janet's workspace off the long, narrow passage was small. She sat behind her desk, her shoulder-length straight light brown hair pulled back, blue eyes focused on me. Just a few years older than I, she radiated confidence and efficiency and with a direct, querying gaze that was taking me in. I was awestruck.

"What can I do for you?" she asked in her deep voice. I took a breath and launched in. "I'm from South Africa," I said, smiling a bit sheepishly, knowing my accent was a giveaway. "I've been here a few months. And I am wondering whether there is anything I could offer to ACOA."

Janet asked a few questions about my background, why I came, what I was doing here. After sizing me up, she said, "There is though something you might be interested in," and went on to tell me about the Southern Africa Committee, which was about to expand its newsletter into a monthly magazine to provide news about a region that was conspicuously absent from the regular media.

"Protest needs to be supplemented by sound information," Janet continued. "Information about the wider struggle against apartheid and the wars of liberation in the Portuguese colonies. Would you like to join us? Your knowledge of South Africa could really help."

Would I indeed? I took down the information for the next meeting two weeks hence and left the office, elated.

I became integrated into the Southern Africa Committee and its dedicated, hardworking volunteers, all with a single purpose of helping to end colonialism in Africa and apartheid. As we planned the new format for the Southern Africa magazine, I was asked to be its editor. "Editor" was a loose term. It was a collective effort by a committee operating on a shoestring, barely able to pay its bills—we were forever one small hop ahead of the printing costs, relying on grants from faith-based organizations and small foundations. Subscriptions added little. My role was to see the process through from start to finish—nagging writers who were invariably tardy with their copy, editing for language and grammar, sending copy to the typesetters, working with a core group late into the night to lay out the magazine—pasting the long strips into columns and using Letraset letters for the headings—and finally sending it off to the printers to be turned into a black-and-white newsprint magazine. At its height we had about five thousand subscribers, mostly academics and activists in the solidarity movement, with some newsstand sales. We sent copies to the offices of the liberation movements of South Africa, Namibia, Zimbabwe, Mozambique, Angola, and Guinea-Bissau in Africa, Europe, and New York, where they had observer status in the United Nations. Much of the content was culled from international newspapers, which paid more attention to the region than the U.S. papers. My father clipped articles from the press in the UK and sent them to me each month in a large manila envelope.

I had arrived in the States believing that if average, peace-loving Americans could only understand the repressive and brutal nature of apartheid, this would spark sufficient sympathy and outrage to pressure their own government, which in turn would pressure the South African government to end apartheid. I was quickly disabused of my naïveté by the other members of the Southern Africa Committee, who viewed U.S. complicity with apartheid as self-evident. This came as a bit of a jolt. Back home I had taken U.S. products for granted: Coca-Cola, Lever Brothers, American gas for my car—it was all just part of trade. But now I was learning that trade wasn't simply trade. I was opening my mind to the fact that United States corporate investment played an important role in expanding the South African economy and bolstering the apartheid system. U.S. and other foreign investment brought increasing capital and, even more significantly, technical expertise that enabled the growth of an efficient modern economy, all the better to invest in. U.S.-manufactured computers were used for the pass system; Polaroid cameras were used to take the photos of the holder of the pass; GM engines were often found in police trucks that arrested anti-apartheid protestors. This support by the U.S. government meant that U.S. corporations were reaping huge profits by investing in South Africa, while South Africa grew stronger and ever more oppressive.

At the same time, I was learning that ongoing wars in countries along South Africa's borders had been launched three years before I left.

I was becoming part of a movement that was global, one bent on isolating the apartheid regime, not just condemning it. In the process, I gained an identity, a mantle I donned comfortably: I was an anti-apartheid activist.

ONE OF THE FIRST PURCHASES ERIC and I had made after moving into our new apartment in Hoboken was a twelve-inch TV set. It cost a week's salary. We turned on the news as soon as we got home (Walter Cronkite vied for our attention with *The Huntley-Brinkley Report*) and checked the pocket-sized TV guide for other programs worth watching. After a lifetime without TV it was easy to become addicts. Blasted out of inward-lookng, local politics into a vast world without parameters, I was slowly learning to absorb and analyze the news from the vantage point of the most powerful nation in the world. Arriving in the United States when we did, at the end of 1967, meant being inducted into the cascading events of 1968, a year that would shape and color the politics, history, and culture of the country for decades to come. I watched, astounded, debates between Black Panthers and white liberals on Channel 13, New York's public media channel, thinking, "Oh my God! What freedom!" These people would be jailed or at least banned back home. It did not take me long to appreciate that "freedom" was not meted out in equal portions. It was a fast-track education and I was sucked right in.

In October 1967, I marched with a hundred thousand others against the Vietnam War. The protestors represented every age, every race, every ethnicity, every economic class—another eye-opener, another mind-extender. Just five months later, President Lyndon Johnson came on the television, his fleshy, solemn face filling our small screen. "I shall not seek, and I will not accept, the nomination of my party for another term as your President," he said. His popularity was at an all-time low because of the war. Protest worked!

Four days later, on April 4, 1968, I turned on the news to hear Walter Cronkite announce the assassination of Martin Luther King Jr.

All hell broke loose. Black ghettos in cities across the nation exploded with anger; looting and burning expressed the sense of helplessness and futility provoked not only by the violent death of a widely revered man committed to nonviolence but by pervasive racism in America. Two months later Robert Kennedy was assassinated. The election of Richard Nixon in 1968 left me angry and apprehensive. I was beginning to adjust to this country, to drive in my first tentative stake, acknowledging that this land could be mine.

Yet there was something missing. The anti-apartheid activism was essentially a movement of activist Americans to which I added my voice. It did not connect me with the struggle back home.

I SIT HIP TO HIP WITH ANC representative Mazisi Kunene, a senior member of the movement, squashed in the backseat of a Volkswagen Beetle. We are returning to New York in February 1969 after a weekend away at a conference on apartheid. For much of the five-hour journey I am a willing listener to the stories he spins about his work, his frequent trips to New York, his mission to raise funds for the ANC through the sale of art. His gentle way, his humor, his roundness, and the growing affection between us as the car speeds south gives me the feeling of finding home. It is known territory. It appears reciprocal, the home connection piquing his interest in me, as someone young enough to mold and draw into the movement. A sister in struggle.

By the time we drive into Manhattan my heart is racing and I feel slightly lightheaded, charged with adrenalin—as if I had just met the man of my dreams. But this isn't about love. It is about having discovered something out there in the world that I can grasp, a new sense of possibility, a connection to home. As I exit the car, Mazisi writes down his number on a scrap of paper and hands it to me.

"Call me," he says. "We have more to discuss. I have work for you to do." I nod and say thank you. We shake hands through the rolled-down window. I pull my bag out of the trunk and head toward the subway. The crisp spring evening air is as inviting as any open veld in South Africa. It is sweet. Life is sweet.

MAZISI BECAME A REGULAR HOUSEGUEST on his visits to New York from London, where he was based, sleeping on the living room couch in our cramped Upper West Side apartment on 104th Street and Central Park West where we had recently moved from Hoboken. Mazisi would invariably walk to the supermarket nearby and return carrying a veritable mountain of food—two chickens, pounds of potatoes, sweet and regular, vegetables of every kind. For the next few hours he would roll up his sleeves and prepare a massive meal fit for twenty. "You never know who might come by," he would say and I would remember the generosity of Africans whose hospitality invariably involved offers of food. "We have to have food to offer." And often people would drop by—members of the movement or sympathetic Americans he had befriended with his charm and allure. Mostly though he was working day and night and wouldn't be home for dinner at all. By the time he left several days later, I had to throw out the leftovers.

I BECAME A WILLING WORKER FOR the movement through my association with him, doing typing and dogsbody labor, but also helping with fundraising, locating African crafts and art for him to sell in the United States, an effort that failed to catch on. He had more success in Europe, where he launched a campaign to sell works donated by known artists.

Our friendship progressed with his visits to New York and with my annual visits to my parents in London. Mazisi introduced me to ANC cadres in both cities as the efforts to raise money continued. I never joined the ANC and he never suggested it. I was comfortable in my unaffiliated status, though I sometimes wonder why. Was I already imaging myself as a journalist, when lack of affiliation would make sense? Was I worried that I, as an obedient girl, would get swallowed up?

I loved his disregard for protocol, his irreverence, and the way he made me laugh. He was already gaining recognition as a poet. His inspiration was his Zulu heritage and he wrote in Zulu. For him African literature held its true essence when written in the original language, whatever it might be. His passion was the epic poem he was writing, *Emperor Shaka the Great*. It would be published in English—his translation—in 1979. This work and the others that followed established him as a great African poet.

On my visits to London we would meet at the ANC office or at his flat near Baker Street or go for walks through the city. On one such walk along Oxford Street, he stopped at a sidewalk cart selling fruit and nuts and pointed to a mound of deep purple grapes. "Two pounds, please," he said, digging into his pocket and bringing out a handful of crumpled notes. The vendor picked three bunches from the pile, weighed them, and placed them in a paper bag. Mazisi took it from him, grinning with expectation. I was taken aback. Shocked! The grapes were clearly labeled with the country of origin: South Africa. I had not bought any South African products since leaving. Here was Mazisi, one of the strongest proponents of the boycott in the UK, who consistently—in the media, at anti-apartheid meetings and rallies—made his "Don't buy South African" pitch. He saw the look on my face and popped a large juicy grape into his mouth, while offering me the open bag. "I think that the boycott is an ex*tremely* important and a brilliant educational tool," he said. "As for me, I do not need to be educated."

I giggled and took a bunch from the bag and together we walked down Oxford Street savoring the burst of sweetness as we indulgently bit into one marble-sized globe after another.

In London five years later, February 1973, I went as usual to visit him soon after landing. He seemed particularly depressed. The awful London weather, typical of late winter, bearing down outside his basement flat made the scene even more dismal. He didn't seem interested in our usually lively catching up. He quickly came to the point. He was engaged to be married, he said. "Given the circumstances," he continued, "it's better that we don't see each other anymore." Circumstances? There weren't any "circumstances" as far as I was concerned. A mutual friend had told me earlier that our friendship had made tongues wag. It was so off point that I never took it seriously and valued our friendship all the more because of the lack of sexual tension. I could do nothing but honor his request. It was the last time I saw him. Soon after, he left his work with the ANC to teach at the University of

California in Los Angeles, reconnecting full-time with his poet self. He would subsequently influence and be revered by a new generation of African writers.

YEARS LATER, IN AUGUST 2006, I was sitting drinking coffee in a suburban mall in Pretoria, waiting for Kendra, who had gone in quest of a pair of jeans. I idly flipped through the daily paper and then stopped, frozen, as a small black-and-white photo of Mazisi stared at me from the upper left-hand side of the page—an older but oh so familiar face. Beneath it was an obituary.

"Mazisi Kunene was one of the greatest figures of South African and African literature," I read. "He made significant contributions to the anti-apartheid struggle from his position within the ANC in exile. Mazisi Kunene was a man and a poet of immense humanity."

Suddenly this affectionate, funny, astute man was there with me again. I recalled how much I had adored this friend, this brother, and how he had influenced my life at a time when I was struggling with self-esteem. He simply acted as if I was already the confident woman I hoped to become. Now he was gone. My regret at never having tried to reconnect with him after the end of apartheid continues to live with me.

8 — We Took Our Cues from the Liberation Movements

G ail Hovey was on a roll. It was the end of April 1970, about a year after I first met Mazisi, and I was learning about a new and quintessential American form of protest: shareholder action. She and other solidarity activists had just come back from a Gulf Oil shareholders meeting in Pittsburgh, Pennsylvania, where they were protesting Gulf's investments in Angolan oil fields. The taxes and royalties that the Portuguese government received from Gulf Oil were significantly bolstering its otherwise failing economy, and thus perpetuating Portuguese colonialism in Angola. Gail sat at the head of a long conference table, occasionally checking her notes, her voice resounding through SAC's unrenovated loft office on West 27th Street as some fifteen of us sat around the table on assorted chairs, riveted by her account. As she talked, her head moved in emphasis, swinging her long brown hair, hanging in a braid down her back.

A national boycott against Gulf Oil was beginning to gain steam. A divestment movement against banks that loaned money to South Africa had already started in the early 1960s and would accelerate a decade later to include corporations doing business there. As a South African I was used to the tactics of strikes, protests, marches, mass meetings, most of which ended in arrests and convictions. But targeting a corporation's shareholders meeting was new to me. As Gail explained, fifty demonstrators had gained access to the meeting by purchasing the smallest number of shares needed to attend, adding to the few bona fide shareholders who were sympathetic to the boycott.

Some wore T-shirts that boldly proclaimed GULF KILLS on the front. They stood out from the regular shareholders dressed in staid business attire.

When the chair called for nominations for the shareholder board, protestors, one after another, jumped to their feet to nominate heads of liberation movements and then describe their bios in detail and read their poems. Angry shareholders yelled back at them: "Sit down!" "Take them out!" "Out of order!" "Where do you come from—Red China?!" Gail overheard one woman say to another: "They are so dumb, they want communism." "Yeah," the other agreed, "they think they can get along without money. Let 'em try!" After two hours of near mayhem, the all-day meeting was adjourned. They had been successful in both disrupting the meeting and bringing the issue to the attention of the shareholders.

Gail and I were slowly getting to know each other as friends, slow because I was intimidated by this poised, self-assured, political, articulate woman who looked with enviable directness at all of us sitting around the table. I met Gail a year after I arrived in the United States when she and her husband, Don, returned from working in South Africa under the umbrella of the Frontier Internship Program of the Presbyterian Church. It was a progressive program designed to engage young people in crucial issues of the day, including race relations, Gail's main interest. To convince the apartheid government to grant them visas and work permits, they needed a cover, so they made arrangements to work at an African school in the north that had been founded by Swiss missionaries at the turn of the twentieth century. Don worked as chaplain and Gail with women in the community. Before they could complete their two-year contract, they were accused by the Department of Bantu Education of "violating the customs and traditions of the country" and had to leave their work assignment early. Now back in New York, they were living in East Harlem where Don was a pastor at a Baptist church and Gail dedicated herself to being a writer and working with the Southern Africa Committee, which she had helped found.

The first time Eric and I invited them for dinner, the men engaged in an earnest discussion about the Vietnam War and Nixon's escalation in Cambodia, big news at the time, with Gail contributing and making sure she didn't let the men dominate the conversation. We had just eaten a delicious meal—my skills as a cook had improved—and I found myself nodding off. This was my escape mechanism when the conversation seemed to rise above my head. Later, when we became closer, Gail told me that I had lain down on the floor under the table "like a pet dog!" (She wasn't the only one of my friends to comment about my sleeping-at-dinner-parties habit. Sally insisted that in South Africa I went to sleep under a grand piano.) "When I first knew you, I thought you were shorter than me," she said. Only later did she realize that, at five feet, eight and a half inches, I had her beat by two inches. And when we embarked on our friendship-for-life in the months following that dinner she also came to realize that I could be funny and sparkly and assertive in my own way. For my part I discovered that this woman I thought was invincible had her own vulnerabilities—as did most of the women of our generation. Discovering that I was not alone in harboring a fragile self-esteem, particularly when dealing with dominating men, was part of my feminist awakening.

THE TWENTY OR SO MEMBERS Southern Africa Committee were mostly Americans in their twenties, white and black, more women than men. Initially I was the only South African in the collective; in time Jennifer Davis became active as well. Like the other solidarity and activist organizations of the time, the anti-apartheid movement had its share of fracturing, dividing activists along race and ideological lines. As a white South African I was not immune to hostile comments directed at me by African Americans who presupposed that because of my whiteness, I had to be party to the apartheid system at some level, and therefore should not be so bold as to be involved in anti-apartheid work in the United States. Some contended that anything related to Africa belonged to the domain of African Americans. This continued throughout the years of anti-apartheid organizing. At first it offended me; I would feel defensive: South Africa is *my* country. How ignorant! But as I learned more about the complexity of American history—the legacy of slavery on the generations that followed, the strength of the civil rights movement, the growth of the Black Power movement—I appreciated how racism penetrated the fabric of American society and cut deep into the culture and history of the country. As in South Africa, white privilege was as taken for granted as breathing air. The struggle for equality and justice was as valid here, even if the context was different, as it was in Africa. In some ways, it was a tougher struggle, both because of the need to challenge the underlying mythology of a democratic America—a just nation where everyone is free and equal—and because, unlike in Africa, blacks in America were in the minority.

I met a number of young black South Africans; most were on scholarships to study in the United States. When they discovered that I was from "home" there were delighted whoops of *Sister!* Back slaps. Hugs. I would be eagerly questioned about where I grew up, what I did, what I was doing here. They were as eager to answer my questions about how they came to be in this country. Many had been underground members of the ANC and PAC and had had to flee into exile when their activism meant certain arrest. Some had done stints in prison. They longed for home, and all they needed to know to consider me a sister was that I was South African and I hated apartheid. At parties we danced ourselves numb with exhaustion to the beat of South African music. I listened to tales of being hounded by the Special Branch and of time in prison. There were hair-raising stories of demonic wardens—"Remember so-and-so when he would do such-and-such?"—withdrawal of food, bouts of solitary confinement for not complying with the strict rules, withdrawal of privileges such as receiving or sending letters. They bent back and laughed raucously, slapping their thighs with the memories they found hilarious. It was the first of many times that I would encounter the way in which impossibly painful circumstances were turned into comedy.

Their laughter was also reserved for their fellow students' ignorance about Africa. "They ask us if we speak Swahili!" believing that Swahili was a lingua franca of Africa, not a language restricted to the east coast. We exchanged other stories: how Americans often asked us, "But what country in South Africa are you from?" There were different countries in South America, why not South Africa? For me, this would often be followed by: "But where are you *really* from?" "South

Africa." Trying to make sense of my whiteness, they would persevere: "Then where are you grandparents from?" "Lithuania." "Aha!" they would exclaim. I was finally making sense. "So you're Lithuanian." I gave up.

African American friends and activists had their own battles to fight. One afternoon I was walking to the SAC office with a fellow member of the committee who was black, talking animatedly, when another young black man hissed as he passed: "Have some self-respect, brother. Get your head straight!" We continued walking, now in silence, my friend's seething fury enveloping us. A few days earlier we had been visiting a friend on the Upper West Side. He was standing in front of me when the elevator door opened and a young girl holding a kitten was about to step out. She froze, clutched the kitten tightly to her chest, her face blanched. Then she spied me and relaxed. A young black man with a white woman companion was either a traitor to his race or rendered nonthreatening.

As activists supporting the liberation struggles we believed we did have our "heads straight." We took our cues from the African liberation movements and their leaders. We avidly read their texts, speeches, and other writings which helped shape our thinking and analysis. When I left South Africa in 1967 I was unaware that wars of liberation were being waged so close to home. Three years earlier, on my trip up the east coast on my way to Europe, the ship had anchored overnight in Lourenço Marques, the capital of Mozambique. To South Africans, "LM" seemed like such a cosmopolitan city, with its Portuguese flair. The beaches were integrated, the cafés were integrated, and South Africans, particularly those from landlocked Johannesburg, used it as their personal playground. Men, bent on the thrill of forbidden sex with African women, snuck across the border to indulge their pleasures without fear of arrest. When I arrived in the United States, I knew nothing about the armed struggles being waged against Portuguese colonial oppression by Frelimo, the Mozambique Liberation Front, or the MPLA, the People's Movement for the Liberation of Angola, or PAIGC, the African Party for the Independence of Guinea and Cape Verde.

All this became more real in February 1969, when I literally sat at the feet of Amilcar Cabral, a personal hero and founder of PAIGC.

One of the benefits of living in the city was the regular visits by leaders of the liberation movements, who had observer status at the UN, to address the United Nations, so we in the movement often got to meet them. Now activists and supporters packed into Jennifer Davis's living room. Jennifer, a full-time research director with ACOA, had become one of my closest friends, one of those friendships that became family in the absence of blood relatives. Her apartment on Riverside Drive and West 86th Street, with its view of the Hudson River, served as a hub for revolutionary traffic passing through New York, providing a meeting space and often a bed for representatives of the movements as well as the South African Trade Unions, and other anti-apartheid organizations and activists. Seated on folding chairs and on the floor, we listened keenly as we learned face-to-face about the progress of their work and the importance to them of our own solidarity work, and we would leave reinvigorated.

Amilcar Cabral's profound analytical prowess and vision of revolution made him the doyen of the liberation movement's leaders. With seeming ease, he could turn complex ideology and political analysis into simple words that gave us the wherewithal to argue, reasonably eloquently and cogently, the importance of supporting their struggle. My copy of Cabral's *Revolution in Guinea: Selected Texts* was held together with rubber bands, the spine cracked and the binding unglued, the pages grown yellow with use and the margins filled with my scribbling. His words slipped into our language, to be retrieved when we spoke about African revolutions. Though I longed for a democratic South Africa, I heeded his caution that people were not fighting simply for ideas: "They are fighting to win material benefits, to live better and in peace, to see their lives go forward, to guarantee the future of their children." It was for this that they waged an armed struggle, he said.

Listening to Cabral was one of those few moments in my life when I knew I was in the presence of a great human being. He talked about the reluctance of his movement to resort to armed struggle, but that the brutality, violence, and destruction of the Portuguese regime left them no choice; he talked about the importance of our solidarity with his revolution and the strength the people took from it; he talked about the new nation that was emerging in the liberated zones, the areas of the country that were under PAIGC control, where schools and health care were being provided to the peasants for the first time. Progress, he told us, was built on a deliberate and careful process of winning over the people. A revolution without the total support of the people, one that was top-down and dictatorial, could never succeed.

Then he turned to a subject that I was hoping for: women's participation. Women were fully engaged, he said. They had needed little encouragement. It was they who insisted on an equal role with men in the movement. The seed of feminism that had been sowed within me when I first read Betty Friedan in Cape Town was taking root. Conversations and heated debates were becoming commonplace among American women drawn to feminism. And here was a man articulating what we were grappling with, but in a revolution in a tiny African country. I wanted to know more. How was it possible to change the patriarchy of African society? Did the fight against colonialism mean that it would be easier to establish a new society that was able to counter deep-seated cultural attitudes? It was hard enough to dislodge patriarchy in the United States. Could this small African country achieve what we could only dream of?

Fresh in my mind was a conversation I had recently had over a drink with a high-level ANC leader, introduced to me by Mazisi, who was attending a session of the United Nations. I had just finished reading a memoir by Helen Joseph, a British woman who, after immigrating to South Africa, had thrown her energies into the struggle against apartheid and been hounded by the security police as a result. She described the women's march on Pretoria on August 9, 1956, which she had co-led with Lilian Ngoyi, Sophie Williams, and Rahima Moosa—four women, White, African, coloured, and Indian. Over twenty thousand women, mostly African, marched on the seat of the government in Pretoria. There they assembled in front of the pillared edifice of the Union Buildings to protest the extension of the pass laws to women. They carried thousands of petitions to be handed to the then prime minister, J. G. Strijdom, and stood for thirty minutes in total silence to emphasize their message. I was twelve at the time.

"I can't believe I knew nothing about this march until recently," I admitted. "Tell me about it."

He remembered it well, he said. "My wife was one of the organizers. She and the other organizers were totally consumed by it. Us men, we got nervous. We weren't sure they realized how dangerous it could be. We wanted to provide security. But when I asked her what we could do to help, you know what she told me?" An annoyed edge crept into his voice. "She told me that if the men wanted to help we could look after the children!" Fifteen years later the memory still rankled. Then repeating the ANC line, he added, "Women's equality is of course important. But first we have to overthrow apartheid so that it is not divisive. Then we can work toward equality for all."

How different an approach from Cabral's insistence that PAIGC involve women as equals in the struggle from the very beginning. After leaving Jen's apartment, a group of us crammed into the backseat of a friend's car and drove through the cold and snowy streets of New York City. The car buzzed with exhilaration as we recapped the evening.

"We must admit he is a good politician," a voice, tinged with skepticism, pronounced from the front seat. "He said just what we wanted to hear about women! No doubt he knows that this is a big issue in America at the moment." Her tone made it clear that she, at least, had not been fooled. I didn't doubt what he was saying. The question for me was how? How to achieve what we in the United States were only beginning to challenge. Her comment irked me for the rest of the ride home.

I regarded myself as both a feminist and a socialist. While I adopted the term "Marxist," I would have had a problem offering a sound Marxist analysis of the world around me. The principles, though, made sense. I was attracted by the notion that workers should own the means of production and benefit from their labor, rather than all the wealth go to their employers, the corporations, the capitalists. Since leaving South Africa I had tried to place the question of justice at the center of my choices and actions, and Marxist principles embodied justice. It extended to my feminism that was becoming an intrinsic part of my worldview. It was not about piecemeal change but about changing the whole political, economic, and social system which was threaded with gender inequality and discrimination.

My new awareness seemed to constantly place me on the edge of fury. My body would stiffen when men hissed or shouted comments as I walked past; I would shout back or give them the middle finger and walk on. Walking the streets of Manhattan could feel like running a gauntlet of male invective and aggressive invasions of my space, my body: The man who jammed himself up against me in the crowded subway, so that even when I realized it wasn't his umbrella against my thigh, I was unable to move. The young man showing off to a handful of ten- and eleven-year-old boys in his charge, who came up behind me and pushed up against me. I shouted at him to get away while the kids laughed, and one of them retorted: "It was only through your coat!"

Walking near Columbia University in a Latino neighborhood where a group of young men hung out in front of a bodega, I felt the usual sense of invasion when offensive mouth-sucking noises and comments followed me. One of the young men called out in a more inquiring tone: "Why are you so unfriendly to us?" I snarled back, "I'll be friendly when you don't single women out and treat us like sex objects." I looked back at him. His face fell as if I had slapped it. What I hadn't noticed was that he was in a wheelchair. I walked on mortified, tears in my eyes, feeling as if I had overstepped a mark although not clear about what that mark was. I began to wonder about the patriarchy that gives rise to machismo. Something more was needed than shouting back. It would take some years for feminists to integrate the new concept of gender into our thinking. We needed gender equality, and to get it, men had to be included in the equation and take on the responsibility of identifying and challenging a culture that gave rise not just to their machismo but to violence against women and girls.

IT IS THE SPRING OF 1972 and I am on my lunch break, sitting with Suzette Abbott on a grassy verge near Columbia University. Suzette is South African; she has been in the United States for about six months. She came to New York as part of the same two-year Frontier Internship program that sent Gail and Don to South Africa.

Later I would learn that she had grown up in a family that resolutely bought the apartheid line, but through her own innate sense of injustice began to see the reality of South Africa. One of the moments that changed her life was a talk she attended by the Reverend Beyers Naudé, an Afrikaner cleric and theologian renowned for his strong anti-apartheid views and activism. She felt challenged to reconcile two incompatible interpretations of apartheid and, as a result, began to reject the warped version of South Africa that had been her reality since childhood. She was horrified by the truth and became radicalized. Hers was a different path than mine to anti-apartheid activism, one that required the courage to denounce all that she had been taught to believe and risk alienation from her family and isolation from the only community she had known. When we met soon after she arrived in New York I instantly felt that tingle of connection I often had with women I sensed were like-minded.

Now, warmed by the sun, we talked about the women's movement. "It's the first time as a white South African that I feel I can legitimately be part of a movement that is important to me," she said.

But if we identify with the women's movement, what are we going to do about it? As a start, we both agree, we should join the many, many women throughout the country who are starting groups. We are serious women. We would form a study group. (We would lose this sense of superiority once the group starts and becomes a hybrid of study and consciousness raising.) Between bites of our sandwiches we begin jotting down potential friends to invite. I am unaware that this would turn out to be one of the defining moments of my life. The group would eventually trim down to a core of five women friends who would in time provide a safe haven from which I could push and test myself: three South Africans, Suzette, Jennifer, and myself; two Americans who were members of the Southern Africa Committee, Janet and Gail. But at this moment taking in the sun we don't foresee any of this.

THE YEAR 1972 CHARTED A NUMBER of feminist milestones. NOW, the National Organization for Women, was gaining strength. In the spring *Ms.* magazine blew onto the scene with its iconic cover: a pregnant woman in the style of an Indian goddess with eight arms, each hand holding an item that reflected the weight of women's work—the housewife's moment of truth. The Feminist Press, founded two years earlier, was fulfilling its mission by reprinting feminist classics that provided grist for another milestone: the establishment of women's studies departments at universities and colleges throughout the country. There were many other firsts: feminist bookstores, battered women's shelters, rape crisis centers, and, after the passing of *Roe v. Wade* in 1973, abortion clinics. Lesbians were coming out and demanding their rights and influencing the women's movement. American and world history was being reexamined, reanalyzed, and retold. Gender-neutral terms—Ms., humankind, mail carrier, fire fighter, police officer—were being adopted, often to be met with derision or amusement before becoming accepted and commonplace.

At SAC, men and women worked alongside each other on the magazine with no discernible tension. The women, who were in the majority, were the ones to assert leadership, Gail and Janet in particular, two very forceful women. Men were active too, but somehow we struck a balance. In many other political organizations, however, women were often relegated to typing, taking minutes, cooking, and other service work and at the same time expected to take on the sexual revolution, which meant, for the most part, being available to men. I felt fortunate to be part of a collective where this was not an issue. My stronger self that emerged from being active in the anti-apartheid movement and the women's movement was helped by finding out that self-doubt was common among women like me.

One afternoon I sat in the backseat of a black Volkswagen Beetle heading down Broadway on the Upper West Side. Barbara and Sally were sitting in the front—both American women who impressed and consequently intimidated me with their unfaltering confidence, their ability to articulate their feminism and general left politics with an assurance that I envied.

"Every day I expect that I will be found out for the fraud I am," I heard Sally say. "I just can't help doubting myself all the time."

Barbara agreed. "Yes," she said. "I feel exactly the same. I do my work, I engage with the world and keep wondering, 'When will they find out that I am putting them on? That I am really a fake?'"

Their words, uttered so casually and convincingly, hung in the car as I tried to make sense of them, sentiments I thought only applied to me. It was an epiphany. Could it be that the insecurities and diffidence that had gripped me were not mine alone? It was a freeing moment. The closer I got to women who were, like me, exploring their feminism, the more I realized that most of us, even those I regarded as the epitome of strength and self-confidence, harbored similar soft underbellies of doubt. Willing to share our personal demons, we could support each other in banishing them. At the same time, my new self-assurance came with a certain arrogance, one that could be downright self-righteous. I expressed it in ways that now make me cringe.

My South African friend Sally became pregnant soon after arriving in Canada. She was twenty-six when she gave birth to her first daughter. When she called me to tell me she was pregnant again, two years later, I responded in a superior tone that I hoped she would find suitable day care as there was work to do, a revolution to fight. I was twenty-five at the time and finding my new legs on feminist terra firma. I gave in to an attitude that prevailed among many of us, I am ashamed to admit, that led some women who had children to feel ostracized and dismissed by the women's movement. (This was not Sally, though: she forged ahead and got involved with the Canadian women's movement from its early days.)

With hindsight, I can understand that my reaction to Sally's pregnancy was due in good part to envy. When I arrived in the United States I fantasized about having my own children, but now I was beginning to have doubts about whether Eric was the man I wanted to be the father of my children. I suppressed this thought, but it surfaced when Sally told me she was pregnant for a second time. Sally had the grace to remind me of this only when my own daughter was born many years later. I remembered none of it, although I could acknowledge how hurtful it must have been. Happily, our friendship survived and mellowed. My marriage did not.

Slowly, with a growing community of feminist friends, I was able to ease the longing created by the holes that remained when I uprooted myself from South Africa. Eric had no such longing. He had left South

Africa and his life there behind. He was something of a Renaissance man, with his love for classical music, philosophy, literature, world affairs, and of course physics and science in general. He delved into these interests, but did not share my sense of purpose to change the world, or at least South Africa. He was more of a skeptic, whereas I was a true believer. Slowly, imperceptibly, cracks began to show themselves in our relationship.

9 — "Well, It's *My* Turn Now!"

I am standing over the stove, sautéing onions, garlic, ginger, and turmeric until they are just the right light brown color for a South African chicken curry. The kitchen is barely that, just a space at the end of the passage, with a narrow stove, a sink jammed next to it, small cupboards above. Spoons, egg lifters, spatulas, strainers, whisks, and a row of pottery coffee mugs dangle from the brightly painted blue pegboard mounted on the wall between the stove and the fridge. The first-floor apartment has one tiny bedroom, a small windowless bathroom, and a living room just slightly larger than the bedroom, each with metal-framed windows that open onto a narrow shaft between buildings. An unhealthy carpet of garbage—paper, discarded clothes, broken household stuff, food containers—covers the ground below.

It is the spring of 1972. The meal I am preparing is for Alec, a Cape Town friend who immigrated to Toronto around the same time we left Cape Town. He and Eric sit at the dining table, a product of street scrounging that now, with its flaps up, occupies much of the living room space. They are deep in conversation, catching up on their various academic exploits, while I continue to cook. Eric is telling him that after four and a half years he can see the end of his dissertation beckoning. He's in a reflective mode, already considering his next steps: where he will apply for jobs, the kind of university post he hopes to get. We had long since put aside the idea of returning to England. The thought of uprooting ourselves again had ceased to be appealing. For both of us—Eric and his research, me and my involvement in the women's movement and the solidarity work—the United States was the place to be.

"We've had to ditch our plan to buy a secondhand car and travel for six months through Asia," Eric is saying, with no apparent regret in his voice. This had been our long-promised reward for our years of frugal existence. For Eric it is no longer feasible: he couldn't opt out of the system for even six months. He has to apply for a job and go for the best offer. "It's like running up a down escalator," he says. "You can't stop. If you do, you are taken down. You lose out." Alec, who is completing a PhD in psychology, nods in agreement.

I had heard this before. This time, my new independent self reacts both to the loss of a dream and to the casual way it's been tossed aside. I throw down the spoon with a clatter and turn to glare at Eric. "Well, it's *my* turn now," I say. "I have worked to put you through university. Now I want something for *me!*" I am amazed by what has come out of my mouth. But I can't stop. "You can get your job. I'm going to travel in Africa."

I pronounce this with such vehemence that I silence the men. I remember a similar silencing a few months earlier when Eric and I were having dinner at the apartment of one of his South African physics buddies, a student at Columbia University. A group of us were cooking together, men and women wedged into the narrow New York apartment kitchen. A discussion—of what I no longer remember—raged around me. I wanted to contribute, but the men were holding fast to their ground and not letting women's voices in. I took the metal spoon I was using to stir a large pot of soup and banged it sharply against the rim of the pot. It clanged like a gong. "I have something I want to say!" I said. Silence fell and the men looked aghast at my outburst. But they listened as I made my point. For one of the first times ever I had asserted myself in an intellectual conversation. I tasted an inner freedom.

"Way to go!" Alec says after a moment, grinning at my outburst. His tone of voice suggests he is impressed by the new Stephanie. Until that moment, I had not realized how tenacious my desire to travel in Africa had become, how it had grown from a teasing thought that flitted in out of my mind to a steadily mounting desire that had to be assuaged.

THE FIRST ORDER OF BUSINESS was to save enough money to

cover the airfare and months of travel. Soon after becoming an official alien with a green card, I had left Two Bridges for a job with American Documentary Films, which distributed films on progressive issues of the day for showings at meetings, classes, gatherings by faith-based organizations, community groups, colleges, high schools. The reels were shipped around the country by Greyhound bus in large gray metal cases.

The office was housed in a brownstone on West 82nd Street. One morning shortly after I started working there, I walked up the stone stairs and rang the doorbell as usual, waiting to be let in. The door was opened by a new person, half turned in animated conversation with someone behind him. I almost gasped. Standing in front of me was an incredibly good-looking young man, with sparkling blue eyes, all the more evident against his lightly tanned face and blond hair. He broke off in midsentence and grinned. We introduced ourselves. John. Stephanie. He was a Canadian from Montreal who had arrived that morning from the San Francisco office. A few days later I was less enamored. We sat around a large table in the dining room at the end of one of our staff meetings. The subject of South Africa came up. "Apartheid is genocide," pronounced John, with all the certainty of his twenty-five years and dogmatic politics. I was irritated. What an ignorant Canadian! I launched into an attack on his perspective that was as dogmatic as his—but of course *I* was right. Apartheid was bad enough. Neither of us gave an inch. After harboring my irritation for a few days, I found myself alone with him at the same table. He began to ask me questions about myself—gentle, interested questions. "Hmm," I thought, "there is another side to this man." I began to seek him out for similar conversations, and slowly a strong friendship grew between us over the year I continued to work there, our first altercation forgotten.

I threw myself into the work completely, but there was one hitch: ADF was in serious financial trouble. Promised royalties were seldom paid to filmmakers; rent was delayed; only necessities, such as paying for shipment of the documentaries—our raison d'être—came before anything else. Checks bounced, threatening notices mounted, and whatever was available at the end of the week was divvied up among the staff. Clearly continuing to work at ADF was not going to get me to Africa. After one year, I reluctantly gave notice.

For the next eighteen months, I worked as a secretary to the librarian at the School for International Studies (now the School for International and Public Affairs) at Columbia University. Besides being able to put away money each month, I could enroll in courses for free. I took two—one in anthropology and one in African history. I had to corral all my emotional and intellectual strength to actually write my first history paper. I was immobilized by flashbacks of my disastrous efforts at UCT. Only when the deadline loomed could I finish it, working late into the night and driven by mild panic. When the paper was returned to me with a bold A in red at the top I almost wept. I walked away clutching the fifteen pages to my chest, breathing hard, feeling a sense of release. Perhaps I wasn't as dim as I assumed. When I got an A for my next course, my confidence was reinforced. I set a plan: I would complete my undergraduate degree at Columbia when I got back from Africa and follow it with a graduate degree in social work, to pursue my interest in community organizing.

First I had to get Africa out of my system. With Eric's encouragement, I was preparing to leave in February 1973. I had saved $2,000, enough to cover my airfare to Africa and my transportation and daily expenses on the continent for close to six months. I wanted to at least discover part of the continent I was born on. I wanted to smell the earth and the air and once again walk on the vast open expanses of Africa. I wanted to feel the wind off the Indian Ocean and the sand between my toes as I walked the beaches. I wanted to counter my faulty education, which skimmed over the continent as a mere space between South Africa and Europe, where "true" civilization reigned. I longed to be among Africans again, to talk with those who were committed to liberation struggles from Africa itself, and explore countries that had pried loose the yoke of colonial rule.

A few weeks before I was to leave on my journey, I was back in Jennifer's living room listening to Amilcar Cabral once again engage with a large group of activists and admirers. He spoke of substantial gains: PAIGC had liberated two-thirds of the country and only a few major towns remained under Portuguese control. When the meeting was winding down, a friend and I approached him. We asked him to elaborate on what he'd said about women's participation in his revolution. In response, he took out a manila envelope from his briefcase and withdrew about a dozen eight-by-ten-inch photographs. He pointed to women in each photo, telling us their names and describing their work. Some were addressing meetings of peasants; some were running health centers; some were teachers; others were mobilizers at the community level. Many held babies in their arms or tied to their backs as they worked. Some had revolvers in holsters strapped to their waists. He spoke with evident pride. When he put away the photographs we thanked him while he maneuvered himself out of Jennifer's low-slung couch. My friend and I looked at each other and grinned: the liberation of women was alive and well in Guinea-Bissau and a major aspect of their revolution.

Then tragedy struck.

It was January 20, 1973. I was in Boston at a housewarming party given by two South African friends, Margie Marshall and Sydney Shapiro. The living room of their recently renovated South End brownstone was packed with South Africans and Americans. We danced and ate, danced and drank, danced and talked. Sid and I danced to the chants of "down, down, down," as we bent our legs to get closer to the ground. He had more than a decade on me in years, but his legs were stronger and I collapsed laughing while he continued his way down. Richard Nixon had been inaugurated that day for his second term as U.S. president after winning by a huge landslide. The liquor helped us ward off an underlying sense of foreboding, so we danced a bit harder, drank a bit harder, laughed a bit harder.

The phone rang around eleven o'clock cutting through the din. Margie went to answer it, listened a moment, then agitatedly pumped her hand, palm down, to get someone to lower the volume. She stood with her ear to the receiver, saying nothing. Then with an anguished "Thank you for letting us know," she said, slowly returning the receiver to its cradle. "That was Bob Van Lierop," she said, referring to a well-known activist. "Cabral is dead. He was shot a few hours ago." She fought for control. "He was assassinated."

We stood like statues, disbelieving. Some began to cry. I continued to stand, unable to move. Anger and sorrow rooted me to the spot. All I could think was that our hero was dead. Africa, and the world, had lost one of its finest visionaries and leaders. We knew that the perpetrators could only be the Portuguese regime. Just four years earlier, in February 1969, they had assassinated Eduardo Mondlane, the president of Frelimo, with a parcel bomb. It was an event that shook the solidarity movement in New York at a time when I was just beginning to learn about the struggles against Portuguese colonialism. This time it was Cabral. How had they managed it?

We would find out the next day. Cabral was dropping off his wife, Ana Maria, at their house on the outskirts of Conakry, the capital of Guinea, where PAIGC had its headquarters. From there he was heading to a meeting. Despite the number of threats to his life over the years, Cabral shunned bodyguards. His motto was "Trust the people." So it was just him, his wife, and his driver when they were accosted, late at night, by three PAIGC members in an army vehicle. They trained their guns on Cabral and ordered him to follow them. Cabral refused. He tried to talk them out of it. A burst of gunfire hit Cabral in the head and he fell backward. The glasses he was never without lay next to him in a pool of blood.

The assassins, discontented party members in search of an accommodation with Lisbon and personal gain, were caught the following day. The Portuguese regime anticipated that by getting rid of Cabral they would bring about the collapse of the liberation movement, replacing the leadership with their puppets. They miscalculated. They failed to take into account how well the foundation of the party had been laid. In response the armed struggle gained strength, not only in Guinea-Bissau but in Mozambique and Angola as well.

Four weeks later, on February 15, 1973, and five years, five months, and two weeks after I entered the United States for the first time, I boarded a plane for the initial leg of my journey back to Africa, to four countries that would give me a glimpse into my continent's diversity. Ahead of me lay Egypt, Ethiopia, Kenya, and Tanzania.

Part Two

10 — "Welcome to Cairo!"

From my window seat, I stare into the pitch-black void as my plane flies toward Cairo. I have entered a state of emotional weightlessness, suspended between the life I have just left and the unknown one I am about to enter. The last few weeks recede into a blur. Preparations filled the hours and days as I became preoccupied with what to take, what to buy, what to ignore, what to let go of as time ran out. My first purchase was a large blue backpack with many pockets which I began to fill with toiletries and antibiotics in case of an attack of dysentery, comfortable walking shoes and sandals, a rain jacket and an umbrella. Clothes vied for space with a flashlight and batteries, a tightly rolled sleeping bag, a towel, notebooks, writing paper and envelopes, a small, battery-operated shortwave radio, a camera and rolls and rolls of film. Books for the inevitable slow or hard times—de Beauvoir's memoirs and her novel, *The Mandarins*, as well the first volume of Anaïs Nin's memoir. At the bottom of the backpack I stowed a dozen current issues of *Southern Africa*. Somehow I managed to get it all in.

The shoulder bag nudging my feet under the seat in front of me contains critical see-me-through items: a list of contacts for each of the countries I will visit, travelers checks, letters attesting that I am a "good" South African, including one from ANC president Oliver Tambo arranged by Mazisi, and my U.S. travel documents. If I had been traveling on my South African passport alone, I would have been persona non grata in most African countries, but my U.S. green card entitled me to a document issued by the Department of Justice that made it possible for me to travel anywhere on the continent.

Though I am outwardly calm on the flight as the hours ticked by, my heart feels as if it will leap out of my chest. During my last days in familiar territory, I had no time to soberly consider what it was I was actually setting out to do: a lone female figure bent under the weight of a heavy backpack, traveling down the east coast of Africa. That would only be revealed as I traveled—as the physical and cultural topography changed, as I encountered unfamiliar languages, dress, and demeanor, as skin tones grew darker. A mosaic of new experiences, sights, and sounds would coalesce, transitioning me from who I was into who I would become.

The plane lands at midnight. I descend the metal stairs onto the tarmac and place one foot in front of another, my left shoulder sagging under the weight of my carry-on bag. Africa stretches south, mile by mile, over mountains and vast stretches of land covered in rock and trees and shrubs; across rivers wide and deep, narrow and dry; through veld and scrub and cultivated fields—food crops, cotton, cocoa, peanuts, coffee—over land that hides oil and diamonds and gold, rich veins striking deep down, to Cape Town, the southernmost point of Africa.

I follow the passengers into a long line that moves slowly until it's my turn. The immigration officer in his less than crisp uniform takes my travel document with a puzzled look. His forehead furrows as he examines the cover of this larger-than-passport-sized document with the words "United States Department of State" printed in big letters on the front. He opens it up to peruse the pale green pages, one at a time, pausing to check every visa—Egypt, Ethiopia, Kenya, Tanzania—and then turns to the back page headed "Important Information," which states that I will not be readmitted to the United States if I commit a felony; if I am a "criminal, immoral, insane, mentally or physically defective alien"; or if I am "afflicted with loathsome or contagious diseases." He calls his superior over. Oh no! Was it a pipe dream to think I could travel on this strange-looking document? What should I do—ask to be put on a plane to Addis or Kenya, where perhaps I would be accepted? Already rejected by Egypt, how likely was it that another country would take a chance with me? I try to remain expressionless. The two men confer in Arabic, unhurriedly paging through my document. Then to my relief the officer stamps my passport with a loud thump. "Welcome," he says. "Welcome to Egypt!"

I collect my backpack and enter into the chaos of Cairo's shabby airport. All is confusion—people on the move weaving in and out of people milling around, mostly men in flowing djellabas, talking, shouting, gesticulating. Squeaky wheels of rusty luggage carts. Porters sizing up the travelers with sharp eyes, eager to grab their luggage for pennies. Taxi drivers lined up like a phalanx, vying for passengers. I choose one who seems less pushy and give him the name of the hotel recommended as good and cheap by a friend. The driver whose English consists of maybe twenty words nods his head in approval. "Hotel good," he proffers. He drives up in front of a grand façade. He removes my backpack from the trunk and follows me inside, his engine still running.

The man behind the counter sleepily mutters the cost of a room: $16 per night. What was my friend *thinking*? My budget of $10 a day will only be doable if I keep counting my pennies. My exhaustion and dilemma bring me close to tears. Should I stay just one night and look for a cheaper hotel the next day? If so, where would I even begin? At this rate I would deplete my $1,500 in travelers checks in no time. I stand frozen. The driver senses there is something wrong.

"Too expensive," I tell him and shake my head as I rub my thumb and first finger together in the universal sign for money. Without a word, he picks up my pack and we return to his car. I sit back as he takes me on a night tour of Cairo, stopping in front of small hotels, indicating with his hands that I should wait while he sprints in. He repeatedly returns, head shaking. Too expensive. Unsafe. Not clean. I am losing faith when he returns to the car, beaming. This one, a five-floor hotel with signs of depleted colonial grandeur, has passed his muster. It is $2 per night, including breakfast. I thank him and he gives me a satisfied grin. "Welcome to Cairo," he says and bows his head slightly in acknowledgment of what I hope is a decent tip. I follow the bellhop into the elevator that creaks its way to the fourth floor. It is well after 2:00 a.m. Exhausted, I get between the worn, clean sheets on the narrow bed and fall asleep.

FOUR HOURS LATER, at six o'clock, I was slowly drawn out of my dreams by a sound that penetrated every corner of the room: the sonorous call to morning prayer from a nearby mosque, echoed by others farther away. I crossed the mosaic tile floor in my bare feet and threw open the shutters for my first view of Cairo: Buildings crowding into each other, most low, some taller. Minarets atop mosques in all directions, sharp against the pale blue sky, competing for the purest call. Carts filled with goods—some donkey-drawn, some pushed by their owners. An occasional battered car, bicycles with shrill bells, and the sound of Arabic, still ringing harsh to my unaccustomed ear, traveling up from the narrow street below my window.

After a breakfast of greasy fried eggs and thick slices of cold toast, I asked the man at reception to write out in Arabic the name and address of the hotel and then stepped out into my new world, feeling Cairo's magnetic pull as I wandered at whim through a maze of narrow alleys that led into wide streets and grand plazas. As I walk by, I am followed by the eyes of men, young and old, some curious, some hostile. I was conservatively dressed, or so I thought, in a skirt that came to just below my knees, a short-sleeved top up to my collar bone, and sandals, but the stares of the men made me feel more exposed than I ever had in a miniskirt in New York.

My self-consciousness subsided as the vitality of this city drew me in. I took in the scenes playing out around me: women in black chadors, selling their wares on the sidewalk, interacting with customers, some diffidently, some boldly; women constantly on the go, some in traditional dress with children in tow, some smartly dressed in Western clothes, though more demurely than my own; young men hanging onto the sides of bulging buses slung low on their axles. At one corner, the driver idled his bus, jumped down, ordered a cup of tea from a street vendor which he downed quickly before hopping back into the driver's seat and continuing on his way. The passengers appeared not to mind. I watched verbal altercations erupt between men, their bodies set to deliver blows, only to be deflated in an instant as they hugged and kissed instead. I was invited to share sweet mint tea with vendors who responded Malesh—"No matter"—when I declined to buy anything. One young man, all politeness, attached himself to me for an hour to show me around the old quarter and then politely regretted that he had to return to work.

After I had been walking and meandering until well into the afternoon, the sun began to disappear. With the encroaching dusk, I decided it was time to head back to the hotel and rest my aching limbs. But I was good and truly lost. Deep in the center of a maze where I could not decipher the street signs or make sense of the numerals. As the wonder of the day vanished, I began to feel stranded, a tiny figure on a huge continent. Tears of disconsolation and loneliness began to trickle down my cheeks. If I asked anyone the way I would break down and embarrass myself. An elderly man stopped in front of me.

"What's the matter?" he asked kindly in clear English.

"Nothing," I said, pasting a bright, false smile onto my face. And instead of asking him the way because I would have dissolved in tears, I added: "I have an eye infection." He nodded and left me to my misery. I managed to gain enough composure to approach a green uniformed policeman and show him the piece of paper with the hotel address. Oh, bless the day, he spoke passable English. He walked me to the corner, turned right, and pointed. There it was. I entered the lobby with its air of aged gentility, its pink and pale yellow walls, high columns and mosaic tiled floor, where tourists and Egyptian visitors milled about to the sound of American Muzak piped in, in the background. I opened the door to my room, fell onto the bed, and sobbed uncontrollably into the hard pillow.

"What on earth compelled me to decide on such a trip? Am I totally *crazy*?" I thought. The continent stretched before me, over five months long. I wanted to remove my pathetic self from this overwhelming, alien place—cut my losses and get the first plane back to New York. But then I would have to face my sorely missed women friends who had entered into the spirit of my travel and thrown me a big sendoff party.

All I could think was: "I want to go home." But what did that mean? Had I not embarked on this journey to be close to home again? Had I not put up a shield between myself and my life in America that announced, "Do not touch: this is not home"?

Home was where I came from, not where I lived. Home was South Africa, Cape Town. But as I lay there feeling sorry for myself, a blanket pulled over my head, it was not South Africa I longed for. Nor was it New York City. Rather, I longed for the new life I had made. Home is where the heart is, and at that moment, my heart was with Eric and my friends.

All I could do was steel myself for my predictably lonely, wretched travels south until I was away just long enough to justify shortening my trip and returning to the comfort and emotional security of my life. As the sharp edge of my muddled thoughts began to soften, I sat up, my cheeks still shiny from my breakdown and looked around my temporary home, a room with its blue-and-brown-hued tile floor, its high shuttered windows, the small table on which my partly unpacked backpack lay, immobile, like a piece of modern art, to be observed, rather than used. I took deep breaths and as they evened out I resolved to do something about this state of affairs. I would have to pull myself together. Tomorrow I would start my trip in earnest.

The next morning, ignoring the call of the city, I returned to my room after breakfast and sat on the edge of the bed, a small notebook resting on my knees, the heavy black telephone receiver in my left hand, my list of Cairo contacts in front of me. I dialed the first number.

"May I speak to Sindiso Mfenyana?" I asked. He was the ANC representative to Cairo who Mazisi said I should call and use his name as introduction. The Egyptian government under President Anwar Sadat supported the liberation movements by providing offices and stipends as well as scholarships for younger members to study at the university. Sindiso's friendly voice cut through my apprehension about initiating contact with a movement I respected and cared about but whose members had more important things to do than entertain lost souls from South Africa and the United States. I introduced myself and mentioned Mazisi's name and told him about the magazine.

"We know *Southern Africa* well," he said, and then added an invitation. "There are representatives from other movements in Cairo this week. Please join us for dinner this evening." Maybe life wasn't so bleak after all. Arriving at his house, I was welcomed by Ruth, his

Russian wife, and introduced to their three-year-old son. By the end of the evening I had invitations for tours of the city and lunches and dinners with representatives from Zimbabwe and Angola as well as a number of ANC members, most of them students.

During the days that followed, I would come to realize that this trip to "experience the continent I was born on" was shaping into a pattern that I had not anticipated. *Southern Africa* was providing an unexpected foundation for that pattern. It had made a mark on the liberation movements and, I would discover, on academics, activists, and journalists and even on such bodies as the Organization of African Unity. To them I was the editor of a magazine that brought the news of their struggles to an uninformed public in the United States. Our collective stood out as comrades in their cause. Being a South African only made me more so. For this I seemed to win their respect and trust. Their assumptions about who I was, I would find, gradually turned me into that person. I began to define a new role for myself. I gave myself a label: Conscientious Observer.

11 — "Visits like Yours Build Bridges"

I had been in Cairo four weeks when Gil Fernandes finally showed up. Gil, the PAIGC representative to both the United Nations and Egypt, was adored and respected by many in the solidarity movement, and I counted him as a good friend. The night of my meltdown, I had fervently wished for his arrival, to provide me with a much-needed anchor. But by the time he did arrive, I was striding out on my own. For the week that we overlapped, I was able to see his Cairo and simply enjoy his presence at a leisurely pace, which was not possible in New York. We took long walks around the city. We ate grilled shrimp at a restaurant overlooking the Nile, strolled through the Cairo zoo looking at the unhappy animals, drank tea at the Hilton Hotel, visited the old quarter. Gil was still in deep mourning over the loss of Cabral two months earlier.

Gil was a particularly effective ambassador for the cause. His manner was one of ease and charm. He won over many of those who were threatened by the idea of revolution, forgetting about its heralded place in expanding democracy and liberty. Gil was a reluctant revolutionary; he abhorred violence but did not question the need for it in order to advance the cause. "I am a simple African man," he would say, in a mock boyish voice. He wasn't, of course. Reluctant or not, he was dedicated to his revolution and helped shape it.

Gil grew up in Bissau. His skill at tennis gave him an entrée into the expats' club, where he caught the notice of the U.S. ambassador, who helped him get a full scholarship at the University of New Hampshire in 1962. During summer breaks he returned to Guinea-Bissau to work with the movement, sometimes at PAIGC headquarters in Conakry, sometimes inside the liberated zones. One summer, as he headed for the border along a winding dirt road, he was in a serious accident and was medevacked back to the United States for a year of treatment and rehabilitation. Luckily, he made a full recovery, except for some loss of flexibility in his neck. "It ruined my tennis," he said, smiling.

He and Cabral took many trips abroad, spending time together on planes, in hotel rooms, and at meetings. Gil listened as Cabral he expressed his thoughts, breaking new ground in his ideology and perspective beyond what was already published.

"I begged him to put his ideas down on paper. All he would say was 'Later, Gil, later.'" Gil shrugged sadly: there was no later.

"Cabral would always insist on going slowly, slowly. He wanted everyone to understand what we were fighting for. He wanted us to be patient. To keep the longer-term goal in mind." Gil shook his head. "Sometimes I just want to give up. Sometimes I wonder whether it's all worth it. But I go on. For Cabral. For the people of Guinea-Bissau," he said. "I could never live with myself if I let him down."

By the end of six weeks in Egypt my legs were strong from the constant walking. I knew where to buy the best street food for a dollar a meal. I was hooked on the delicious array of fresh-squeezed juices. I had my favorite places for coffee and pastries, particularly *balah el sham,* the syrup-soaked doughnuts that reminded me of *koeksisters* from home. Sometimes I went on walks by myself, sometimes with other South Africans, students or activists working full-time for the ANC. I visited the pyramids and rode a camel with one South African, drank coffee with another in cafés frequented by men who seemed to have hours to while away. I got used to the word "comrade"—*camarada* in Portuguese—a term that had little to do with any communist party or Soviet-style nomenclature and everything to do with a sense of affinity and mutual respect that arose from being committed to the same struggle. It was one step closer to inclusion than "sister."

And then, just as I began to feel accepted as a comrade, I bumped up against the complexities of race and gender. A few days after interviewing Edward Ndlovu, a high-level leader in the Zimbabwean struggle, he invited me out to dinner. Before we placed our order, Edward looked at me with intent. "We need to have a serious and

open discussion," he said. Uh-oh, here it comes, I thought. *Damn.*
There were few invitations to dinner without another agenda lurking
just below the surface. I looked back at him, expressionless.

"Despite what I think, I am not about to tell you how attractive you
are." He chuckled at his attempt at humor. "What I want to know is
this: Have you written any books?"

I shook my head, mystified.

"Are you writing a book at the moment?"

"No. Of course not. I would have told you." I was puzzled. "Why
do you ask?"

"Well, there is a rumor going around the southern Africa community about you being suspect."

Suspect? I stared into his face, trying to decipher his expression—
disdain? anger? mocking? sympathy?—while a sick feeling spread into
my abdomen. Being suspect—being considered a spy the real inference
of the word "suspect"—could result in ostracism in a flash for South
Africans, particularly white South Africans. In the past, infiltrations
had led to the exposure of activists, safe houses, and secret plans, even
assassinations, so constant vigilance and tight security were necessary.
But this also meant that baseless accusations could lead to witch hunts,
spiked by rumor and paranoia. A person once tarred with the brush of
suspicion found it virtually impossible to scrape it off.

"Our source says that you are trying to ferret out information."
Edward raised an eyebrow to indicate he was asking a question. He
was a tall, imposing person, and he leaned back in his seat as if to
better observe my reactions. How to respond? If I said no, he would
not necessarily believe me. In exile communities, rumor takes flight
with particular velocity. I began to wonder whether the doors that had
so readily been opened for me would now be slammed shut, reverberating down the length of East Africa as word that I was "suspect"
traveled ahead of me. Edward explained that talk was circulating that
I had written an offensive book about the liberation movements; that I
was writing another condemning Africans who marry white women;
that when a particular ANC member refused my request to stay in his
apartment—presumably as a nefarious ruse to gather information—I
had become extremely angry. I was dumbstruck.

"Does Sindiso believe this?" I asked, mortified by the possibility that the ANC representative would question my bona fides.

"No," said Edward, "He doesn't. But we have to get to the bottom of this."

My relief was marginal. I knew that even if the leadership vouched for me, the rumblings from lower-level militants could do harm. We were quiet for a moment as I tried to think who could be spreading such nonsense. Then it struck me. A few days before, after an evening at Sindiso's, I was woken from deep sleep by energetic banging on the door of my room in the B and B I had moved to a few days after arriving in Cairo. I was up in a flash. Was there a fire? An emergency? I tied a *kikoy* wrap around my waist, over the large T-shirt I slept in, unlocked and cracked open the door. I stared into the bloodshot eyes of an inebriated comrade who had been persistent in his advances earlier that evening and who I had equally persistently rebuffed. A man knocking at a woman's door in the middle of the night was bad enough under any circumstances, but in Cairo? I told him to wait downstairs. A few minutes later, fully clothed, I confronted this man, who was swaying on his legs in front of me. The night watchmen curled up in the corner ignored us.

"There is someone you *have* to meet!" he instructed.

"Don't be ridiculous. It's one o'clock in the bloody morning. I was asleep."

"No," his voice urgent, if slurred. "It's really important that you meet him right now. He leaves Cairo at six in the morning."

Then he should also be asleep, I thought to myself. "Forget it, it's too late. I'm going back to bed."

His anger was ignited. "He has good information for you! You'll be sorry!"

"Too bad," I retorted, turning to go back to my room.

"Then I insist that you have dinner with me tomorrow evening."

I told him with much irritation that I had another engagement and I walked off, leaving him muttering as he swayed out the door into the night. It took me a while to get back to sleep as I conducted a tirade against men in my head.

I related this incident, naming the comrade in question. Edward burst out laughing, shaking his head at the behavior of the younger militants. That was that. I never heard another word and no one's attitude changed toward me. But I reassessed my situation. I had been too naïve in believing that the interest of the men I was meeting derived from who I was, not from what I was, namely a young woman traveling alone. At the time many white women were traveling in Africa. Such travel was an anomaly in the local culture. If African women traveled alone, it was likely out of necessity, not to seek adventures. Many visitors to Africa were insensitive to this, as I would find in my travels, where arrogance and thoughtlessness trumped awareness. There was, for instance, the time I overheard a Tanzanian airline officer who was making out a ticket for a young American woman ask whether she was "Miss" or "Mrs." "I am 'Ms.,'" she shouted rudely at the utterly perplexed man, who could not have heard of this appellation only recently adopted in the United States.

In casual contact with the opposite sex, including a few of my South African comrades, I tended to wait for the crunch, the claim that I had no idea just how irresistible, beautiful, amazing I was. Or declarations that I was the woman he'd always wanted to meet, if only we'd met before he married. And so forth and so on. I needed to spend more time with women.

Maria de Jesus was the first woman I got close to. As a representative of the MPLA in Cairo, she worked as a translator for the Portuguese news program that was beamed to southern Africa. We got into the habit of going for walks together, meandering through the city and along the Nile. We ate in local restaurants where she introduced me to grilled pigeon with hot sauce and once I was able to banish the image of those ragged feathered scavengers in Central Park, I found them quite delicious. Sometimes we treated ourselves to mint tea at the Nile Hilton, sitting on the terrace overlooking the magnificent river. She told me that she used to feel guilty about accepting invitations to dinner at the Hilton, indulging in expensive food when her people were so poor and oppressed. But when she told Agostinho Neto, the president of the MPLA, how she felt, he took her hand and said, "My dear Maria, we are not struggling to be miserable!" She began accepting invitations.

Maria's father was a Portuguese plantation owner in Angola; her mother was a plantation worker. When Maria was three, her father sent her to Portugal to be raised by his wealthy family and receive a European education. The widespread poverty of Lisbon troubled her. Once, when she was seven, she insisted on taking food to the street children who ran ragged in the neighborhood. The next day she did so again. On the third day, a thought struck her: they would always be hungry and she wouldn't be able to feed them every day. Something bigger than charity was needed. It was the beginning of her political awakening. At fifteen she returned to Angola, where she reconnected with her mother. She was unprepared for the wretched living conditions there, and the tyrannical rule of the colonial government. At first she felt alienated from her homeland, believing herself to be more European than African. It was her mother who set her straight. As we sat looking at the Nile she recalled her mother's words: "Your father has taught you many things. I want to tell you what is even more important: this land is ours. Go and tell that to the world."

She began to hang out with the intellectuals and political activists in Luanda who would later become leaders of the MPLA. Then she married a Swiss national and moved to Switzerland, where she experienced exclusion from his social circle. She pined for Angola and became determined to return to Africa to work full-time for the liberation of her country. She decided that when her daughter turned twelve and was old enough to understand her mother's choices, she would leave Switzerland. "My daughter is proud of me. She writes me beautiful letters. I miss her so very much."

It was hard to believe that Maria was some twenty years older than me. Vivacious, attractive, funny, romantic, iron-willed, she was like a beacon of light that drew me into her sphere. Her commitment and courage were unwavering. I reflected back on conversations about courage I had had with friends before I set off on my travels: "You are so courageous to travel by yourself," they would say. "I would never have the courage." Many of these were friends whom I envied for their self-confidence and the ease with which they negotiated intellectual life. It took no courage to travel down East Africa, my compass a list of contacts I had acquired before leaving New York, propelled by expectation and possibility. Courage was a label reserved for those fighting to overthrow colonialism and minority rule, for those ready to risk death for their cause, for those who left their children in the care of others, not knowing when—or whether—they would see them again. That was courage.

"You know, Maria," I blurted out on one of our walks, "At times I feel awkward with the comrades. You know, being a white South African, arriving in Egypt out of the blue and hoping that somehow people would accept me. It feels rather audacious."

"Ah, but your face!" she countered. "Anyone who meets you sees immediately how trustworthy and concerned you are. There can be no doubt."

Maria accepted me as an African, as a comrade. She helped me feel more secure, my feet rooted to the continent that stretched before me all the way down to South Africa. I felt poised, equidistant between America, my home of the last few years, and South Africa, home-home, the place that held my roots. The sense of this rooted-ness increased as I continued my journey, my step steadier, my doubts diminishing.

In a letter to my women's group shortly before leaving Cairo, I wrote:

> For the last few days I have been feeling superbly free. Almost constantly high! I feel so in contact with myself. I find I am able to be far more forthright and open with people as a result. I have to account to no one. Every day is my own and I can decide afresh what I want to do. I am enjoying being by myself far more than I could ever have imagined. I roam the streets for hours at a time, getting lost, figuring my way out of the maze. I laugh at everything that goes wrong, and I am endlessly patient with the total disorganization of this city. No doubt within one week of returning to the States I will be my old harassed self. But stronger, I think.

When it was time to say good-bye, Maria took both my hands in hers and said: "It has been important for all of us that you came. Visits like yours build bridges. When we next hear about the atrocities in

South Africa we'll say, 'Remember Stephanie!' And we'll all look at each other and say, 'Yes, if there's one Stephanie, there must be more Stephanies.'" Then she kissed me on both cheeks, Portuguese style. "Stephanie, I will never forget you," she said as we hugged. It is I who never forgot Maria. Nor the confidence she helped instill in me.

12 — A Bona Fide Journalist

I walk out of the Organization of African Unity building in Addis Ababa into the bright May sunlight and the rarefied air that, at eight thousand feet, leaves my legs weak and my breath short. I hold a press credential that will allow me to attend the summit meeting of the African heads of state to mark the OAU's tenth anniversary. I place the credential slowly, almost ceremoniously, around my neck as if I am presenting myself with an award. I am no longer simply a volunteer editor of a small collective magazine. I am a bona fide journalist with a press credential to prove it. I have a purpose beyond being a South African making her way down the east coast of Africa, dreaming of home.

This is my second visit to Ethiopia. After arriving in Addis from Cairo I boarded a bus and headed north over the high mountains, getting off at Lalibela to see the rock-cut churches that date back to the twelfth and thirteenth centuries; visiting Gondar, the capital of Ethiopia from the mid-seventeenth century for over two centuries, with its extraordinary Fasilides Castle; making a side trip to an Ethiopian Jewish Falasha village in a chariot-style donkey cart (a ride that went on for so long I began to worry I was being kidnapped), where I was welcomed by women and shown their small round whitewashed mud-walled synagogue, a metal Star of David attached to the top of the roof; arriving finally at Asmara, the capital of Eritrea, which was on the cusp of a long struggle for independence from Ethiopia. I was a woman alone, absorbing, day after day, evidence of a glorious ancient culture about which I had known absolutely nothing.

Back in Addis I stepped out of tourist mode to meet with a senior officer of the OAU's Decolonization Section. As I began to introduce myself I saw the latest issue of *Southern Africa* on his desk. I pointed to it in explanation of who I was. He picked it up and leafed through it, commenting on how much his committee appreciated our work, while I itched to reach across his desk and grab this issue, which I had not yet seen. He assumed that, as a journalist, I would be returning for the two-day heads of state summit and the two-week deliberations that would follow. It was the first I had heard of it. Of course, I said, hoping that Janet could work her fundraising magic to raise the cost of my flight back to Addis from Nairobi, my next destination. My journey was fast shifting from a personal to a professional one.

I head for the meeting hall hoping to find a friendly face from Cairo. Instead I find dark suits, ties, and shiny shoes competing with the flamboyant, brilliantly dyed, flowing male attire of West Africa and the crisp white djellabas of the north. A helpful official tells me I can find the liberation movements at the exhibition hall nearby. Loud hilarity greets me as I enter. I stand just inside the doorway watching the energetic busyness as exhibition posters are hammered into place, displays set out. There is a buzz of English and Portuguese and the universal language of backslapping, hugs, and laughter as militants from one organization reconnect with militants from another. There is nary a woman among the twenty-five or so delegates. If only Maria were there—we could roll our eyes at the glaring absence.

I walk toward the displays, which range from new textbooks with bright illustrations that PAIGC produces for children in the liberated zones who are attending school for the first time to weapons that the Angolans and Mozambicans had captured from the Portuguese army. These latter are centrally displayed on a raised platform: a U.S.-made mortar; part of an American-made training bomber, known as the Harvard, that the Portuguese army uses extensively; and a parachute with a MADE IN USA imprint. I take out my camera so I can record evidence of this blatant U.S. involvement on the side of the Portuguese. By now, all eyes are focused on me. A light-skinned *mestiço* Angolan in a khaki Nehru suit comes over. He is older than the others, thinner and shorter.

"Hullo," he says, "My name is Paulo Jorge." We shake hands as he introduces himself in good, accented English as the director of MPLA's Department of Information, based at their headquarters in Lusaka. I introduce myself and hand him a copy of the magazine. His face lights up. "This is a *wonderful* magazine," he gushes as his comrades crowd around him. "We fight over it when it arrives in our office. Everyone wants to read it first!"

He then takes me in hand and introduces me to his delegation and the delegations of the other movements. A few I already know from New York and Cairo. By the time I leave three hours later I have helped set up the exhibition, I have interviews promised, even a possible one with MPLA's president, Agostinho Neto.

THE FOLLOWING DAY THE SUMMIT was officially opened in Africa Hall by Emperor Haile Selassie of Ethiopia. He walked slowly, erect, and with obvious difficulty to the podium. (His forty-four-year despotic rule would end in a coup less than a year later.) Despite the microphone, his frail voice barely carried across the assembly hall. From the journalists' gallery I looked down upon some forty leaders of a new Africa emerging from centuries of colonialism. Before me were presidents, both the bad and the good, many in national dress, whose faces were familiar from photographs. There was Julius Nyerere of Tanzania, trying to build an equitable socialist country, as was Kenneth Kaunda of Zambia; Léopold Sédar Senghor of Senegal, a poet and self-proclaimed president-for-life; Jean-Bédel Bokassa of the Central African Republic, renowned as a tyrannical dictator; Félix Houphouët-Boigny of the Ivory Coast, one of two African leaders willing to maintain relations with the South African regime; Hastings Banda of Malawi, the other collaborator with apartheid; Anwar Sadat of Egypt, whose controversial rapprochement with Israel appalled me; Yakubu Gowon of Nigeria, who took power through a military coup and managed to crush Biafra's efforts to secede; President Idi Amin of Uganda, dressed in his signature bright blue military uniform, an oversized caricature of a leader, more so in contrast to the childlike proportions of Haile Selassie. The five Portuguese colonies— Angola, Mozambique, Guinea-Bissau, Cape Verde, and São Tomé/

Principe—as well as Zimbabwe, Namibia, and South Africa were conspicuous in their absence as independent countries, although not inconspicuous in the way they were lauded by one speaker after another, some of whom I suspected didn't really give a damn.

After the speeches, I headed for the press gallery. The journalists were almost all European men. A few African men. Two French women, the only women journalists besides me, dressed Paris-smart-casual and enviably self-assured. A Yugoslav correspondent sought me out. He was based in Nairobi, he informed me, and had seen me talking with the liberation movement reps. Could I introduce him? Whatever misgivings I had about being thrown into the deep end of the press pool, I felt pleased that I was the one with connections.

I hardly slept on the days that followed. I gathered information. I gathered stories. I fended off approaches from liberation movement cadres, young diplomats, and other journalists. I spent more and more time in the exhibition hall. At some point during the second week, Paulo suggested we go for coffee at a nearby hotel. I was beginning to really like this trim, neatly dressed man, possessed of a coiled inner energy, a way of cutting through bullshit, and a total absence of macho-tinged vibe. Paulo held himself slightly aloof from the rest of his comrades, while asserting a natural style of leadership. His attention did not wander as I answered his questions about the magazine and the solidarity movement in the United States. Then his demeanor became more serious.

"Stephanie," he said, a strained look creasing his earnest face, "You have no idea how difficult our revolution is." He shook his head as he spoke. "Last year the Portuguese launched a huge offensive. They dropped herbicides from planes and destroyed crops over a vast area. The peasants were driven out of their villages in panic. Old people, mothers, their children . . . " His voice trailed off.

I had heard that the Portuguese military was using defoliants against the civilians in Angola, but now napalm? I immediately thought of nine-year-old Kim Phúc Phan Thị, running naked down the center of a road in Vietnam, her back on fire from a napalm bomb.

"People starved because they had no food and no place to grow it," Paulo continued. "Many of us who were working outside were called in to help. We spent days walking to get there. And then to see the hunger and the vacant eyes, and the potbellied malnourished children…" He paused again. "It broke our hearts, but it made our determination stronger."

They slept little and the food they brought didn't last long. "We felt we had failed our people. We had to talk and talk and talk to convince them that their sacrifices were worthwhile." He took a sip of his coffee, which he had barely touched. "How can they believe us if their stomachs are empty and their children are crying from hunger?"

Paulo looked solemn, his spirit residing in some distant place. And then more lightheartedly, he said, "I was away from my work in information for seven months. When I got back to Lusaka the whole department had collapsed and I had to build it up again."

We sat in silence. I couldn't think of anything to say, feeling the outsider I was. I looked up and saw Paulo looking at me intently.

"Stephanie, would you like to visit Angola?" he asked, breaking the silence. "We could arrange for you to spend a week or two in the liberated zones."

I waited a moment, taking in the offer. It was huge. "Paulo, I would very, very much like to visit your country," I replied

"Okay, then," he said in a voice that brought our coffee break to an end. "I will arrange for you to have an interview with President Neto. I will let you know when."

PAULO'S OFFER SHOWED HIS ACCEPTANCE of me as a serious journalist. For a brief moment I had been welcomed into their circles. I would return to New York while they would discard their civvies for camouflage uniforms, retrieve their weapons, and march for miles into the interior of their countries to continue waging their relentless wars. Now I had the possibility of seeing it firsthand. At the same time, I fell in love with the idea of being in the midst of so many delightful, dedicated, smart, funny, serious, committed revolutionaries. I fell in love with the idea that I had become a journalist. I fell in love with being on the continent, with being surrounded by Africans who treated me as a fellow African, a sister, a comrade, and who assumed I was as committed to ending colonialism and apartheid as they were, even though I was not risking my life to do so. I began to fall in love with the new me. It was a seductive feeling, one that had found its way further into the confident self that had begun to emerge in Cairo.

And then I fell in love.

13 — "We Can't Stop Until It's Over"

After leaving Paulo I entered the crowded lobby of Africa Hall, where a reception filled the large space. For a moment I felt at a loss in the dense sea of people until I was able to maneuver my way toward my liberation movement comrades. The Guinea-Bissau group, uncharacteristically somber, was clustered around a man I did not recognize and who appeared to be the source of their dampened spirits. He was a short man, stouter than his comrades, his demeanor verging on imperious. He was introduced to me as the head of their delegation, Victor Saúde Maria, the director of PAIGC's Department of Foreign Affairs. I knew his name; he was one of the inner circle of leaders. When I was introduced as a South African journalist from New York, he looked me up and down and smiled the oh-so-recognizable predator smile.

"I saw Gil Fernandes in Cairo recently," I said in a chatty manner, trying to deflect my discomfort. "He told me you would be here and suggested that I ask you for an interview."

"Excellent, excellent. How about tomorrow at eight thirty?" I agreed. Another Guinea-Bissau arrival strode purposefully toward us. Energy returned to the group of militants. The PAIGC and MPLA comrades showed their obvious affection with hugs, backslaps, and arm punches. After a while I became aware that he was standing just outside the group, observing me intently. I became self-conscious, laughing a little louder than the jokes and teasing warranted, talking a little more earnestly than usual. One of his mates, realizing that we hadn't met, led me toward him.

"This is Antonio Lopes," he said. "Tonio is in charge of our exhibition. He's a terrific artist. You will see what he produces tomorrow."

I introduced myself. I took in his height, his strong slim muscular body, his dark complexion, which set off the unusual blue-green of his eyes. I began to make small talk, floundering and tripping over my words. This is absurd, I told myself. I no longer felt self-conscious in the presence of these militants, so why now? We exchanged information about ourselves in the superficial way that is the norm at large gatherings. Slowly the formality receded. I learned that he grew up in Bissau; that he had been a pilot in the Portuguese army and deserted, which led to a six-month prison sentence in Lisbon. Then he joined PAIGC. He was granted a scholarship to study in East Germany. He was an engineer. "I haven't practiced for a long time," he said.

"Where are you based?" I asked when the conversation seemed to lag.

"Mostly in Boké." I knew of Boké, the small Guinea town (sometimes referred to as Guinea-Conakry, or simply Guiné, to distinguish it from Guinea-Bissau and Equatorial Guinea) close to the border with Guinea-Bissau where PAIGC had a military base. "Also in Conakry." I asked if he traveled a lot. I was hoping he was part of the diplomatic corps, like Gil.

"Not at all." He was here because he could draw—he pointed out the schoolbooks on display that he had illustrated—and was needed to help create the exhibition. "I seldom travel. I am a good soldier. I do what I'm told." He gave me a wry smile.

As Tonio and I continued to talk there was an almost imperceptible change in the dynamic. We found ourselves stepping closer to each other as if the ambient volume had slowly been turned down. Then Tonio was shaking my hand and saying good-bye.

The next morning, I was in Victor Maria's hotel room for the interview. It was my first interview in my new profession. I took out my notebook and glanced at the questions I had prepared. Then I removed my tape recorder from my bag and set it on the small table before us. He placed his hand over my hand. I withdrew it. Already tense, I was unnerved by his gesture. I steadied my voice as I told him

I had met Cabral in New York; that it was not only Guinea-Bissau's loss, but Africa's and the world's.

"What has this meant to your struggle?" I asked.

He became serious. He talked about the war, about recent victories, about PAIGC's plan to declare independence later that year. "We have liberated two-thirds of our country," he said, repeating what Cabral had told us at Jennifer's apartment. "We are in control. The Portuguese have the towns, but even in these areas there is wide support for our struggle."

PAIGC had recently shot down six Portuguese military bombers. Among the dead was one of the Portugal's top army commanders. Victories such as these showed that the assassination of Cabral had not slowed the armed struggle down—it had given it more purpose. Victor Maria was a practiced interview subject, and I could entice little that was fresh from him, little of the passion that sparked the conversations with Gil and Maria in Cairo or, more recently, with Paulo Jorge. I felt unequal to the task. When I switched off the tape recorder, he looked at me. He seemed to be sizing me up. I waited for him to say something inappropriate. "Would you like to visit the liberated zones of Guinea-Bissau?" he asked, "I can arrange it."

I was momentarily nonplussed. Angola *and* Guinea-Bissau. "That would be interesting," I responded noncommittally. I was hesitant—his come-on vibes had been unmistakable. What strings would be attached? The interview ended, and he headed for the meeting hall while I went in search of Tonio. My first question was whether he thought Victor Maria might be serious. "Yes, definitely," he replied. "If he has asked you, he means it." I felt a stab of excitement. He asked me to have dinner with him. Over our shared plate of *doro wat* and lentils, using our fingers Ethiopian style, our conversation was relaxed.

"You know," he said, "sometimes outsiders think the revolution is romantic . . . a valiant struggle for justice . . . " Tonio paused, grasping for the right word. "It is ex*haus*ting. Nonstop. We can't stop until it's over. However long that takes."

"Cabral is dead," he went on, with the same faraway hurt look in his eyes that I had seen in Gil's. Tonio had been nearby when Cabral was killed. He had seen him lying on the ground, the blood pouring from him. "I went berserk, mad even. I flew into such a rage I wanted to kill someone. My comrades had to restrain me."

I put my hand over his and we sat saying nothing more. His jaw was clenched. There were tears on his cheeks and tears appeared on mine. Then he shook his shoulders as if to chase away his bleak thoughts. "Are you married?" he asked, breaking the silence. I wasn't sure what to say. "Yes" was no longer an uncomplicated answer. As I gained more distance from New York, both physically and emotionally, I was no longer the Stephanie who married Eric. In South Africa we had shared much—our view of apartheid, our friends, our dreams. In the United States, less so. Eric's focus was physics. Mine was social activism, particularly around apartheid. Now far away from Eric I felt like a bird that had left the nest and was now finding its wings. I could never return to that safe place. A new relationship based more on friendship than love was emerging through our letter writing, where we were able to describe our feelings and thoughts more eloquently than we had been able to face-to-face. Whether we wanted to, or even could, reinvent our marriage, I was no longer sure. "Yes" was the short answer. I asked about his wife. He told me he had met her at university in East Germany.

"We have been apart for such a long time that I don't think our marriage can survive. It will be many years before we can test it again. Besides, she is living with another man although she says she still loves me. I just don't know any more." I nodded. I didn't know any more either. Then he smiled and stood up. He put out his hand. "Let's go dancing," he said.

We were drawn toward the music coming from a nearby club. I danced, giving in to oblivion as a live band played pulsating rhythms. I hadn't danced since I had left the States and I was enjoying myself. Tonio danced with more control.

"You are the best dancer here," he said. Unlikely—there were some pretty fantastic dancers around us. As the evening wore on, the band began to play slow, close-dancing music. "I could fall in love with the man," I thought as we slipped into a natural harmony. I was beginning to feel despair at the notion that I was unlikely to see him again, when he said in a firm voice: "I've been thinking. Next time I travel, you must come and meet me. When it will be, who knows." Then after a moment's silence, "No, better still. In all the years I have never, ever taken time off. I will ask for leave." And I will make the time, I thought. When the band began packing up, it was almost 4:00 a.m. We did not have to pose any questions. We found a taxi and headed for his hotel. I leaned my head against his shoulder. He turned toward me.

"You know, if you look at your individual features," he said tracing his fingers around my face, then along my nose, around my lips, "they are not particularly beautiful. Your mouth, your nose, they're okay. But, ah, when you take them all together, then you are very beautiful."

I instinctively touched my apparently not particularly attractive nose. I looked back at his crystal eyes, contemplating how beautiful they were, and said, "*You* are the beautiful one."

He shook his head. "No," he said. "Never."

The next morning at 7:00 a.m. I stepped out of the hotel elevator into the reception area where two Namibian friends were in conversation. They looked at me astonished. I knew they were wondering who had scored. I was secure in the knowledge that they would never guess. Anyway, if they did, it didn't matter. This was different. I was falling in love with this revolutionary.

"Revolutionary." The word nagged at me. What did it mean to fall in love with a revolutionary? And "fall" was the apt word: I was tumbling, losing my footing, plunging, toppling, plummeting into intense, unanchored emotions that consumed me after just one night with this man. Time and timing were factors. Time, when constricted, leads to speeded-up responses after Cupid's arrow has found its target. I had been away from New York, from Eric and my friends, for close to three months. In this new environment, which nurtured my self-esteem, I was ready for such an encounter. No strings. No guilt. No regrets. As a feminist questioning the role of women in relationships and society in general, the issue was not so much who I fell in love with but what role I played in the relationship.

What was it about these movement revolutionaries that captivated young women in the solidarity movements, both black and white? Were we having affairs with them because of the allure of the revolutions they were engaged in? Many of the comrades were taking advantage of this allure. The sexual revolution was in full swing at the time, but the women's movement was fast gaining ground, and those of us who identified as feminists were feeling both freer to express ourselves and wary of the expectations that the sexual revolution imposed on us. The women's movement led us to question the principle of fidelity and to experiment with open relationships. We were trying to change the definition of committed relationships, married or not. We had been socialized by a patriarchal system, which we were now finding stifling and unequal. Months before I left for Africa, my feminism had steered me to the position that an open marriage with Eric was the only way to be consistent with my principles. Later I would recognize that these "principles" had more to do with a failing marriage than my own personal revolution. "Open marriage" meant an open door through which we could both exit. Most women drew one line that we would not cross: no relationships with men who had partners, married or not. When it came to Tonio that line got rather fuzzy. I rationalized it. He had not been together with his wife for years. She was living with another man. Hence, without a single qualm, I could convince myself that this situation was different.

The following day I helped dismantle the exhibitions before hurrying off to interview Agostinho Neto. Paulo had finally been able to pin him down—I was granted fifteen minutes at four o'clock to discuss with him a possible visit to Angola. I told Tonio, who was engrossed in taking down the Guinean display, that I would return to the exhibition hall after the interview.

I sat, somewhat nervously, across a small table from this respected leader in his hotel room. Alberto, the head of external affairs at the office in Dar es Salaam, took notes discreetly. In his slow, measured way, Neto plied me with questions.

"Why Angola?"

Having prepared for this question, I replied, "Because the United States, thanks to your oil, regards Angola as being within its sphere of interest. The U.S. media covers little of this."

"Can you walk long distances?"

"Yes," I replied in a positive voice. (Well, I would have to do some serious training once I got to Dar es Salaam. I imagined long runs on the beach.)

"Can you get your expenses paid to the border?"

"That will not be a problem," I assured him. (I was confident that Janet could work her fundraising magic once more.)

"How long do you want to visit?"

"As long as the MPLA can put up with me! Two or three weeks perhaps?" I didn't think I could ask for more.

"I'll put in a request for a month" he said. Request? What he said surely must go, although it might well be up to the military to assess the most appropriate time. I gave him my contact details in Dar es Salaam and added that I would call in on the MPLA office as soon as I reached the city. Then some small talk. How did I like the conference? Was I getting the material I needed? Had his delegation been helpful to me? We could have a longer talk in Dar, he said. I thanked him.

"Not at all. I am sorry I have kept you waiting." He smiled again his slow, friendly smile. "I too was kept waiting by heads of state."

And that was that. Fifteen minutes sharp. Alberto accompanied me out of the room. He assured me that I had made a good impression. He looked at me with a slightly puzzled expression. "It can be very dangerous. Aren't you afraid of the Portuguese?"

"No, I'm not. Angolans live with that reality every day. I am prepared to take that risk." He seemed satisfied with my response.

"I will see you in a few weeks in Dar," I said as we shook hands while I wondered whether he asked male journalists the same question.

The invitation to Guinea-Bissau was also starting to look positive. Victor Maria asked me to send a formal request to him at PAIGC headquarters in Conakry once I was back in New York and suggested October or November as a good time. I wondered how I could fit both trips in. I would have to figure that out when and if the time came.

Each step away from President Neto's hotel was a step toward my new life. But could I do it? My writing and publication experience was limited to say the least. Self-confidence and doubt oscillated in step with each stride as the two invitations began to solidify in my mind, first as fantasy, then as dream, and finally as a plan.

Meanwhile I had to find Tonio. He was not at the exhibition hall, not at his hotel, and there was no message at mine. This was our last night. I began to feel frantic. Exhausted, I returned to the hotel, slept for an hour, and headed to the dining room. Boisterously occupying a large table surrounded by empty beer and wine bottles was the PAIGC delegation.

"Come and join us!" Victor called, beaming and beckoning me over. "We are celebrating! PAIGC scored a major victory!"

I glowered at Tonio, who stood up and walked over to me. "I am sorry," he said. His manner was correct and matter-of-fact, showing not an iota of emotion. I knew that he had to be circumspect in front of his people. Bugger his people, I thought. I was swayed by emotions that rode wildly on the knowledge that I might never see this man again. I held out my hand for him to shake it.

"Good-bye," I said, still hanging onto cool. I then said my good-byes to all the PAIGC cadres around the table. Some rose to shake my hand or give me a comradely hug. I went over to shake Victor's hand and congratulate him.

"Thanks for everything. I will be in touch," I said. He stood up and we air-kissed, one side, then the other.

"Good," he responded. "I will wait to hear from you."

I returned to my room and dozed fitfully. I woke with a start. I had forgotten to call to say good-bye to a British contact who had been helpful to me on both my visits to Addis. I went downstairs to the lobby to make the call. The man behind the desk handed me a note written on a sheet of hotel notepaper. "I love you," it read. His handwriting was spidery and slanted forward. "You are all what I dream about. Travel well. Love, Tonio." I called him.

"Can you come?" he asked. I went.

Our lovemaking had an edge of desperation. We had found each other too late. At two o'clock I had to leave. My flight was in a few hours. On the street we kissed formally as any friends might. I got into a taxi, waving as the car drove off. Waving good-bye.

14 — Can I Take My Inner Calm Back with Me?

I emerge, scrubbed clean from a shower after a day in the center of Dar es Salaam, the capital of Tanzania, the last country on my trek. I close the door of my friend's beach house, and step onto the sand of Bahari Beach. The evening air is chilly against my damp hair. The dark is about to descend, a quick transition between day and night, accentuating the crests of the white waves against the navy blue sea. I am wearing an orange and pale yellow striped dress I bought in Nairobi; made from two kikoys it flows down to my ankles. At the edge of the sea I engage in a half dance, my arms stretched above my head as the soft cotton sways sensuously around my body and swirls and billows in the light gusts of wind.

The sounds of the sea are universal, the melody of every beach, whatever the size and wherever the place, differing in volume and scope in tune with the tides and the winds, whether sheltered by high mountains in Cape Town, or open sweeps of sand, flat and seemingly endless, as in Dar: The rushing hiss of buildup until the wave breaks, the brief silence as those next in line surge for their turn to crescendo and crash. Frothing white waves, at times wild and rough, break on the sand. Or at other times, smooth and gentle as silk. The water turquoise and bright, or deep blue and dark, sometimes the color of lead. Tonight the sea is gentle; it is the color of lead. The hoarse rustling of the wind through the fronds of the palm trees sporadically joins the sound of the ocean.

Shells of different sizes, colors, and shapes are scattered over the sand. Frilly green and brown seaweed provide a dark rim along the high-water line. White crabs scatter sideways in front of me, blending in so perfectly that they appear to vanish as they skim across the sand. Some little creature beneath the surface is sending up spaghetti-like spirals of sand that curl into six-inch mounds. I bend over one hill and dig furiously to try and surprise the little worker, but it eludes me.

The sand is gritty, crunching under my toes. As I walk toward the receding tide, the texture changes to fine, smooth, mudlike. With each step, my heel sinks—squish—holds it for a split second so that I have to tug ever so slightly to raise my foot again to step forward. I walk and walk, past the beach houses, past the hotel's thatch-domed shelters that provide shade from the midday sun. The sky is overcast, a little rainy, but it is perfect because it is the beach, an endless stretch reflecting the moods of the changing sea. I emit a sigh of satisfaction. I am content.

I slow to a stop. I feel rooted, balanced in time. No past. No future. Just this moment, the sea and me. Rain begins to fall in heavy drops. The moment fades away, and I retrace my steps along the sand, back to the house, faster this time, the drops pockmarking the now gray sand and etching splotches onto my dress. I sit on the small veranda as the palm trees bend and sway before the incoming storm. I am calm and content. My trip is ending. Just one more week.

Can I take my inner calm back with me? My throat constricts at the thought of again being surrounded by American accents, American culture, the bustle and noise and boisterousness of it all. New York is not home. Home is where I feel strong and independent, where I blend in with the physicality of the geography, the varied landscape— where my emotions are in balance. In Tanzania I am close to the south, close to home-home, which I can now believe will truly be free one day. I feel a magnet constantly drawing me south, increasing its pull when I smell the earth, when I walk on the beaches, when I am with other Africans, particularly South Africans.

When I left Addis, I was eager to go farther south, to countries that, in my southern state of mind, seemed more "African." After four weeks in Kenya, mostly as a tourist, I traveled by bus from Nairobi to Moshi, just over the border in Tanzania, within view of the snow-topped Mount Kilimanjaro. Then on to Dar. The bus bumped and rattled into the terminus on the edge of the city. I breathed in the early morning air, which hinted of the humidity to come, a mix of dust and vegetation and diesel fumes, and waited while our wiry driver scampered to the roof of the bus and began to unceremoniously toss down luggage—bags, suitcases, cardboard boxes, African cloth bundles tied with string, and my dust-clogged backpack—to the passengers gathered below, all of us exhausted and stiff from the long hours on the crowded bus. I adroitly maneuvered the heavy load onto my shoulders and back—a skill acquired after much repetition—and went in search of a working phone. I rummaged through my handbag for my travel-tattered notebook with telephone numbers of friends of friends who had offered me beds. I dialed each number, only to get no answer or learn that they were away. I stared at my pack on the ground and felt momentarily lost. Steeling myself against the despondency that had sucked me in in Cairo, I took a breath and dialed the MPLA office. Within forty minutes a car arrived to whisk me away over bumpy roads to the MPLA office.

Once there, I was motioned to a chair and told to rest. A cup of tea appeared. Friends from Addis emerged one by one. Paulo Jorge looked strained and preoccupied, his body tense. He briefly took both my hands in welcome. Others, including Alberto, welcomed me like a long-lost friend and then returned to their work. The atmosphere at the exhibition hall, with its leisurely pace and time for chatting and laughter, was nothing like the earnest activity surrounding me. After more calls, I found a contact at home and the driver delivered me there. For the next few weeks, while in Dar, I spent time with MPLA comrades. My trip to Angola was never raised. I delivered a letter requested by Neto in Cairo and heard nothing. Patience, I counseled myself.

Dar was a city that attracted exiles: expat teachers at the university, health practitioners, development practitioners, many in search of a country that they believed was building socialism. Americans, Brits, and Europeans were there in large numbers. In the five weeks I was in Tanzania I began to find a community and make women friends, including Jane Ngwenya, one of the representatives of the

Zimbabwe African Peoples Union, one of the two liberation movements fighting against the Rhodesian regime, with offices in Dar. As
we became friends I realized how much I missed the closeness of
women: the laughter, the understanding, the silences that were not
distances that needed filling. Although I sustained my friendships
in New York City through frequent letters back and forth, I needed
the immediacy of face-to-face connection. I began to look forward to
long conversations with this forceful feminist—not a label she would
have assigned to herself. Jane bemoaned women's subordinate status
in the Zimbabwe liberation struggle. She entered protest politics in
1960, the year of the Sharpeville massacre and the march on Cape
Town, when her children were very young. Her husband resented her
decision, particularly after she was arrested, and she was dismayed
when the women in their community were even more critical of her
activism than the men. "It's very sad," she said. "They just can't see
how much they are subjugated by men."

Facing arrest once again, she fled into exile. She had no option but
to leave behind, with heavy heart, her two teenage children.. She now
worked with the movement in Tanzania, where she found that the
attitudes toward women were not very different. "Many of the men
around me refuse to accept me as a real leader. They are threatened by
a woman in authority," she told me. But what really incensed her was
the movement's decision not to involve women in the struggle until
after victory. "It is nonsense. It has to be an integral part of the revolution we are waging in Zimbabwe," she said. "If we don't fight such
attitudes now, it won't happen."

In a letter to my women's group I wrote:

> Jane and Maria couldn't be more different in personality. Yet both
> have made deep personal sacrifices for the struggle. I cannot help
> but be inspired by their strong commitment and the direction they
> have chosen for their lives. Both left their children in order to do
> so. We could talk intimately, because although from such different
> cultures, from such different backgrounds, the common ground
> of being women aware of the oppression of women, the need to
> struggle as women for change, brings us together. The solidarity

of women *is* very strong. It can cut directly across cultural barriers and class barriers. Tell *that* to those assholes who accuse the women's movement of being merely a middle-class phenomenon. And Christ, I have heard enough of that!

After Zimbabwe gained its independence in 1980, Jane was appointed deputy minister of Manpower Planning, Development and Labour, a position she held until 1984. Soon after independence in 1975, Maria was assigned to Sweden, Angola's first woman ambassador. Neither survived politically as their governments moved to the right and corruption and oligarchy became the rule of the day.

I WALKED THE CITY DAILY. Here in the southern part of East Africa, in the slow-moving city of Dar, with its sultry heat, its market smells, its friendliness, the tropical feel accentuated by the many palm trees, I was content. In Dar, a city of Africa and Africans, I felt African regardless of where my grandparents hailed from.

On my first visit to the ANC office, one of my countrymen was surprised when I introduced myself. "I took you for an Angolan," he laughed. "You are with them so often, I just assumed." He had also assumed that I was *mestiça*. By now I was tanned a deep brown. My black hair was short and frizzy. It was not an implausible conclusion. But it appeared to make no difference when he realized his error. After all, many whites had joined the ANC; some were in the leadership.

I also visited the office of the Pan Africanist Congress. Like the ANC, it was recognized by the UN and the Organization of African Unity as a legitimate movement. *Southern Africa*'s coverage of PAC was more limited than that of the more popularly supported ANC. The PAC had broken away from the ANC, with an ideology of pan-Africanism emphasizing Africa for the Africans. They viewed multiracialism, a tenet of the ANC, as safeguarding white interests and pandering to white bigotry. It was not an ideology that I was comfortable with and wondered what reception I would get. No need. I soon got into an animated conversation with the young African at the front desk. When I told him I was from Cape Town, he called to the back office. "Hey, man, *kom hisso*"—Come here—"There's a sister of yours to meet."

A young coloured man came through the door, all smiles of welcome. Again the chit-chat, why I was here, where we were from.

"Ah, Cape Town, the beautiful city," he said. "I lived for a few years in Athlone."

"My father had his law practice in Athlone," I responded.

As these words exited my mouth I realized that I was reinforcing what they already assumed: I was black. No one would expect a white lawyer to practice in Athlone. I felt like a fraud. But what could I say? "Sorry, comrade, you're mistaken, I'm really white." I didn't want to sound as if I had taken offense by the race miscasting, so I said nothing. I knew that the exile grapevine would fill him in soon enough.

I NEEDED TO SEE MORE of Tanzania and returned to tourist mode, once again traveling alone, by bus. I went to Lake Victoria, second in size only to North America's Lake Superior; to Mombasa and the island of Zanzibar off its coast; to the Serengeti National Park, where I watched the array of African game from a Land Rover as golden light played on the vast plain, feeling like a mere speck on this terrain.

I enjoyed traveling by myself. Alone I could commune with my surroundings and my own thoughts and reflections: I did not have to accommodate myself to someone else's needs or wishes. I could test myself, absorb the texture of the life and culture around me, whether walking through the hustle and bustle of a capital city or relaxing into the pace of the rural areas. Two or more people traveling together presented a self-contained capsule, but as a single person, I was often taken under the wing of friendly strangers. I had help finding hotels, cheap places to eat, places to visit off the beaten track. I had invitations to share food, to be taken on guided tours of a town or village. I would sometimes find myself being protected in unexpected ways. Like the younger woman who sat next to me in a crowded bus for hours. Every so often she would stretch her hand over to tug down my skirt, to try to get it to cover my knee. She was embarrassed for me, her new friend, who was dressed inappropriately. Or the older woman with me on the bus from Addis to Asmara—she did not like the way the men were looking at me, so when the bus broke the journey at a small hotel high in the Simien Mountains for the night, she insisted I share her room while feeding me *injera,* which she had brought with her, rather than let me eat where the men were eating.

Unfortunately, a white woman in Africa traveling alone had a different meaning for men. My efforts to claim I "belonged" to someone else by telling them I was married meant nothing as my husband was not with me. I held back the comments I was quick to blurt out in New York but felt the same seething. Had I really thought anything would be different? Why should it be? Patriarchy and sexism are global. I kept my antennae out to spot situations that might become uncomfortable. In Zanzibar, a young local I met at my hotel offered to show me around the island the next day. As soon as I agreed, his attitude switched from congenial to swagger and conquest. I balked and told him, probably a little too brusquely, that I had changed my mind. He was astounded, not knowing what he had done to turn my yes into a no. Such caution, however, meant I avoided situations I couldn't handle.

Back in Dar, I set off to the MPLA office. Paulo greeted me in his friendly manner, but when I asked about traveling to Angola, he became evasive. It was clear: they must have concluded I was not up to the task but were too polite to tell me. Alberto followed me as I walked disconsolately out the door and asked me to join him for a drink later. Camaraderie with Alberto had been slow to develop when we were first in Addis. I had assumed it was a language issue, but with a group of MLPA comrades one evening he commented, in perfect English, that he was surprised that I was drinking tea. "I thought Americans only drink coffee," he asserted.

"I'm not American," I told him. "I'm South African. We ex-British colonials drink tea."

"Ah, now I understand you," and then added with a smile, "I was wary of you. I thought you might be CIA." We both laughed. I kept on being considered a spy in one way or another.

Over glasses of local beer later that evening he confided in me. The movement was going through a crisis. One of the top leaders had broken away to form a new faction and a plot to assassinate Neto had been uncovered. They were not allowing any journalists to travel inside until the situation improved. I was grateful for his explanation. I had to remind myself that it wasn't always about me.

Years later stories would surface about the extent of the MPLA's disarray and the atrocities committed against its own people—shades of the authoritarian, corrupt government that would follow in the decades after Angola became independent in 1975. But back in 1973 I was too willing to believe the best of the movement. For now, though, I had to put my dream to rest while at the same time acknowledging that my trip, after almost five and a half months, was over.

My disappointment at not going into Angola was tempered by a letter from Tonio, written in his characteristic broken English. After reiterating his feelings for me, he wrote:

> You must write Victor if you want to come. I have speaked with him and he tell me that you looks very serious and he is waiting for your letter. Now the numbers of aeroplanes who we have shoted down is 18. Our struggle goes very well and I am sure that you will like to come here. Only it will be a pitty because I will not be able to accompane you.

Victor, and by extension the PAIGC, *was* serious about my visit.

TIME ON THE CONTINENT HAD PASSED like a sand-filled hourglass. At first the grains seemed to slip at a sluggish pace from the upper bulb to the lower. There was a suspended moment of equilibrium before the grains appeared to speed up until, and with a final spurt, the time was over. I tried to hang onto those last vanishing grains. The previous months had reinforced my sense of home. I had stood in the open spaces of Africa, felt its breezes, swum in its oceans, walked its beaches, looked into the far distances of its seas and open veld. These fused with memory and history and a sense of place that was grafted onto my being from the day I was born. The memory of the country of my birth, how it shaped who I became, merged with a new appreciation of the humanity that was Africa and its people— and influenced how I was affected by the colors of the sky and the tangy sweet smells of the earth.

How could I ever have imagined that by getting to know the continent better I would have my fill and then let it go? The idea of a social work degree had completely dropped off the list of things I wanted to do. Africa, not just South Africa, had become more firmly embedded in my life than before. Rather than muting my nostalgia, the trip left me with a renewed longing for home. I had reconnected with my South African self. I was African regardless of my European heritage. These identities established themselves acutely during my travels through the continent of my birth, of the birth of my parents. I heard the continent's call for me to return.

15 A Conscientious Observer

arrived back in New York at the end of August 1973, the hottest,
muggiest month of the year. It felt like a foreign country. Africa
had settled into me, attaching itself like an extra layer of skin fused
beneath my physical one, so that once more I was the outsider, the
immigrant, the unrooted. I was startled by the brashness and noise
of the city. Too many high buildings shortening my vision, too many
people on the sidewalks, all rush-rush, too many cars sending up a
cacophony of honking, engine revving, and expletive-laden yells out
of rolled-down windows. I felt like I had ventured into a metal box
and strangers were banging on the walls from the outside with metal
spoons. I climbed out tentatively, inch by inch, as I became reaccli-
mated to a city that I remembered thriving in—a city I would have to
learn to love again.

My women friends were delighted to see me, and I was as delighted
to see them. One took me to an ice-cream store for a welcome-home
treat. I stared at the large colorful tubs and my mind reeled with the
plethora of choices. How could one possibly decide? The perky assis-
tant behind the scrubbed-clean counter, her blond hair neatly pulled
back, her uniform without a wrinkle, handed me different flavors to
savor, a separate spoon for each dollop. The spoons were stubby, made
of a sturdy white plastic. I dropped the offending items into my handbag, unable to throw them away. I finally ditched them days later. A
sign of reentry.

About a week after my return, I got together with my women's
group and sat with Gail, Janet, Jennifer, Suzette, and three or four

others who in later years would peel away for various reasons. My body refused to relax. I had much to say, but I had grown unused to being with these friends, who, during my six-month absence, had continued to gel as a group without me. They had life-changing events to report: Gail had adopted an infant son; Jennifer had separated from her husband; Suzette, whose husband had abandoned her just before they planned to return home, had decided she would settle in the United States; Janet McLaughlin, who married soon after I first met her and was now Janet Hooper, was pregnant with her second child. Their news had reached me through their letters, but hearing about it in real time tugged me back into my life before Africa—the new dividing line between what I was then and what I now hoped to be. Only when I could add stories of my trip and find them listening with keen interest and empathy did I begin to feel re-anchored and less of an outsider. This was family, family was home, home was the comfort of sharing intimacies with some of my closest friends in the familiarity of Jennifer's living room.

I had missed one male friend as much as my women friends: John from American Documentary Films, whose humorous letters had me laughing as I traveled. He was now engaged in trade union organizing for the Oil, Chemical and Atomic Workers union, working in the warehouse of a pharmaceutical company that his small action group had successfully unionized. He moved boxes, drove a truck, and tried to thwart a decertification campaign. John was as close to me as any woman friend. He listened. He was thoughtful. He empathized. He gave good advice. I confided in him freely. He had one distinct advantage over my women friends: as a man, he understood and could convey the perspective of men, often useful when I was in angst about a current affair. Our conversations, free from the subtext of sexual tension, invariably happened over a beer, cuddling close as lovers in the wooden booths of the dark cavernous West End Café on Broadway. I loved him like a brother.

Reconnecting with my friends was relatively easy. Reconnecting with Eric was not. Our letters had appeared to break new ground, to open up a frankness that had been subsumed by our lives before I left. It quickly became apparent that it was easier to bare one's soul on the anonymity of a blank page than to communicate face-to-face. The glue that had held our relationship together—our love, our interests in classical music and literature, our shared past—was not enough keep us from becoming unstuck. In the months that followed we began a painful and protracted disengagement after eleven years.

Slowly I began to enjoy New York again. I knew how to negotiate it, how to reestablish the rhythm of my life there. Throwing myself back into the work of the magazine helped the reintegration. The news of an invitation to Guinea-Bissau was greeted by the collective as an achievement not only for myself but for the magazine. I published my first articles, a report on the OAU conference, an interview with Victor Maria. During the long flight back to the United States, I had mulled over possible angles for the trip. I didn't want to join the many journalists and filmmakers from around the world who had visited the liberated zones briefly to confirm that PAIGC was in control of over two-thirds of their country. What if I focused on one issue—the role of women—peering through this one window for a view into the revolution as a whole? That way I could combine my two areas of political engagement: the women's movement and the anti-apartheid, anticolonial struggles. It would be a chance to bring alive the photos Cabral had shown my friend and me at the meeting in Jennifer's apartment shortly before his death. Another thought began to take hold, first as a quiver, then as a full-blown idea: I would write a book in order to explore this theme in depth. I drafted a letter to Victor outlining my idea, emphasizing that it would bring more exposure to their cause than a few articles. Shortly before Christmas I received a reply from Victor:

> Concerning this eventual visit we have reached the conclusion that you should come. We think that it will be possible for us to receive you next January or February. Now it depends on your time table, if you can make it or not. Anyway, let us know in time your plan. This will facilitate our work for preparation of your visit.

With the intervention of Gil, I was able to postpone the visit to April. Family foundations and faith-based organizations that had supported *Southern Africa* magazine came through with funding. Bob Van Lierop, the African American filmmaker who had visited both Guinea-Bissau and Mozambique to record the revolutions, took me in hand. He took me to an army-navy store downtown where he selected appropriate gear, emphasizing the need for camouflage and sturdy boots. My single-lens reflex camera was still in good condition. I bought a new telephoto lens, stocked up on film, bought a tape recorder, packs of batteries, and dozens of cassette tapes. These were the heaviest items in the backpack that was accompanying me to Africa for the second time. I renewed my travel document. And I began to train, going for two-hour walks along the Hudson River chanting to myself "Hup-two-three-four! Hup-two-three-four!" to keep up a brisk pace.

I telegrammed the PAIGC office giving them my arrival date and time, and just six and a half months after returning from Africa, I boarded a plane for London to spend a few days visiting friends and avoiding my parents. I knew that they would have worried themselves sick if they knew I was inside the war zones, so I gave them a bland reason for my travels—visiting Dakar and Conakry to interview PAIGC leaders or some such. It would have been hard to maintain the subterfuge if I saw them face-to-face. Besides, my father, now fully ensconced in the British Trotskyist movement, was wont to attack my "liberal" (read non-Trotskyist) politics. I did not want to open myself up to his arguments when I already felt as if my trip to Guinea-Bissau might be over my head. Avoiding him meant avoiding Leonie. My six-year-old niece, whom I would love to have seen, would be incapable of keeping my presence a secret from her grandparents.

As soon as I landed at Heathrow I headed to Hermione Harris's house in Highbury Hill. Hermione was a soul mate; we had met in Cape Town when she spent a year working for an anti-apartheid organization that I was connected to. No sooner had I put down my suitcase and paraphernalia for my trip than I succumbed to flu. My rheumy eyes grew small in my aching head. I felt miserable. I slept the first day through buried under a comforter. Later that afternoon Hermione appeared at my door with a telegram. Telegrams seldom contained good news. I ripped it open:

in reference to your letter of february 19th we inform you that we have never received a request on your part to visit our country stop also no positive response could possibly have been given on this question stop being impossible to receive you in the coming months it is not useful to come to conakry stop salutations paigc

Was this a flu-induced hallucination? I read it again. My life and my hopes disintegrated like tempered glass fracturing into a thousand pieces. I dragged myself to the phone and tracked down Gil in Geneva. I could not still the panic in my voice. He was unperturbed. "It must be a bourgeois element—some backward bureaucrat in the party!" he teased in his calm, reassuring tone, promising to find out what the glitch was. "Maybe Victor was away when your telegram arrived."

I settled in to wait as my flu receded, unable to appreciate the beauty of the London spring that was bursting out around me. The intermittent rainy days better suited my mood, gray like my worry that my new career as a journalist was stillborn. I kept up my training regimen at the local park but without much enthusiasm. My hup-two-three-fours were more like a wound-down record than an energizing chant. Every few days Hermione and I would walk up the hill to Highbury Barn to treat ourselves to one of those ubiquitous English breakfasts at the local café. I would down fried eggs sunny side up, bacon, sausages, grilled tomato, baked beans and toast. along with copious cups of weak English coffee, to try to still my anxiety as I awaited the telegram that would seal my fate. When the envelope did slide through the mail slot two weeks later, it seemed to shimmer like Day-Glo paper. My fingers fumbled as I opened it: "visit finalized stop confirm arrival date stop will be met at conakry airport." I let out a yell of relief that brought Hermione rushing down the stairs, and we jumped up and down as we hugged. Two days later I was en route to Conakry, the capital of Guinea, the former French colony, independent since 1958, that had provided support to PAIGC from the start.

Part Three

16 — "I Will Not Have to Prove It Again"

My dream—before me for so long—has possibly an hour more to live. I dreamed myself into a situation where I have to prove strong and capable and competent. Where I don't speak the language, but where sensitive communication is paramount. I believed, and no doubt still do, that I have to prove *myself*. I think it is the last step I must take. If I prove capable, I will not have to prove it again.

I wrote this to Gail from my room at Conakry's Hôtel de l'Indépendance. The hotel showed signs of former grandeur, a reminder of the charmed life of the French colonizers. But now, like the capital itself, it was in disrepair. Wanting to stretch my legs after the long flight, I had taken a walk around the environs of the hotel and continued the letter with brief descriptions of what I had seen. The poverty. The crumbling buildings. The smoke wafting from cooking fires on the balconies of apartment buildings. Signs of progress since independence were slim. But this was the nature of post-colonialism. Letter writing was a good exercise, keeping me connected to friends before being catapulted into an unknown sphere beyond their support and comfort.

I looked out the window at the African landscape, stately palms alongside gnarled trees whose genus eluded me, set against a reef and a shimmering sea, the vista broken by hilly islands. Through the window came the mingled scents of earth and salt sea. Birds chirped. Breezes blew. It was cool and only slightly humid. I took in deep

satisfying breaths of Africa, a scent like no other. Even here on the
west coast it felt right.

Until it didn't. I had been told by the PAIGC official who met me
at the airport to expect someone shortly after lunch to discuss my
program. Lunchtime came and went. I continued my letter writing.
I read a little, wrote in my journal. Dark began to descend, and with
it doubt. Had I misunderstood? I remembered the caution of one
journalist who had been confined to his hotel for ten days before setting off. Was this my fate? Had I been forgotten? I lay on the bed and
slept fitfully, trying to doze away my travel fatigue. The next morning
there was still no word. After breakfast, I headed down to the sea that
beckoned from my window, notifying reception where I was in case
someone came for me. I spread a towel on the narrow beach and lay in
the sun. All worries drained into the warm sand. Give a Capetonian a
beach and we can wait out anything. I became sanguine. This is a revolution. They have other priorities than me. At lunchtime, I gathered
my things and headed back. No message. The beach calm deserted
me. I once again felt abandoned.

The space in my head that allowed anxiety to enter also allowed
doubt to take hold, despite my letter to Gail. I had willed myself into
a place that was unknown to me and impossible to envisage: Just me
and a real revolution. My anxiety had little to do with the possibility
of physical adversity and danger. I believed—possibly cavalierly—
that PAIGC could protect me. I had confidently envisioned roles
for myself: journalist, intrepid recorder of life in the war zone, book
author. Now alone and frankly scared in a faraway hotel room, I
wasn't so sure that I was up to the task.

When the phone buzzed after five, I was physically jolted. I picked
up the receiver, trying to steady my hand. José Araújo, head of the
Department of Information, introduced himself and politely asked if
he could bring someone to meet me. I opened my door to a smiling
mestiço man and a woman about my age, ebony dark. Her assertive presence filled the room. Araújo introduced Teodora Gomes,
a member of the party's Regional Commission. She was close to
my height, with a straight back and a strong, muscled body, a dark
blue turban twisted around her head. Araújo explained in excellent

English that Teodora was on her way back to the interior after attending a conference in Algeria. I would be accompanying her the next day. I grinned like a Cheshire cat and nodded back at her wordlessly.

"Can we see what you have?" Araújo asked, looking toward my backpack resting on the floor. I unpacked the results of the Army-Navy shopping spree. Two pairs of green military pants. Four green T-shirts. Green jacket. Light brown French lace-up canvas boots, ankle-high. Poncho. Water canteen. Flashlight and batteries. Toiletries. I pointed to a smaller black padded bag with my camera, telephoto lenses, and film. Notebooks and an array of pens and pencils. Bob had organized me into packing as lightly as possible.

"*Botas?*" Teodora asked and I guessed she meant boots. They had been buried under other clothes. I picked them up for her to examine more closely. She nodded her approval.

"We use the same ones," Araújo said. "Do you have another pair? One won't last the long marches." I hadn't thought of that. "You won't need the poncho. It is not the rainy season."

He told me to put aside the clothes I wouldn't be taking to the *mato* (literally "forest," but the word used for "war zone," which I would adopt). They would be kept for me until my return.

"I need to mention one thing," he added. "The Guiné government gives us permission to bring journalists into the interior through Conakry. They do not give permission for journalists to write about Guiné. We have to guarantee that."

I shrugged. It was not an issue for me. "I understand," I replied.

"We will come for you tomorrow at ten," said Araújo shaking my hand. "Get a good night's sleep. You won't sleep well for many days." Teodora shook my hand. She didn't smile. She was still sizing me up. But I couldn't stop smiling once I closed the door behind them. Anxiety and doubts vanished.

The next morning they arrived promptly. Teodora was in military uniform. I was in my green T-shirt, army pants, and canvas boots. I was on my way. On the drive to Boké, unable to converse with my companions, who spoke no English, I allowed myself to dwell on the possibility of seeing Tonio. He would have no inkling that I was heading to his country at that very moment. I replayed memories of our time in Addis as I headed mile by mile toward Boké, his base when not in the *mato* or in Conakry. Since my return to the United States he had written once. A postcard from Algeria, a photo of Algiers on one side and circumspect words on the other.

> Dear Stephanie, Times go. A big distance sepears us, but every day you are near me because our friendship iz great. Many greetings from your friend, Tonio

There was no need for circumspection. I had told Eric about my relationship with Tonio. I was similarly circumspect when I replied to his postcard, though, telling him my trip had been approved. I was hesitant to send letters to him via the PAIGC office. I had no idea how personal mail was handled or if he had received it.

The four-wheel-drive vehicle rumbled into the small dusty town of Boké near the border with Guinea-Bissau and stopped in front of a row of low brick houses. Boké had a PAIGC military base and was a pass-through point for all entering the south front. Hot and sticky and covered with a layer of red dust, I followed Teodora across a cement courtyard, past cooking fires tended by women whose children played nearby, to a room just large enough to hold two single beds, each draped with a mosquito net, that Teodora and I would share. Back in the common area I was introduced to the dozen or so militants milling around. A few spoke English, and they plied me with questions about who I was and why I was there. Teodora watched the interactions intently, insisting on translations.

"She wants to be sure we don't say anything to you that she wouldn't approve of," one of the cadres laughed. Here was my first chance to flex my new journalist muscles and begin to ask questions. Hit by the enormity of what I was about to embark upon, my mind went blank. In my head I fumbled with possible questions and they all felt trite. What was needed was easy conversation with those few who could speak English and let it flow. But my sudden attack of shyness tripped me up. The only question that persistently presented itself was: "Can you tell me where Tonio is? Could you tell him I am here?" Unable to suppress it any longer I explained to one of the English speakers, in what I hoped was a neutral tone, that I met him in Addis the year before.

"Oh, Tonio!" he smiled, assuring me that yes, he was in Boké. "He never comes to this house, though. Perhaps you will see him on your way back."

I felt on the brink of desperation but reprimanded myself. This will not do, Urdang! You are here on a serious, important, professional assignment. No room for romance. Banish such thoughts. Just then, the sound of a jeep coming to a noisy halt in front of the PAIGC house next door reached us. "It's Tonio!" one of the militants called out. He went to fetch him. He entered the house—the same determined walk, the same slight distance from those around him—to cheers and friendly backslaps. Then he saw me.

"Stephanie?" he said, pronouncing my name with emphasis on the middle syllable—"Steph*funny*." We tried to act as if we were incidental acquaintances whose paths just happened to cross. We shook hands. Said hullo. How are you? Good to see you again. When he could, he grabbed the opportunity to say in a quiet voice: "I have not been here in months. *Months*! I just came with no reason." He didn't know I was coming. He raised his voice and in a perfectly relaxed tone, asked: "When are you leaving for the front?"

"Tomorrow."

He turned to Teodora and told her he had to deliver something at the other side of Boké. "I'll take Stephanie with me," he said. "I can show her the town."

"No," she answered resolutely, with a slight frown. I suspect my attempt at controlling my emotion hadn't escaped her. He bristled with annoyance. I couldn't help an inward smile. She was no push-over, Teodora, and she took her responsibility for me seriously. It would not be the first time I would encounter her tough-mindedness and disdain for male posturing. We chatted for a few minutes more. Then Tonio strode purposefully out the door.

The next day Teodora and I set off early for Guinea-Bissau. After a few hours, the large lumbering Russian-built truck carrying us and a group of militants slowed down and came to a halt on the bank of a wide river that was, at that point, the border between the two countries. Through a bluish haze, I could make out palm trees and forests on the far bank: Guinea-Bissau. I felt a jab of emotion. Teodora jumped down from the truck and I followed. Teodora spoke several languages—Portuguese, Creole, French, Russian, and a few local languages—but none of them English. I felt diminished by my English and useless Afrikaans. For the moment, a few words in common and hand signals would have to do. Teodora pointed to a small ferry making its slow way toward us from the opposite bank looking increasingly dilapidated as it neared. The truck had to negotiate its way through the mud of the receding tide, but it finally boarded the ferry which would transport us from the one Guinea to the other and we followed on foot.

As it chugged its slow way across the river, aiming for the road on the opposite bank, Teodora and I stood next to each other, supporting ourselves against the flimsy rail. We were dressed almost identically. Dark olive green pants and short-sleeved cotton T-shirts. She wore black leather Adidas-type running shoes. I wore my canvas boots, the same as those on the feet of the soldiers with us. The similarities ended with our uniforms. Teodora's thick hair was covered by a mottled emerald green and black turban, neatly twisted about her ebony face. My curly hair was cut short. Looped onto Teodora's military belt, so that it rested against her right hip, was a black leather holster holding her revolver. Slung over my shoulder was a black leather case holding my camera. Teodora was a participant in her revolution. I was an observer. A conscientious observer.

When our driver maneuvered his vehicle off the ferry and onto the Guinea-Bissau side of the river, I looked around, almost expecting some dramatic sign of change. The trees were the same, the birdcalls were the same, the heat was the same. Teodora tapped me on the shoulder and pointed. *"Povo do Guinea-Bissau!"* she said. People of Guinea-Bissau. An elderly, wiry man followed by a girl of perhaps ten years was walking out of the dense forest. They balanced large bundles of chopped wood on their heads. It could have been a scene from any West African country, but I could not shake my romantic thoughts: not just people of Guinea-Bissau, but people of the revolution! As I waved at the two, a grandfather and granddaughter perhaps, who now stood by the road watching us pass, I wanted to know how their lives had changed. I would have to wait to find out from others.

My interpreter, Espirito Santo da Silva, a teacher at a school in the liberated zones, was waiting for us at the base camp where we were to spend our first night. Espirito was Cape Verdean, with a light brown Afro and light brown skin that showed his mixed Portuguese and African heritage. Born on one of the islands off the west coast of Africa, he had lived for a time in Europe. He spoke English as well as the Creole that was common to both Guinea-Bissau and Cape Verde, but none of the indigenous languages; Teodora would be the go-between for those. The small dictionary I packed was a godsend. But what I failed to consider at the time was how his absence as a teacher for a month would affect his students. All I thought was that I was going to promote their cause, so why shouldn't they pluck an interpreter from wherever he was based to be at my side constantly for over a month? This was more than a tad presumptuous on my part.

We set off from the base shortly after dawn, urged on by an impatient Teodora, eager to complete the last leg of the journey possible by road and begin the march on foot to her base. I was told to sit up front next to the driver, while everyone else—Teodora and Espirito Santo, the militants of the Força Armada Liberação (FAL), who would provide security for us, a few young peasant women—piled into the open back of the truck, amid ammunition, medical supplies, boxes of condensed milk and dried soup, and live chickens, their legs tied together. The truck swayed and dipped. I pressed my straightened arm to the dashboard (there were no seat belts) as the driver picked a zigzag path between large potholes and cracks at a pace that no doubt could have been easily overtaken by militants on a march. The din was terrific. The engine roared, the truck rattled, branches overhead swished and scraped against the roof of the cab and the sides of the truck. Every so often a thin branch whipped through the window to sting my arm. Suddenly: *"Para! Para!"*—Stop!—came from the back, accented by frantic banging on the roof of the cab and shouts in Creole. The driver slammed on the brakes, grabbed his rifle from the ledge behind him, and jumped down. Some of the soldiers stood up in the back of the truck and took aim. I looked around in horror. Portuguese? Shots rang out. I gripped the dashboard. Then large birds took to the air. The driver returned to the truck and we proceeded, having failed to help alleviate the food supply problem in the liberated areas.

Darkness fell. Wouldn't bombers be able to spot our headlights before we could hear the planes through the din? Then a shout from the back: *"Avião! Para-para-para!"* The drumming on the roof of the cabin was more urgent this time. The driver switched off the lights and cut the engine. Everyone in the back jumped down and crouched against the truck. I was told to stay put. In the silence, I too could pick out the distinct whine of bombers overhead. The sounds faded. I breathed a sigh of relief.

One of first questions Teodora had posed when we were eating dinner in Boké was: "Can you walk?" She "walked" her index and middle finger across the table for emphasis. "Oh yes," I said, explaining that I had walked hours every day before leaving in preparation for my visit. Teodora was unimpressed. Her fingers picked up speed. "Ah, but can you *run?*"

She had reason to be unimpressed. The first day's long march left my legs weak and my body tired. My efforts to get marching-fit in the United States were not enough. To reach Teodora's base, the farthest point on our itinerary, we marched seven to eight hours for the first four days, setting off in late afternoon or early morning to avoid the worst heat of the day. After that our marches were three or four hours for side trips from her base. Later, on the East Front, the marches were shorter, and by then I was super fit.

The bombers came often, sometimes several times a day, and even I began to pick out the first hum of the small planes above the ambient sounds that were a backdrop to the site we might be visiting. Every settlement, whether village, school, health post, or base, had trenches dug into the orange-tinged earth, five feet wide with steps cut into the earth on either side. The *povo* and militants alike ignored the hum in the distance and continued their work. Their nonchalance did not extend to me; they sent me to the trench at even a faint sound of a plane. I felt a little silly alone in a trench while life went on around me. There were exceptions. On the second day in the *mato,* the sound of bombers was loud and close. Teodora grabbed my hand, pulling me behind her as we sprinted across a clearing for the nearest trench. Villagers came flying out of huts. Women stopped their pounding. Children were hastily scooped up by whoever was the first to get to them. About twenty adults and six children pressed together in our trench.

"Comme ça!" instructed Teodora, demonstrating. I followed her lead and squatted uncomfortably with the others, our heads down, arms bent at the elbow braced against the walls for balance. Crack! Crack! The bomber spat two of its bombs, the deafening sound reverberating through the air. Two more followed. Closer still. The militants angled their heads in the direction of the sound to figure out where the bombs might have fallen. From the tone of their voices, they might have been discussing an everyday affair. Except they *were* discussing an everyday affair. About a mile away, they agreed. To my ear it sounded more like yards. Two more bombs exploded. Then the drone of the bomber receded. A militant walked over from another trench. "Okay, you can come out," he said. "The plane was one of the small ones and can only hold six bombs." Then he added, looking at me. "Stay near the trench. The *Tuga*"—the Portuguese—"don't warn us in advance when they are going to bomb us!"

We learned the next day that nothing had been hit. This was the first of a number of attacks I would experience. If we were near a village we would run to join the villagers in their trenches. If not, we'd hide under trees, hoping for the best. The shout of *"La luz!"* when marching at night was a call to switch off our flashlights. PAIGC's recent successes in downing planes meant that wary pilots flew high, staying out of range of PAIGC's land-to-air missiles, often disgorging bombs randomly. They could still do damage. On one of our marches we passed a charred hole ripped out of the forest floor. A schoolchild on an errand had been killed there a few days before.

The one trepidation I brought with me to Guinea-Bissau was the *pranchas*, the makeshift bridges that spanned river beds, narrow, uneven, lacking any support. I had seen Bob Van Lierop's photographs of militants crossing *pranchas*. The thought of traversing these flimsy constructs gripped me with terror. I would experience mild vertigo when anything protruded above the ground, even a low wall.

As a child, I had practiced walking on a two-foot-high four-inch-wide brick wall that edged the driveway at the back of our house, but that was as good as I got. A few days into Guinea-Bissau, the path through the forest veered toward the left, and there, in a clearing, was a dreaded *prancha* over a narrow but deep dry riverbed. "Oh shit!" I said softly to myself. I stared in horror at the mess of rough boards and poles and branches with nary a supporting rope or rail, just wide enough for single file.

"Espirito, I can't do this," I hissed at him as he was about to stride out. My voice was constricted. He turned to me, slightly bemused.

"Oh, it's not hard. Just follow me." He took a sure-footed step forward and was on his way. I continued to stand stock-still. Give me bombs any day. Just not this. Teodora came up behind me and immediately took in the situation. She took my arm in her hand. Her body was strong and firm, like a rock—no, like a boulder. A moving, steady boulder. With handles. "*Comme* ça," she said as she began, slowly, slowly to move crab style, across the *prancha*, holding tight onto my upper arm, my body close to hers. We moved as one. A step to the left, stop. The right foot joined the left foot. Another step to the left. The right foot joined the left foot. "*Ne regarde pas en bas!*" she instructed in French. "Don't look down!" Not a chance. We inched across. When we reached terra firma once more, she smiled at me as if I had just completed a Herculean task, which is what it felt like. With each crossing I gained more confidence, finally progressing to walking behind her, lightly holding her hand. I was triumphant.

TEODORA GREW UP IN AN *assimilado* family in a small town in the south where her father was a shopkeeper. *Mestiços* or Africans deemed "civilized" enough because of education and entrepreneurship—like Teodora's father—could be awarded the status of *assimilado*. With it came certain privileges—such as Teodora's ability to attend a Portuguese school—but not full Portuguese citizenship. When Teodora was a teenager, soldiers arrived in her town, rounded up ten well-known PAIGC supporters, and shot them to death in full view of the townspeople. Her whole family, refusing to be cowed, made the decision to join the guerrillas in the *mato*. She was still a teenager when PAIGC sent her to the Soviet Union for a one-year course in youth organizing. Later, she returned to study child psychology. Once back in Guinea-Bissau she rose fast in the party hierarchy and was appointed regional political commissioner.

Teodora expected her directives to be taken seriously, and they were. When men eyed me with too much interest or pointed to me with a "Who's *that*?" she pulled herself up to her full height and looked them in the eye. "That is my friend," she would say, and they backed off. For her parents, marriage was a woman's main goal in life. Not for Teodora. "For me, marriage meant a life of hardship." She saw too many unhappy marriages, too many subservient women. Education was her escape route. "I realized that the more ignorant and economically dependent a woman was, the more she was dominated. With education I could defend myself."

Teodora's generosity was a consistent backdrop to our weeks together. She insisted I sit in the most comfortable seat, that I get enough sleep. With shades of my grandmother, she piled my plate high with large portions of rice and whatever went with it at that particular meal. If I protested, she chided me for not eating enough. My grandmother did the same, adding, "Wot you don't like mine food?" Teodora's thoughtfulness reminded me of the generosity I had encountered in Africa the previous year. Here though it came in a war zone, where life was relentlessly taxing. The anonymous lift in the dark that hoisted me through the deep mud of a riverbank toward a waiting dugout canoe. A militant catching sight of my boots, still muddy after I had washed them in a stream, and then filling his canteen with water and meticulously washing away the residue. A gift of three fresh eggs from an elderly skinny peasant woman who carefully nursed them in the palms of her hands throughout a three-hour district meeting. A gift from a nearby village of a large gourd full of ripe mangoes. A chicken—despite the scarcity of meat—brought by a member of the village council who traveled a long distance to the school we were visiting so that she could present it. The child sent up a tree to shake oranges off the branches, four of which were offered to me in a worn piece of cloth. Fresh oysters steamed just right by a young cadre who had also made sure that the gift of eggs was soft-boiled and ignored my protestation that they should be shared. The care taken so that I had the best seat, that I was not sitting in the sun, that I got plenty of rest.

I was once mortified when I was given the sole can of Portuguese sardines. I was seldom hungry even after long marches, and all I could think was that I would soon return to the abundance of America, while my companions would continue to live their spartan lives, marching at times on empty stomachs. To resist would be considered rude and ungracious, so I said nothing and ate everything put before me. The food was mainly rice, rice, rice with a sauce over it. I found myself craving white bread and baloney sandwiches, cuisine I normally found inedible. We seldom had fruit or vegetables. On one occasion we came across a mango tree, the fruit not yet ripe. Yay, *fruit*! I ignored my mother's words to me when, as a child, she warned me never to eat unripe fruit and happily ate the green mangoes with my companions. As a result, I was completely immobilized with stomach cramp for half a day and had to miss a visit to a nearby village.

It was a relief every now and then to come across someone who spoke fluent English, to be able to delve a little deeper and not ask Espirito to explain and re-explain. One particular evening at a base where we were spending the night I got into conversation with a high-level commander.

"How do you manage the conditions in the *mato*?" he asked, genuine interest in his voice. "It must be hard for you." By then I had experienced different sleeping arrangements: canvas camp beds, floor mats, thin foam mattresses, bed frames constructed from logs strapped together with mangrove vines. Buckets of water, sometimes heated over fires, but usually cold, served as my bath, a luxury I indulged in every two or three days. I got proficient at conserving water, using a cloth dipped in the bucket to wet myself thoroughly, then wiping away soap with the same cloth and finally using the scoop provided—an enamel cup, a small bowl, a calabash—to rinse off. I would save water enough to wash my undies. It worked well—except for the time I entered a reed bathing enclosure to find two buckets of fresh water covered with leafy branches where about twenty-five bees happily buzzed. I retreated fast, my horror and fear exhibited on my face. A group of women standing nearby broke into peals of laughter. Okay, I couldn't act like a scaredy-cat white woman. Intellectually I knew that the bees wouldn't bother me if I didn't bother them. We would have to share. I carefully removed the branches and began to wash with slow movements. The bees ignored me. It was the shortest bath I ever took.

I responded to the commander's question with a somewhat nonchalant shrug. I really didn't mind. I adjusted easily, slept soundly most nights after the physical exertion of a march. The commander added: "It's like the camping the Europeans do. Except that for us, it isn't camping for recreation. It's our life. And it's gone on for years and years." He laughed wryly. "And will go on for many more."

It turned out he was wrong.

17 — "There's Been a Coup!"

One of Teodora's treasured possessions—along with her revolver and the portable manual typewriter that she worked on at her base—was a small, black, scratched-up shortwave radio. It accompanied her everywhere. Each evening a group of cadres would cluster around to listen to the news from Lisbon. The evening of April 25, 1974, was no exception. Teodora turned on her radio and, with her intense frown, fiddled with the tuner to get more than static and hisses and occasional words. Then suddenly the clear voice of the Portuguese announcer cut through the evening air. After a few minutes I saw a look of disbelief on the faces of those around the radio. They began shouting to the others to come and listen. I watched as they stood in stunned silence, listening intently to the voice emanating from that tiny radio, their faces flushed and incredulous. The announcer was talking in rapid-fire Portuguese. I heard the words "Marcelo Caetano" and "Antonio Spinola," but I couldn't understand the rest. Only when I pulled at Espirito Santo's arm was I able to pry him loose just long enough for him to tell me what they had heard.

"There's been a coup in Portugal!" he said, briefly glancing my way before turning back to the radio. What on earth was happening? A coup? By whom? Good guys? Bad guys? That very day we'd been in the trenches while planes dropped bombs on us. Was the coup staged by people in the military even further to the right than Prime Minister Marcelo Caetano? I could only wait.

Then, when the newscast ended, everyone talked at once. Excitement competed with disbelief and loud voices argued each other down. Espirito Santo explained that young army officers had overthrown the government, that Caetano had fled the presidential residence and was seeking refuge, that General Antonio Spinola was the interim leader, that the coup was intended to end fascist rule, and that people were dancing in the streets throughout Portugal. Those around me weren't dancing. They weren't convinced that Spinola, an exemplary officer of the fascist regime who at one time was governor-general of Guinea-Bissau bent on crushing the resistance, could represent anything but a right-wing coup. Or at the very least, more of the same.

Portugal's economy was built on bleeding its colonies of resources. The Portuguese government imposed taxes, created a system of forced labor, and limited access to services. Health services were for the families of the Portuguese administrators and settlers and education was for their children alone, except for the small number of *assimilados*. When PAIGC was founded in 1956, the infant mortality rate in the rural areas was six out of ten; the illiteracy rate was 99 percent. Peasants were forced to sell their crops for a pittance and then use this income to pay taxes to the administration. France and Britain were forced to give up their colonies when demands for independence swept through Africa in the late 1950 and early 1960s. Not so Portugal: with the poorest economy in Europe and a massive poverty problem itself, Portugal relied on the resources from its so-called overseas territories to sustain itself.

When armed struggle became the only option in the 1960s, the Portuguese believed they could bomb the liberation movements into submission. Instead the guerrillas became steadily more successful, and this had consequences in the home territory. By the time of the coup, two-thirds of the Portuguese army was embroiled in the colonial quagmire, and the wars were draining over 40 percent of the national budget. With soldiers dying or returning disabled, there was growing opposition from Portuguese citizens. The rumble of discontent grew to a roar. The government fell in a day: not one shot was fired on April 25, 1974.

Teodora's radio continued to bring word from outside. The new government pledged to negotiate with the colonies for independence.

Over the next few days, the bombing raids became less frequent and then ceased altogether. I smiled when I first picked out "Camarada Victor Maria Saúde" and "Camarada Gil Fernandes"—previously labeled *terroristas*—from the news reports. It was a sign of a seismic political shift after half a century of fascist dictatorship. When I arrived in the liberated zones I had assumed that the war would go on for many more years. Who didn't? I began to ponder its effect on Africa. The West, which coveted South Africa's resources—gold, diamonds, precious metals—had little interest in undermining that regime. In contrast, Portugal had become an embarrassment to Europe. No, I told myself, apartheid was there for a long, long time. I would have to be satisfied with the victory I had just witnessed.

Meanwhile, my visit continued as planned: three weeks with Teodora and Espirito Santo in the South Front, a break in Conakry and Boké—and, finally, some truncated time with Tonio—and then, with a different guide and interpreter, Fina Crato and Mario Ribeira, ten days in the East Front.

18 — "We Have to Fight Twice"

I n Guinea-Bissau we say that women are fighting two colonialisms: one of the Portuguese, the other of the men." This phrase, attributed to Cabral, was repeated in the South Front with Teodora and again with Fina in the East. Strong stuff to my ears. What did it mean on the ground for women's lives? How had women's lives changed as a result of the revolution? War or no war, I was on a quest to find out.

Bwetna N'dubi was one of the first women I interviewed. She was waiting for me at Teodora's base early one morning when I emerged sleepily out of my tent. I had first met her the previous day at a rally of a few hundred people. The long march had tired me out. Teodora was already sitting at a small table in the clearing, picking steadily at the keyboard of her typewriter while Bwetna patiently waited for me on a chair nearby. She had walked for two hours to reach me but looked fresh and composed when we sat across from each other, my notebook resting unevenly on the makeshift table in the screen tent made from mosquito netting and a structure secured by sturdy branches. The effort to protect the office–dining area–meeting room from the ubiquitous mosquitoes was foiled by the many holes in the netting.

I was immediately attracted to this woman in her late thirties, her serious manner reinforced by her tall and erect countenance. Her taut body was evidence of hard work in the fields and the long distances she marched as a member of the regional council. A PAIGC directive insisted that at least two of the five members of all the elected councils had to be women. I could not gauge how widespread this was as I had to rely on Teodora for women to interview, and I knew she would choose the most vocal women, the ones most likely to be members of such councils. After the customary inquiries about health, family, the walk to the base, followed by my explanations about why I was in Guinea-Bissau, all translated from Bwetna's Balanta into Teodora's Creole into Espirito Santo's English, I turned on my tape recorder and began to pose questions. Her answers were lengthy and I had to ask her to take more frequent breaks to benefit from all she said. This was a consistent problem. Women would rush on, barely taking a breath in their desire to tell me their stories. I would try for a balance between their eagerness and my wish to lose as little as possible in the translation.

Bwetna's peasant family was typical. Her parents were illiterate and, like the majority of peasant children, she had no education. The vicious downward spiral of poverty and exploitation meant hungry children and hungry families. The administration clamped down on any glimmer of protest with an iron-clad hand. "The *Tuga* paid us what they pleased for our crops," Bwetna told me, using the common Creole word to refer to the Portuguese. From a young age Bwetna watched as her father was whipped by the *Tuga* when he was unable to come up with tax money. As Bwetna told me her story she rubbed her fingers and palms together in a jerky way, as if she was trying to erase the memory. The skin of her bony hands was cracked and calloused after many years of pounding rice and other hard domestic labor.

During my time in Guinea-Bissau I was prone to reflect on differences with South Africa. The apartheid regime was oppressing and destroying the lives of its own people. Portugal was an occupying force. I am aware that comparisons between levels of suffering are meaningless. They might have been different, but the brutality, violence, and trauma were all too real, whether forced to grow crops for a pittance in a Portuguese colony or forced to work for a pittance to sustain the apartheid economy; whether rounded up as a child into forced labor gangs or deprived of childhood in the absence of parents, facing malnutrition and death from hunger and poverty. Different tactics; similar disastrous impact.

The colonial administration needed labor—to build roads, dig trenches. They simply grabbed it whenever and wherever they chose.

Bwetna was eight or nine when the first white men she had ever seen came to her village and rounded up a group of boys and girls, including her. The parents watched helplessly as their children were taken away to work on the construction of a road that ran through a nearby forest. The girls' task was to collect water and carry sand. They were not paid. They slept in the forest. The only food was the rice they brought with them and Bwetna remembered being always hungry, always exhausted. The children were beaten if they tried to escape. Bwetna was a scared little girl and cried a lot. I had read enough about Portuguese colonialism to know about these conditions, but to listen to the stories was something else. This was child slavery. It was gross violence against children.

"Has your life as a woman changed because of the mobilization?" I asked Bwetna. Her face lit up. When the first PAIGC mobilizers came to her village, they insisted: "We want women to participate as well." She was now an elected member of the regional council. "I have more responsibility than many men." But it wasn't easy, she said, emphasizing her point with a drawn-out *n'tchia,* a squeaky sucking-in-air sound that came with scrunching up one side of her mouth. "*Ai,* men don't like this. They have had to learn to accept us as equals in our struggle. We women have to join together so that men can't tell us that we can't do the work they do. We have to fight twice—first to convince women, and then to convince men that women must have the same rights as men."

An uneven smile played around Bwetna's mouth when she talked and illuminated her face in a flash when she found something pleasing or amusing like the idea of fighting twice. She was luckier than most, she said. Although she had to be away regularly from her home and her husband, he "stays home and takes care of everything."

I heard versions of Bwetna's story from other women I interviewed, whether they were Muslim, animist, or Christian, from a village or a small town. I knew that these changes could not sit well with all women, and certainly not all men. However, women assured me that *their* fathers, *their* husbands, *their* brothers supported the revolution and therefore for them, no problem. They were encouraged. *Other* men however…

"In my case it was no problem," Njai Sambo, a member of her village council told me. "Although both my father and my husband accepted what the party says about women, I know men who have refused to allow their wives to join the struggle. They feared that if their wives went to the camps, other men would take their women. Women had to do what their husbands said."

As I waited for the translations to reach me I had time to absorb what the women were telling me. I felt that tingling sensation that comes when captivated by a story, a statement, good material for my book. What I was hearing from African peasant women, who in all likelihood had never crossed the borders of Guinea-Bissau, resonated for me as a Western feminist. They were talking out of their experience, so vastly different from mine and most American women. And yet in their understated way they were speaking our language. Patriarchy was not only a Western concept.

I was getting what I had come for. I was getting my stories. And so I adjusted my tape recorder, made sure the batteries were working, wrote notes at a furious rate. I welcomed the painful details, I welcomed the assertiveness, I welcomed the turn of phrase. At the same time, I couldn't deny a sense of inadequacy that would pop up unbidden. I knew I had to banish such fears, banish thoughts that I was a "play-play" journalist. PAIGC had trusted me. I had no choice but to do my level best to be a serious one. This only got worse when I had trouble pinning Teodora down to an interview in the South Front. Without her reflections, I worried that there wouldn't be enough breadth for a book. I became anxious, and this made me selfishly unsympathetic to Teodora's situation: how trying it must have been to arrange the interviews, to make sure I was safe, all the while needing to get on with her own work, particularly now that the war had stopped. I couldn't help it; I was turning into a difficult journalist, one of those pushy ones who leave a bad feeling behind after they returned to whatever country they came from. Finally, about two days before we were to return to Boké, she relented.

As she began to talk, to grow more expansive, it was clear—to my relief—that she was really enjoying herself. She emphasized that the struggle for the liberation of women was multifaceted. Women had to participate together and equally with men. But there was the internal struggle as well: women had to convince themselves that they could be free, and that they were equal to men in every way, in social life, in political life. This was the tougher issue, she said, one that would take a long time to achieve. And finally, women had to convince not only themselves but the men as well. Only then could we hope to transform society.

Predictable or not, her views fit so well with the views of American women who considered themselves socialist feminists. Hearing Teodora say it, within the context of the ongoing struggle, heightened my own commitment to feminism. I found her words particularly compelling because I was trying not to impose my own perspectives and steer clear of the heated debates and analytical and theoretical writing that marked feminism in the West at the time. So I chose to avoid questions that might be culturally contentious, ones that I thought were of more relevance to Western women at this juncture.

Others had fewer qualms. About two years later, a journalist I knew from the solidarity movement visited independent Guinea-Bissau and gave me the recording of her interview with Teodora. I once again heard Teodora's forceful voice expounding on the advances for women. Then this question: "In the United States lesbians represent the cutting edge of the women's movement in their activism and struggle against discrimination and oppression. How is this reflected in the women's struggle in Guinea-Bissau?"

The interpreter's English was fluent. I suspected he had studied in Europe and might have been familiar with such concepts. After he translated the question there was silence. Then Teodora asked him to explain. He rephrased the question. He translated. Teodora still needed clarification. Back and forth they went. I didn't need to understand the Creole they were speaking. Teodora's perplexed tone told it all. Then finally she got it.

"Oh no," she responded. "We don't have that problem here." I laughed out loud. "Not in *our* culture" was the subtext of her words. I recalled the young man I had met at one of the bases in the south when I was with Teodora. He was in his early twenties, no more, dressed in the regular camouflage army uniform but somehow managing to give it more flare. His walk and his mannerisms could not be mistaken: he was gay. I observed him for the day we were at the base. He mingled with the other men and women with ease. No one appeared to react to him at all even though there could have been no doubt about his sexual preference. I didn't ask about him—I felt it would be intrusive. What would Espirito's response have been? Teodora's? A lost journalistic moment.

At the same time, I saw Teodora's denial of the "problem" for what it was: a blindness to lesbian and gay presence in Africa, something that has, at the time I write this, become a heinous violation of human rights in many parts of the continent, egged on by a fundamentalist U.S. right wing.

Teodora's analysis in 1974 confirmed my desire to believe that if a revolution confronted the status of women it would have a greater chance of success. I wonder, looking back down years and decades, how I could have viewed revolution and life as such simple equations: revolution = women's liberation = people's victories = success.

19 — "You Will Leave from Bissau"

I t is the beginning of June 1974, seven weeks since I first ferried across the river into Guinea-Bissau from Guiné. I am heading across the dry open African veld to the Vendoleidi base in the East Front, our last stop in Guinea-Bissau before heading back to Boké and Conakry. With me are Mario Ribeira and Fina Crato, who have been my companions on this second trip into the liberated zones. Chatting easily among ourselves, we are walking at a slower pace than I have become accustomed to, no longer in single file. The sense of urgency has dissipated. The bombers are no longer a threat. The war is over.

Mario had recently returned from Sweden, after five years of study, and was keen to discover for himself the changes that had happened during his absence. He was not disappointed. Conveying this to me in fluent English was, frankly, a relief. About my height, he was slender like all militants. That he was multiracial was clear from his light skin, thick black beard, and soft curly black hair that was always topped with his khaki cap. He grew up in Guinea-Bissau; his paternal grandfather was German, his grandmother was Cape Verdean, and his mother was African.

Virtually tied at the hip for ten days, we got to know each other well. I appreciated his lack of rhetoric—no pat phrases about the revolution—and his careful translations. Together we reflected on and analyzed what we were seeing and hearing. He was more than a translator. He was a kindred spirit, a man who understood the importance of women's fight for equality. With Mario I could let go (mostly) of the little barbs of doubt that had on occasion surfaced during my interviews in the south, wondering how much Teodora was influencing the outcome. I felt more comfortable with my assumptions and observations.

I was the first journalist that Fina, age twenty, energetic and open-minded, was accompanying. She too was fascinated by what she was hearing, interjecting her own forthright perspectives on men, male attitudes, and the need for change. As a team of three we interacted seamlessly, Mario providing a communicating bridge between us. Fina did not, like Teodora, hold a senior political position, and so had no political agenda to push. I watched her interact freely with the women we interviewed, her small body poised to take in what they were saying, an African print scarf on her head, her hair in stout braids sticking out from under her scarf. The older women appeared to harbor no reserve or hesitancy at being asked questions by such a young woman. With them, as with everyone, her broad mouth was quick to break into a grin, her eyes twinkling mischievously. There was both a toughness and a softness about her, and I thought she would go far in the new Guinea-Bissau.

Fina was born in 1954 on Como Island, a large island in the south-east. She was two years old when PAIGC first began mobilizing the villages. Eight years later, sitting in the sun outside her house one morning, she heard a drone in the distance that grew louder and louder. She ran inside to her mother, shouting excitedly.

"Mama! Mama! Planes are coming."

"Oh, stop your nonsense," her mother shouted back, "You're always making things up."

A few minutes later, the planes could be seen getting bigger and bigger as they approached. The sound was unmistakable. The villagers ran out of their houses into the open. They had never seen planes so close before and stared up at the sky with curiosity, smiling at each other and exclaiming, some waving at the metal birds. Then bombs began to rain down on the upturned faces. One, then another, then another. They rushed for shelter. Many were killed. Many more were wounded. It was the beginning of daily raids that continued for months. They began to adjust their lives. By five o'clock in the morning the women were up, preparing food. By seven o'clock everyone was ready to leave the village. They hid in the mangrove swamps, where they would remain the whole day, water up to their waists. The *Tuga* then began to bomb at dawn, this time using napalm. This was before its use in Angola that Paulo told me about. "The villagers were very inventive," she said. "They would take the empty napalm canisters and make spoons and combs and such things."

AS WE ENTER VENDOLEIDI I can see that military discipline has been replaced by elation. People are out in the open, no longer listening for the drone of bombers, no longer the more earnest, somber atmosphere I had found at the bases I visited. It could have been a different country. Cadres were quick to say: "You'll see, you'll leave from Bissau!" Perhaps, I thought. Would the new Lisbon government give up their source of raw materials in their colonies so easily? Could they even afford to? But here at the base and all over the liberated zones, the war is definitely over. I watch two young soldiers in green and brown camouflage uniforms, cleaning their AK-47s, meticulously rubbing the disassembled parts with oil. For the last time?

The Guineans are free. So are the Angolans and the Mozambicans. Now it is left to Zimbabwe, Namibia, and South Africa to purge the blight of minority rule from the African continent.

WITH MY TRIP COMING TO an end, I could allow myself to succumb to another emotion: I will be seeing Tonio once again. Waiting in Conakry between my trips to the South and East Fronts, we had managed to spend time together alone. One afternoon he picked me up at the hotel and drove me in his jeep to a restaurant on a pier that jutted out to the sea, where we ate grilled chicken and drank local beer and watched the setting sun. I felt becalmed watching the small fishing boats as they set out or returned with their catch as the sun set, the clear sky streaked with orange and red. Just two lovers holding hands, gazing at the horizon. He was in a reflective mood. "Don't be romantic about the revolution. There is *nothing* romantic about it."

At the time, he was certain that the war wasn't over. Too much was yet to be resolved. "I have given eleven years of my life to it." I did a quick calculation. He was twenty-five when he joined PAIGC. "They should have been happy, full years—the best years of my life, hard years. Not that I regret it. Never. But in the end the sacrifices are for the next generation." He separated his hand from mine, as he drew back into himself. "We are nearly all men. We drink, think, talk, live the revolution. All our talk is about tactics, politics, strategy. It absorbs our lives. There is little real humanity." He stared out to sea, caught up in the thoughts he was expressing. "Sometimes something happens and a memory stirs in me and I remember what I should have been. But there is no time to ponder it. Only now that I am with you, I am very aware of the sacrifices I have had to make. Talking to you, someone I can really talk to, brings back feelings and thoughts I have cut out for a long time."

We sat silent. Then he turned to me. His voice was almost defiant. He reiterated the plan to meet. In Algeria, perhaps. Or Brazil. A much-deserved break, he said.

On the way back to the hotel we were caught in the first rain of the season, which burst in torrents out of a now wild and merciless sky. It was soon after the May Day celebrations, and the banners that stretched across the road broke and wrapped themselves with frenzy around the poles. Scarcely able to see even inches ahead of us, Tonio stopped the open jeep under the shelter of a bridge to wait out the storm, and I watched the plummeting rain bounce back off the dry, hard earth, giving the impression that it came from both above and below.

Now, as I am about to leave the East Front I have time to fantasize: Tonio and I basking on the beaches of Brazil, eating at restaurants overlooking the sea, making love; or in Algeria, a country that had long intrigued me; or even on the beaches of Portugal itself, a destination I had long boycotted. My thoughts of a holiday mutate into fantasies of a more permanent life. The year between my trip to Africa and this trip to Guinea-Bissau had further eroded my marriage. This trip clinched for me that it was irrevocably over. I am free to consider a different future. Why not live in Guinea-Bissau now that it was about to be independent and contribute to national reconstruction? With the prospect of Mozambique's independence, majority rule in South Africa would surely come closer, by leaps and bounds. Until I can return home, why live in the United States when I could live in Africa?

But I had a community in the United States that had taken the past nine years to build. I had crafted a family from my close South African and American friends. Leaving would mean unhitching myself from the anti-apartheid movement that moored me to that interim home. There was still the strong tug of my community, my friendships. Yet beside me a militant walked, easily shouldering my most precious possession, my backpack, which contained all my notebooks, tapes, and rolls of film. They represented my new career as a journalist. I wanted my writing to meld with my activism, an activism that was part of my life in the United States. Back and forth I went: Guinea-Bissau, Tonio, the United States, my community. Then I began to play with a compromise. What if I were to divide my time between New York and Bissau? See how it goes with Tonio. Skills of every kind would be needed. I could be of use. *Bingo!*

Tonio's marriage played no part in my fantasy. He and his wife hadn't spent time together in years. Tonio told me in Addis that he didn't know if he still loved her. It was me he loved. That was all I needed to know. Twigs snapped underneath my now worn down canvas boots as my pace quickened with these thoughts.

A few days later we drove into the PAIGC compound in Conakry. My brain was spinning. I was high from my trip to the East Front, which had rounded out my material for my book, high from witnessing the historical moment of the coup from inside Guinea-Bissau, excited by the talk of negotiations and the thought that all the Portuguese colonies were on their way to liberation, and high at the thought of seeing Tonio again and planning the future years together. I looked out of the window of the small building where I was changing out of my uniform for the last time, removing my worn, mud-caked boots, peeling off my dust-clogged socks. Across the clearing I spotted him in earnest conversation with another comrade. I pulled on my civvies as hastily as I could and headed out the door. I was ready to fling my arms around him. I couldn't give a damn about what others would think. He saw me and strode purposefully in my direction, looking intently at the ground as he walked. Something in his posture made me assume a more restrained stance. A few feet before reaching me he raised his head slowly until our eyes met.

"I vont that you meet my wife," he said, formally shaking my hand. His face was blank, no smile.

"Your *wife*?"

"She arrived yesterday. As soon as negotiations were announced, she left East Germany and came to be with me."

My limbs turned to lead. I could say nothing more. There was nothing to say. Others came up to greet me, all excited by the turn of events. The animated buzz felt like a swarm of ecstatic bees threatening to sting me. I wanted to swat them away. Inside me a spark was dying little by little. I saw a European woman walking toward the group that had gathered around me. She had a sweet face, curly blond hair to her shoulders, and a shy smile.

"Meet Sonya," Tonio said. To her, he spoke German. Close to Afrikaans I could pick out some of the words. He was explaining that I was a journalist. In truth, that was all I was now, a journalist. We shook hands. Her hand was soft.

That night I joined a group at a local restaurant. The mood was celebratory. The Guineans drank beer and ate succulent grilled chicken and fish with gusto. I picked at my food and acted the part of the cheerful, carefree visitor, laughing when others laughed. I cast sideways glances at Tonio's wife. She was quiet and seemed overwhelmed by it all. I felt a glimmer of sympathy. It was her first visit to Africa. We had no common language, but as the only whites and pretty much the only women, we smiled at each other. Each one of her smiles, gentle as they were, sent stinging shards into my heart, still consumed with Tonio. The band blared out West African music at top volume. With lively abandon, I danced with the men, one then another. No longer able to resist, I asked Tonio to dance. We headed for the other side of the packed earth dance floor. Shielded by the other dancers, we pressed close against each other and moved slowly to the music. I was just able to contain the wrenching sobs that threatened to break out.

"There will always be Antonio and Stephanie," he said into my ear. "Always." We danced closer, and he momentarily held my head tightly to his chest. A daring move. Then he was the correct PAIGC militant again as he pulled away. "I have to give my wife a chance. She loves me." There was no hint of apology in his voice. Of course it was the decent thing. I begrudgingly respected him for it. "I have to find out whether I still love her. Whether we can build a life together. It is only fair. She has waited so long."

Of course it is only fair.

LOVE? WAS IT THE REVOLUTION that had propelled my feelings? Perhaps I was simply romanticizing these valiant, courageous, selfless people who had committed their lives to the struggle. Tonio embodied these qualities for me. I wanted to believe that it was Tonio the man, not the revolutionary, who had sparked my love.

There was a difference between looking into a revolution from the outside, and being on the inside looking out. I was on the outside—the conscientious observer. To Tonio, revolution meant the daily grind, the continual hard work and lack of personal life. To me, his sacrifices were heroic; to him, this was just something that had to be done while one's youth passed, year by year, and a normal existence that meant family, stability, community—home—remained elusive.

So when we met—I from that unattainable outer world and Tonio the very embodiment of the revolution—it was not surprising that the connection was volatile. But sustainable? The brief and magical relationship in Addis the year before and then in Guiné added a frisson of excitement to my travels. I lived a life that tended to defer to my heart. I had no regrets on this score. That didn't mean I denied my mind, the part of me that had come in a professional capacity to view a revolution. Although I was crushed when my fantasy dissolved, I knew I would have to move on. I had a book to write.

I was to spend a few more days in Conakry, interviewing leaders about their responses to the end of the war and their vision for a future that was tantalizingly imminent. José Araújo, the head of the Department of Information whom I had met when I first arrived in Conakry, agreed to set up final interviews. These would round out my trip nicely, ending it on a positive note, which would not have been possible before the coup. I couldn't believe my good fortune, that I had actually been in the war zones at the time of the coup. I was witnessing history in action.

I forced myself to get up early to prepare my questions. Once more at the Hôtel de l'Indépendance I could look out my window at the sea. I felt calm as I concentrated on my task, so much so that I literally jumped when the phone rang. It was reception telling me that José Araújo was waiting for me downstairs. Excellent, I thought. He would have my itinerary for the next few days. I grinned at him when I saw him waiting for me in the foyer. He didn't grin back.

"You must pack your bags," he said. "Your flight leaves in three hours." His voice sounded curt; not his usual friendly welcome. "Plans have changed. We are very busy. It is best that you leave right away."

I looked at him dumbfounded. What was going on? Why the sudden change in my program? I guessed that the powers that be had reviewed my program and decided that my presence and the need to cater to me was no longer a priority. I had no other explanation, and Araújo would give me none, so I could do nothing but pack my bags.

At the airport I passed journalists who were just arriving, with their confident strides and bags heavy with audio and film equipment ready for the interviews they would be conducting. I could not help feeling envious, even jealous. On the other hand, my bag was heavy with tapes and notebooks and undeveloped film. I had material and stories that these journalists and reporters, rushing in for a few days to write about the sudden change of fortune, could not get. It was okay that I was leaving. I had done what I came to do. I now had to take the final step.

20 — "Now I Need to Believe in Myself"

I am once again in New York. With a specific task ahead, I feel more rooted. The re-entrance is smoother. I try to put Tonio out of my mind, but it takes a while for the rawness to heal. I find an apartment to share, set up a desk in my room, and settle in to make sense of my notes, transcribing tapes, figuring out A Book. I support myself through writing articles and as a guest lecturer at universities and colleges all over the United States, in both African Studies and the Women's Studies departments. I talk at meetings of feminists, solidarity activists, and whoever else is interested.

My first presentation is arranged by Suzette at a women's center in Brooklyn. In the car on the way there, she shows me the flyer she designed for the event. It is striking and professional, the sort of flyer announcing someone with important, erudite things to say. I am nervous enough and somehow this flyer threatens to do me in.

The smallish room is jam-packed with about seventy women sitting on chairs, cross-legged on the floor, leaning against the walls—all looking eagerly at me, ready to take in what I will say. I launch into my talk, picturing the women I have interviewed, the scenery, the long walks, my interactions with Teodora and other leaders, and after a few stumbles I find myself speaking effortlessly from the pictures in my head. I come to the end. The applause is spontaneous and sustained, the questions from the audience show real interest, the vibes are positive—what a relief! Gail and Suzette hug me and proclaim the event a great success. But on the ride back home Suzette asks, "What was wrong with the flyer? Why didn't you like it?" There is hurt in her voice.

"It's wonderful!" I reply. "It just scared the living hell out of me!" We can laugh now that the talk is over. I will find that I never overcome my pretalk nervousness, those proverbial butterflies fluttering about in my stomach. More like a swarm of bees trying to escape my chest than delicate butterflies.. Once I launch in, the apprehension usually dissipates. I once admitted this to Prexy Nesbitt, a good friend in the movement who had arranged a series of talks in Chicago. "If you were *not* nervous, I would be worried," he says, speaking from his own experience. "The nervousness comes with a rush of adrenalin that gives spark to your talk. Without it you could succumb to blandness."

In the ensuing months I refine my talk, adjust it for different audiences, and find myself enjoying my role as a lecturer and storyteller. By the end of the year I have settled down to seriously work on my book. I start. I stumble. I write. I am done in by massive writer's blocks. I question why I ever thought I could write a book. I question my sanity. What I can't do is quit. Not after the welcome I got from PAIGC. They believed in me and arranged a trip worthy of a serious journalist, one they trusted to tell the story right. Now I need to believe in myself. I owe it to them.

John takes on the role of sorting me out. We drink more beers at the West End Café. He does more than cheerlead, refusing to let me wallow in self-pity, but instead asking probing questions that help me break through the blocks. This is the first time I am tackling something that relies on an ability to both write and analyze. It is the first time I am being called on to actually finish something, unlike my truncated university career. He helps me crack open the blocks, which assure me that at least for now, I can do it. When we part I am ready to return to my electric typewriter for a burst of energetic writing, my fingers flying to keep up with my thoughts.

IN SEPTEMBER 1974 GUINEA-BISSAU becomes the newest member of the United Nations, its colorful green, gold, and red flag joining the phalanx of flapping pennants that line the front of the UN building on First Avenue. Gil Fernandes has been named ambassador extraordinary and plenipotentiary to the United Nations. One crisp fall afternoon we go for a walk in Riverside Park on the Upper West

Side of Manhattan. The sun in the clear blue sky lights up the leaves, yellow and red. The scenery, the feel of the air, the mingled smell of New York could not be more different from Africa. This is a wonderful time of year in the city, when the intense heat of the summer dissipates, the air is crystal clear, and the Hudson River is blue and sparkling, nature's gift before the cold of winter settles in. I turn to Gil walking beside me. He looks serious, even a bit annoyed.

"Anything the matter?" I ask.

"Remember," he begins, and he looks sideways having to twist his body slightly because of his old neck injury, "you were told in Conakry that you only had permission to write about Guinea-Bissau, not Guiné?"

"Yeees," I reply cautiously, trying to figure out where this is going. Of course I knew this. José Araújo had impressed this upon me when he came to my hotel room in Conakry.

"Conakry is really annoyed with you."

I stop walking. Gil turns to face me.

"But I didn't write about Guiné!"

"Well, they read your letters. They thought you would write critical articles. You should have known better."

The blood drains from my face. Suddenly that rushed departure from Conakry falls into place. How thick could I be? In South Africa I would have known instinctively not to write anything in letters that wasn't for the eyes of the security police or the government. After seven years of living in a democracy I had lost this intuitive sense. I thought back to the mildly disdainful remarks I had made about Conakry in my letters to friends. It seems that the powers that be in Conakry were more impressed with me as a journalist than was warranted.

"I'm sorry," I say, my voice as small as I felt.

"I just wanted you to know," he says, with his not-to-worry shrug.

But of course I do worry. At first I am humiliated but then I become angry: How could Conakry assume I would break my assurances to PAIGC? How could PAIGC buy into this bullshit? It's just the sort of thing South Africa would do—reading mail, expelling journalists. I push it aside, but I can't let go of the sinking feeling I have let PAIGC down.

NINE MONTHS LATER, IN JULY 1975, it was Mozambique's turn to see its flag raised at the UN. Joaquim Chissano, one of Frelimo's top leaders, headed his delegation and joined us at a party to celebrate the victory. He looked even slighter than he was as he danced with an elegant six-foot member of the Southern Africa Committee, his legs moving fast and rhythmically to the African music blasting from the player. Next to him danced Sharfudine Khan, the well-loved and respected head of the Frelimo office in New York. Sharfudine, an observant Muslim, had refused to dance at many a party over the years. "I will dance when Mozambique is free," he assured us. Now he was fulfilling his promise. We stood around him and laughed, clapping in time to the music, applauding both him and his country.

THE PAGES OF MY DRAFT piled up. And as they did, it was clear that I needed a section on the liberated Guinea-Bissau, now independent for over a year. I applied for a visa and was relieved to find that the Guiné incident had not rendered me persona non grata. And so, just short of two years after I was rushed out of Conakry, I headed back to Guinea-Bissau.

This time I did not need a special travel document. I was a citizen of the United States. I applied in 1974 when my South African passport was about to expire. I doubted it would be renewed. Besides my work in the anti-apartheid movement, a book based on papers I had written with a colleague for the UN Centre Against Apartheid had been found "objectionable" in South Africa and banned. When the letter arrived with the date of my induction as a U.S. citizen, I wrote to Prexy, my African American friend from Chicago, about my ambivalent feelings: By becoming a citizen was I distancing myself from "home"? Is there a contradiction between being an activist in the struggle against apartheid and becoming a citizen of a country that props up that system? He calmed me down with his reply:

> How hard the process of joining this country must be for you. You
> are deeply and totally an African woman. And you must bear in
> mind, when you say their silly "I pledge's" and "I swears" that the
> day will come when, with thousands of others, you folks will stand

again on Table Mountain. It is one of my deepest dreams, you
know, S, the dream of being with you folks when you walk back
into your own land and your own history.

Many years later, in 1994, Prexy would be one of the international
monitors for South Africa's first democratic elections.

I was pretty cavalier about the whole business. The naturalization
ceremony didn't help: the tacky miniature paper flags I was handed
before the ceremony with "Made in Korea" stamped on the sticks;
the imperious judge who delivered a lecture to the three hundred or
so inductees, extolling the United States as the greatest country in
the world and admonishing us to appreciate the new freedoms we
would be enjoying, and then, before we took the Pledge of Allegiance,
warning us that officials would be walking down the aisles to make
sure we were reciting the pledge. I dutifully repeated the words even
though I could not share the elation of most of those in the hall with
me. While appreciating the democracy compared to the police state I
had grown up in, I continued to question the claimed freedoms. What
about racism? What about poverty? What about women's inequality?

In November 1976, when I voted for the first time in my life, I was
unexpectedly moved by the notion that I could vote for a presidential
candidate of my choice. I thought of the disenfranchised population
in South Africa and treasured the freedom to cast my vote. I have
voted at every opportunity since, whether local or national. With
this first election, I had to acknowledge it wasn't "just" a passport—I
was making a commitment to living in the United States and being a
responsible citizen. What I didn't feel was blind patriotism, especially
the frequent assertion that "America is the best country in the world."
I wonder how many other countries these patriots have known.

ONE SATURDAY NIGHT A FEW WEEKS before I am to leave for
Guinea-Bissau I am at a party with John. We have had a little too
much to drink. Our defenses down, we say, why not? Neither of us is
involved in a relationship. John and I are so close, why not, in these
days of the sexual revolution? We spend the night together. The next
day he is off to New Orleans for a two-week holiday to indulge his

love for jazz. While he is away, I am surprised to find that the ground has shifted. I can't stop thinking about him, missing him. It is clear that I am in love with him; I have probably been in love with him for a long while. I am eager for his return. As soon as he does we head for a catch-up at the West End Café. I want to take his hand; I want to sit close to him; I want to tell him, my beautiful lover from two weeks back, about these new feelings, but he gets in first, eager to tell me about the affair he had in New Orleans. I move away from him. I sit in silence. He finally picks up that there is something the matter. I tell him. We talk for hours. He admits that he feels the same way as I do. That he has for a long time. But he thought he was following my lead, treating our night together as a transient moment and so was protecting himself. Our relationship speeds up on the fast track, spurred on by knowing we will soon be apart for the months I am in Guinea-Bissau.

21 — "She Doesn't Know What She Fought For"

swing my camera bag over my shoulder and behind me so that my back can take its weight. With my free hand, I grasp the door frame of the old plane, a former Portuguese troop-carrier that now bears the gold, green, and red flag of the new African republic. I descend the rickety metal ladder from the plane, rung by rung, until my feet are on terra firma, independent Guinea-Bissau. I exult inwardly as I follow the other passengers across the runway toward the small, shabby airport terminal. A North African agronomist, African and East European diplomats, two Danish filmmakers, PAIGC militants, and an elderly peasant woman have all shared the bumpy flight from Dakar to Bissau this Saturday morning in May 1976. The heat presses down from above and rises up from the dark, tarred surface to envelop us. I remember how the country's climate had been described to me: hot and very hot. Today is very hot. Yes, I am back, but more than that: I feel as if I am part, if only a speck, of the achievement. I am ready to settle in for the next two months, ready to reconnect with my continent of "home."

The next few days I find many of the cadre I had got to know during my previous visit and I am welcomed like a returning friend. Teodora is now a high official in the government, and Tonio and Victor Maria are now ministers; others are members of Parliament, judges, department heads. Only Mario is missing, and I am sad to hear that he is out of the country for medical treatment. A few years later I learned that he died.

The Ministry of Information has set up an itinerary for me so that I will see not only Bissau and other towns that were out of bounds during the war but places in the liberated areas that I had marched through on my previous visit. I can now visit by car or fly. I spend most of my time in Bissau, absorbing the pace of the small city, walking from end to end, visiting the homes of friends now settled there. Slowly I peel off my New York and American outer layer and meld with my South African and African self.

My first trip to the south is a quick trip on a six-seater plane; before, I had marched eight hours a day through the *mato* with Teodora. Beneath us are huts, rivers, forests, palm trees, mangroves, and villages spread out like a tapestry map come alive in tones of brown and green—the rich textures of earth, foliage, human life. A similar scene must have greeted Portuguese pilots as they reconnoitered for targets, instantly transforming a tranquil countryside into a nightmare as their bombs scorched the vegetation, gouged holes out of the fertile earth, and reduced huts to smoldering cinders, leaving civilians dead and wounded. Two years earlier I had been on keen alert for the sound of those bombers. I am the one surveying the scene from above. An apparent tranquility is no longer threatened because it comes, now that the war is over, with something more profound: peace. Were the new freedoms promised nestled among the scene I was surveying below? The answers I will get in the weeks I am there are disturbing.

The plane bumps down onto the Catio airstrip, a dirt clearing in the midst of rice fields, palm trees, and huts. Children come running from the huts to greet the plane, their thin brown legs moving fast, their small bodies exuding the thrill they feel at this arrival from above. Planes like this one are now a novelty, not a threat. I spot Cau Sambu, regional party secretary, the charismatic leader I had met in the South Front. No longer in camouflage, he stands out in a long pink djellaba that sways as he walks toward me. He has a lot more weight on his tall frame than he had when I first met him. Most people I remeet have.

The last time I heard Cau address a meeting he had kept his audience captive until his voice grew hoarse, his long speech filled with stories and metaphors, sometimes encouraging, sometimes admonishing, promising a new life once the war was won. All the while I sat on a makeshift bench built out of three rough poles strapped together with vine, built for us dignitaries—Teodora, the other regional leaders, and myself. The days of marching long distances and eating minimally had rendered me skinnier than I had ever been. I sat out the hours of the meeting, eyeing with longing the soft ground the women were sitting on, while I constantly shifted my weight to no avail until my butt was bruised and aching. This time there are chairs and a table. Cau stands for a speech radiating the same energy and vigor I remember from my previous visit for close to one and a half hours. My interpreter, Bari, fluent in English and about my age, translates ably as Cau describes the conditions of the country, reporting on decisions made at the recent meeting of the National Assembly (elections were to take place for a new assembly in a few months), and emphasizing the need for vigilance against counterrevolutionaries as well as the need to protect what had been gained during the armed struggle. If a fisherman has a canoe full of fish and one fish goes bad, he cautions, then it is necessary to throw that fish away immediately or it will turn the lot. I feel some foreboding at the suggestion that justice be taken into the hands of the average citizen. Afterward, a number of villagers stand up to express glowing praise for Cau and the ongoing revolution. But not all are enamored. An elderly man slowly gets to his feet. He has on a long, worn djellaba and a small woolen hat, the same iconic one that Cabral always wore, more befitting a New York winter than the hot season in the tropics. The people do not have enough tools to cultivate rice, he says, and without transport they can't get what rice they do harvest to the market. "When are our lives going to improve?" he asks, looking directly at Cau as the crowd murmurs agreement.

I am already aware of the transport situation in the country. Not enough new roads are being built. A shortage of both trucks and gas means produce isn't getting to the market. With the imminent arrival of the five-month rainy season many villages face being cut off by water. I have heard that in some areas rice had been stuck in storage since 1974. The country that Cabral extolled for its perfect conditions for growing rice—an abundance of water as well as low-lying fields— is having to import, not export, their staple with foreign exchange they do not have. Cau assures the naysayer, in a tone of voice that makes little attempt to mask his irritation, that patience is needed, that everything cannot happen at once. The man shakes his head, unconvinced. His patience has worn thin.

This man's words and his courage to stand up and speak stays with me and I feel apprehension. My mood lifts as we drive through an avenue of mango trees, the dark orange fruit hanging tantalizingly from their branches. Beneath lies a carpet of splattered fruit where ducks are having a grand time waddling from one mango to the next, their tipped-up backsides swaying from side to side as they happily jab.

Sitting in the garden at the back of Cau's small brick house in the center of the town, Bari and I are treated to a bucket of the fruit, the creamy flesh ripe to perfection. We dig in. Once again, I find myself mentally comparing South Africa to the rest of the continent, and South Africa usually wins this contest. The beauty. The vegetation. The fruit. The people and their humor. But right now Guinea-Bissau's mangoes win hands down. I feel as contented as the ducks as I devour one after another until my face and fingers drip with the thick sticky juice. But the familiar African landscape sparks my yearning for South Africa, nostalgia ripples like a brook headed downstream, headed south where South Africa's turn is next. *When* is the only question.

Finally, when we can't possibly consume even one bite more of mango, we enter Cau's small living room. A gaunt woman is standing in the center of the room. She smiles the broad smile of someone recognizing a friend. I try to place this frail, slightly stooped woman who I first take to be elderly. Only when my eyes adjust to the dim light do I recognize Bwetna N'dubi. As we hug I can feel the ribs of her skinny body beneath her blouse. What has happened in just two years to the strong, muscular Bwetna I had met in the liberated zones, the self-assured member of a regional council, with her straight talk and confident walk?

We head back into the garden and Cau joins us. When Bwetna begins to respond to my questions, he cuts her short before Bari can translate. Her voice becomes hesitant, her responses cryptic, just a bland, everything's-just-fine. She looks down at her lap. Only when Cau is called away does she open up. Her tone is stronger, her sentences longer, her voice more emphatic. She fought hard in the struggle, she says. Now she has nothing. Not enough food for her family. No money to buy clothes. She has been sidestepped. The people who had not participated in the struggle are being given the jobs and the local leadership positions. All those years of struggle have, for her, come to naught. "Total, complete disillusionment," Bari tells me. "She does not know what she fought for or why she believed in the revolution so fully."

There is nothing I can say, other than smiling back at her, trying to convey empathy. I go to find my bag and take out the eight-by-ten inch black-and-white photograph I had taken of her in the liberated zones. Her delight gives rise to a bright smile, the old, slightly crooked smile that had won me over when we first met.

AS MY TWO-MONTH STAY gathered speed, I became progressively more perturbed by the gap between the lifestyle of the leadership and the extent of the poverty around me. My critical side surfaced after a delicious meal of grilled fish and Portuguese wine at a simple Bissau restaurant. The cost of the meal far exceeded the monthly income of an average peasant family. I was there with members of the leadership, including Tonio, who was now minister of planning, and as we stood together outside the restaurant having probably imbibed a little too much wine, I admonished Tonio for living like a king. I thought his salary of $500 per month huge in comparison with the $31 per month minimum wage for agricultural workers and $35 per month for other workers. Peasants' incomes were far less, if they could even be quantified monetarily.

"What do you want us to do?" he snapped back at me. "Do you want that everybody live like the poor people in our country or do you want that *everybody* has a good standard of living?"

It reminded me of Maria's words in Cairo, quoting the MPLA president: "We are not struggling to be miserable." Tonio continued, his face showing his annoyance. "We are a totally uncorrupt, a totally honest and non-exploitative government. That is very important. There are few African governments like ours. And we cannot do everything at once. The ministers have responsibilities that no one else has, and it is *not* a big salary."

I was still thinking about the wage gap, not of amount. I shook my head.

"You don't understand," he said.

"Oh, I understand very well," I retorted.

"Then you are *stupid!!!*" he snapped back and walked toward his car.

"Maybe you should not compare yourselves to ministers of other African countries, but to your own people," I continued, hurrying to keep up with him. I was now well seated on my high horse. He glared at me, and once again informed me that I was being ridiculous as he, always the gentleman, opened the car door for me. Like all the ministers, he drove a new white Volvo. Unlike most of the other ministers, he drove it himself, though I suspect the state would have provided a driver if he wanted one.

Our tangle over wages was not the only disagreement. A few days later we got into an altercation over the use of Soviet planners to help Guinea-Bissau with a three-year plan for urban development. The Soviets' lack of Portuguese and limited knowledge of the country made me question their competence to lead such an endeavor. They had of course supported the liberation struggles. African leaders, among them Oliver Tambo, president of the ANC, tried carefully to tread the path of neutrality between East and West, stating that they would have gladly accepted support from Europe and North America if it had only been offered. But the West was too busy labeling them terrorists.

"The Soviets are the experts," Tonio responded. "They will provide technical expertise, which we desperately need." He saw it as a simple case of development aid. "Planning is planning," he stated firmly. I saw it as something more sinister, a sign that Guinea-Bissau was losing out in defining its own path to the future. What could the Soviet "experts" possibly know about the conditions in this small, impoverished country in Africa, just beginning to work at national reconstruction. I shot back: "There is no such thing as disconnected, objective planning." He dismissed my argument with a shrug and said no more.

The tension between us had, I knew, more to do with the "us" than with the state of the Guinea-Bissau economy. The memory of our relationship still gave rise to occasional sparks of sexual tension. Nevertheless, he did have a point. Their salaries were not large. Tonio and many of the other ministers and high-level civil servants lived in modest houses and in modest style. Neither did he lord his status as minister over anyone, something I witnessed on a number of occasions.

One afternoon he wanted to show me the forest where he hunted on Sundays, as he continued to do once he relocated from Boké. As we drove toward the forest, we were stopped at one of the frequent roadblocks stationed outside of Bissau. As identification, he showed his party membership, saying simply "Membro do Partido," rather than other IDs that would have emphasized his status.

We walked a short way into the forest, dense and dark green, trees both spindly and large, as if they had been there for millennia. I was transported back into the *mato*, listening for bombers. At the time Tonio had felt trapped by the revolution, one that he was fighting for the next generation. He thought it would go on for many more years. Did he feel trapped in a different way as a minister with heavy responsibilities? It was not a question I could ask. We were both careful to keep our distance, avoiding delving too deeply into our personal lives or asking deeper questions about his life as an official.

Despite our occasional altercations, I knew that Tonio was unlikely to be corrupted. When I revisited the country in the early 1980s a Guinean friend remarked: "Tonio could make a really effective minister. Unfortunately his hands are tied. He is totally dedicated and very honest. Racism holds him back." Racism? How was that possible? Tonio had grown up in Bissau; he was African to the core and had never considered himself anything else. But in this new post-liberation environment, he was deemed insufficiently African because of his mixed European and African descent.

During this first visit to independent Guinea-Bissau, and the ones that followed in the 1980s, I became steadily aware of the shoots of corruption and repression that were pushing up like determined weeds through the cracks in the revolution, entangled with failed hopes and distorted visions. The Portuguese colonies had moved from wars of independence to the realpolitik of the wider world. In time the revolution would fail horribly in Guinea-Bissau under a series of ever more corrupt regimes that abandoned the revolutionary vision of Amilcar Cabral. The cohesion that existed between the ethnic groups, one of the achievements of the revolution, would split apart at the seams. Guinea-Bissau dissolved into an eerily Shakespearean morass of political intrigue, assassinations, conflicts, betrayals, and brother-against-brother duplicity, all overladen with a lucrative drug trade that ran through the government, the army, and the police force like an electric wire, leaving the population destitute.

FAST-FORWARD BRIEFLY TO 2003, when I was working for the United Nations. I got a call from the Guinea-Bissau mission. Teodora was in town and wanted to meet. I suggested a restaurant nearby and headed there half an hour later. We had no translator other than a Spanish friend of hers and somehow, as we always managed, we communicated. But much was lost. What I did understand was that Tonio had been shot to death four years earlier, assassinated. He was found in the forest where he had gone to hunt. The same forest we had walked in? I wondered. The perpetrators were never found. Around the same time, Victor Saúde Maria was assassinated. Victor had fled to Portugal after a power struggle with João Bernardo "Nino" Vieira, president at the time, and then returned from exile to found a new political party when a multiparty system was being negotiated. He was still leader seven years later when he was killed. Nino, Amilcar Cabral's star young military strategist during the war, was assassinated in 2009. By then Guinea-Bissau had the dubious distinction of being deemed one of the world's leading narco-states. This was quite a feat for a country of 1.6 million people. Its many tiny uninhabited islands and coastal inlets provide a perfect transfer point for Latin American cocaine on its way to Europe. While Spanish haciendas built by Colombian drug barons grace Bissau, the people of Guinea-Bissau are impoverished. Sixty percent of the people live below the poverty line. Amilcar Cabral's dream ended in tatters.

22 — "This Very Day Is South Africa's *Pidgiguiti*"

I am sitting on the bed in my room on the second floor of the *pensão* in Bissau, a notebook propped up against my bent legs; with no desk in the small room, my knees will have to do. Light comes in through french doors leading onto the veranda of the old colonial-style building, which could have been transplanted directly from Lisbon. It is owned and run by a friendly older Portuguese couple, who had decided not to flee with their compatriots. It is clean and inexpensive, well suited to my budget.

On this particular day, June 16, 1976, I am scribbling, crossing out, scribbling again, trying to craft something that will be both meaningful and entertaining for the rally I had been asked to address in the stadium that evening. My shortwave radio plays in the background as I wait for the BBC World Service bulletin. I hear the familiar few bars of jaunty martial music that signals the news is about to begin and put down my pen to listen. Seldom does a day go by when I fail to catch the late-afternoon news. It is my lifeline to the outside world. This time, the tone of urgency in the broadcaster's voice catches my attention.

"At least twelve people are reported to have been killed in a series of violent clashes between black demonstrators and police in several South African townships. Angry youths threw stones and beer bottles at police, as a protest against the compulsory use of Afrikaans as the main teaching language in black schools turned violent." The announcer continues: "There are known to be at least two black children among the dead and two white men."

The Bantu Education Department had recently issued a regulation stating that Afrikaans would thenceforth be the language of instruction for many subjects taught in secondary school. But Afrikaans was widely viewed as the language of the oppressor, a language Africans do not generally speak or want to speak. Protest was inevitable. I find myself holding my breath, waiting for more details. My country! My home! So far away.

An African woman reporter describes what's happening. Soweto is the center of the protests. Tens of thousands of young people are out in the streets, being dispersed by tear gas, being shot at. I remain immobilized. These are *children* under attack. I begin to sob uncontrollably and abandon any attempt to prepare for my talk. By the time I am picked up and driven to the venue I have regained my composure. I and a thousand or so others listen to speeches about the need to transform the country so that all can benefit, about the obligation for every citizen to take part in the process of reconstruction. PAIGC's rallying cry, *Nô pintcha!*—Forward!—repeated in unison by the crowd, punctuates the speeches. My turn comes. I speak in short sentences so that the young woman who is translating my words can do so easily. I tell them I am honored by the invitation to address the people of Bissau in a free Guinea-Bissau, saying that I and the world have learned so much from their revolution. Then I repeat what I had heard that day on the radio about the struggle in my own country. Students are rising up in South Africa. They are confronting the police. They are making their demands. They are not backing down.

"Your victory over Portuguese colonialism has given inspiration to the struggle against apartheid," I continue. "It shows that successful revolution is possible. Your victory will mean South Africa's victory." I get to the end: "What is happening in South Africa today, this very day, is South Africa's Pidgiguiti!"

The crowd sends up a roar of approval. They hear the reference to Pidgiguiti—the massacre in 1959 of fifty peacefully protesting dockworkers that sparked the beginning of the armed struggle—and they get it, even before my words are fully translated. *Nô pintcha!* they yell. Their solidarity is clear. For the first time since listening to the BBC earlier that day I am smiling.

Back in my room, I once again turn on the news. A follow-up broadcast identifies the first child shot in Soweto. His name is Hector Pieterson. The children who are being killed are not anonymous. Hector is a real, identifiable child. A mother's son. A father's son.

With no television, the mental images emerge as if from a mist: young protestors facing their tormentors long enough to lob whatever is available to them from the ground. Rocks and stones. Beer bottles. It is a new kind of response to the police. In Sharpeville the protestors had been shot in the back while fleeing. These young people are not fleeing. They are standing their ground. They are saying *Enough!* at great risk to themselves as no other generation has done before them. The resistance, the protests, the uprisings are now unstoppable. It looks as if the tipping point that my father predicted sixteen years earlier, at the time Sharpeville and the march on Parliament in Cape Town, has arrived. It does not escape me that these uprisings have come just under a year after Mozambique raised its new flag on Independence Day. No matter what the future holds for independent Guinea-Bissau, Mozambique, and Angola, their victories have intensified the resistance in South Africa. Victory over colonialism to South Africa's east and west is helping crack the system of apartheid wide open.

As I take in the news during the days that immediately follow, I feel both more connected and more disconnected. Connected I understand viscerally why these protests are happening. The oppression and discrimination, the denial of basic human rights by a tyrannical police state has reached a breaking point. The protests over the imposition of the Afrikaans language pried open the flood gates. Disconnected because I am here, not there. I'm not even in the United States where my friends will be following the events in real time and watching footage on the nightly TV news. "Why am I in Bissau at this moment?" I ask myself. This country has already won its struggle. It is not *my* struggle. I feel my exile acutely. Why did I leave? I should be back home.

During the days that follow, wherever I happen to be, walking down the street, visiting or interviewing comrades, I am constantly asked: "What is happening in your country?" "What's the latest news?" I relate what I have gleaned from my shortwave radio. I reiterate that their victory, the victory of Guinea-Bissau, is providing inspiration to the people of South Africa. They nod and say they hope victory will come soon. *Nô pintcha!* In South Africa the rallying cry is *Amandla!*—Power! And the responding cry is *Awethu!*—To the people! At this moment I understand that power is closer. Much closer.

23 — "I Am Proud of You"

I return to the United States and move into a two-bedroom apartment in Washington Heights, near the Cloisters. John moves in with me. I continue to speak around the country to cover my share of the rent and general living expenses. I visit a city for two or three days, give a lecture to a class or two, run a seminar, give a talk at a women's center. I sleep on couches, on spare beds, occasionally on the floor. I visit parts of the United States that I could not have seen otherwise. It is a vast and varied country, and it grows on me. Good Americans, I tell my sometimes skeptical friends from England or South Africa, are the best people in the world. My talks are not always met with approval. At UCLA I speak at a graduate seminar in the African Studies Center. "Your anecdotal presentation has been most interesting," the professor says patronizingly, insinuating that my report has little academic value. I feel myself flushing. He has exposed my true self—I'm a fraud! A Ghanaian woman studying for her PhD pushes back her broad shoulders and her voice cuts through his. "This is a presentation that we should all pay close attention to," she berates him in a voice as large as her physical presence. "Ms. Urdang is talking about *Total. Social. Transformation*," and with each of the three words she brings her fist down on the seminar table and thumps out her emphasis. He has no comeback.

AT THE END OF 1976 when I was in London visiting my parents, I gave a talk at the Institute of Race Relations. After they immigrated to the UK, Joe had immediately joined the Fourth International and leapt back into Trotskyist activist politics. Even though I was far less cowered by him, our relationship was still too fraught with the weight of history for me to appreciate the joy he must have garnered from being back in the fray, his mind once again engaged in the discussions, the debates, and analyses without having to fear the apartheid regime's repressive hand.

A year earlier when I was visiting, we had had a row in the living room in their small house in Hampstead Garden Suburb. For me, the good thing was that we *could* have a row, one in which I felt secure and unfazed by his attempt to dominate the conversation. I had retrieved the voice he had repressed during my childhood and adolescence. He could no longer expect me to think as he thought, no longer make me feel inadequate if I didn't. My trip through Africa, and then to Guinea-Bissau, my awakening as a feminist, my living apart from him across the "pond," the generally positive reception to my writing and my talks all came together into a woman, now thirty-two, who was considerably more secure and confident in her own two shoes. The argument had started when he dismissed my comment about how the revolution in Guinea-Bissau had transformed peasant men and women. "There can be no revolution if it is based on the peasantry," he snapped at me. "Guinea-Bissau must industrialize, and quickly. Otherwise there will be no workers, hence no dictatorship of the proletariat. Without this there can be no socialism." I remained cool and held my ground against what I found to be an unacceptably rigid ideological stance. I felt irritated, angry even, an anger all the more satisfying because of the years of feeling intellectually oppressed by him.

Nonetheless, all was not in the past. I could still find his influence overwhelming as I discovered when I stood up to begin my talk at the institute. He sat in the last row of chairs, in my direct line of vision, with his right arm draped over the back of the chair next to him, his knees facing the opposite direction. I read his body language as a mixture of boredom and superciliousness. As I spoke, my eyes were drawn again and again to his impassive expression, and I had to force myself to continue my lecture without faltering. When appreciative applause filled the space, my eyes were instinctively drawn back to him. He was clapping as hard as anyone, a broad smile filling his face.

After the talk my parents joined a group of friends—South Africans and Brits—for dinner at an Indian restaurant. From the other end of the long table I watched my mother and father throw themselves into the discussions that animated our group. Joe was alive, his face flushed; he was on a roll. "He's really enjoying himself!" I thought, amazed. After dinner, my parents and I headed for the tube station back to their house. Joe did something he seldom did: he put his arm over my shoulder as we walked. "That was a wonderful evening," he said, still energized. "It reminded me of my youth in South Africa and the intense arguments and discussions we would have about politics." Then he turned to look at me. "That was an excellent talk you gave. I am proud of you. I look forward to reading your book."

He never did. At the age of seventy, in September 1977, he suffered a massive stroke: fourteen months before *Fighting Two Colonialisms: Women in Guinea-Bissau* was published, thirteen years before Mandela walked to freedom. I flew to London. I sat for a day in his hospital room with my mother and Leonie, watching as my father faded. At one point, he stared straight at me, clarity in his eyes. I faltered, not knowing whether I should go to him and hug him. Would my presence alert him to the fact that he was dying? I lost the moment as his eyes went blank again. Late that night after we had been encouraged by the staff to go home and get some sleep, the phone rang. He had died. Alone.

Looking back from the perspective of the age he was when he died, I see a man who was an idealistic, committed young attorney; who opened his practice in a black area, maintaining it until the government drove him out; who rejected the financial benefits of a law office in the center of the city. I see a man who made a difference to that community, helping them negotiate the trials and trauma imposed by the Group Areas Act. He was a man who walked his talk. As such he was rare among white South Africans. He was true to himself and he made the difference he could. It is good, after all these years, to be able to understand and respect that. I only wish I could have told him.

WHEN I RETURNED TO NEW YORK from Guinea-Bissau, in the wake of the June 16 student unrest and the months of protest that followed, South Africa was all over the news. The sight of African youths being shot at, whipped, arrested, and tossed into police vans seemed to shift the way Americans responded to apartheid and to South Africa. It gave my writing impetus as I settled in to finishing my book while *Southern Africa* magazine continued to grab part of my time. We were energized by the student uprisings and appalled by the repression that came with it. We devoted many pages to the thousands of arrests, with over a thousand killed, to the U.S. complicity, which wavered not one bit. One story moved me particularly. In it we quoted the South African photographer Alf Khumalo, whose photo of Hector Pieterson, the first child to be killed, being carried across the arms of another student, his horrified sister running alongside, became a symbol of the resistance and the repression. Khumalo described how, on that first day, the marching children, whose numbers had swelled to about twelve thousand, began stoning the police. The police began shooting live bullets, not warning shots. "What frightened me more than anything was the attitude of the children. Many seemed oblivious to the danger. They continued running toward the police—dodging and ducking." This was for me, for us, the very crux. The children and youth were willing to die rather than continue to live under oppressive rule. Once people are willing to die, there is nothing a repressive state can do to stop the resistance. These youth were putting into action Mandela's speech from the dock at the end of the Rivonia trial: "A democratic and free society is an ideal for which I am prepared to die."

In 1974, South African students had already held rallies to celebrate the overthrow of Portuguese colonialism in neighboring Mozambique and Angola. Posters and banners declared, "Frelimo fought and regained our soil, our dignity" and "The dignity of the Black Man has been restored in Mozambique and so shall it be here." The message was clear: if Mozambique could do it, so could South Africa. In 1975, South Africans celebrated independence in Mozambique and Angola on campuses and in the townships—and then came the protests in 1976. What I had intuitively shouted out in the stadium in Bissau was not rhetoric.

Through all this, and into the immediate years of heightened resistance in South Africa, the pages of my book steadily mounted.

Sometimes I wrote easily. Sometimes it was excruciating. I'd get stuck over one particular chapter. I would slip a piece of paper into my typewriter and stare at it, willing the words to flow. Nothing. Instead I would take to my journal.

> I am at a block. I am disgusted with myself and feel I am spine-less. I can't break through that grey, gaseous cloud that holds the chapter in its interior and keeps me out. I feel fragile and incapable. And tired. The book stretches on so, and I can't see the end. Once I finally break through the worst will be over. I despise myself for allowing myself to give in so. Instead I eat. I read the newspaper, I read books—with growing fascination—such as *Flying* by Kate Millet. So honest, but so self-indulgent. But as I write I feel self-indulgent myself somehow. It is only another form of talking to oneself. An acceptable form. For if I walked around talking aloud my thoughts, people would think I am mad. Instead I can banish myself with my typewriter and write as freely as I wish. Except I can't write my book.

John came home one evening to find me in an especially distraught state. "What's the matter?" The gentleness in his voice infuriated me. I yelled back: "I can't write anymore! Why did I think I could?"

He picked up the three hundred or so typewritten pages and sat down next to me on the edge of the bed. And then he asked: "Why do you think you are reacting this way when you have almost finished?"

I answered by grabbing the pile of pages and flinging them onto the floor in a tantrum worthy of a two-year-old. He bent over and carefully picked them up, restacking them in numerical order. He returned to his place next to me with the pile on his lap, his hand over them so I wouldn't fling them again.

"Tell me what you are writing about at the moment."

I explained that it was the chapter on the women leaders and it all seemed too banal.

"Do you think you are finding it difficult because, unlike the peas-ant women, they might read your book?"

I stared back at him. He had hit the nail on the head. I was worried that they might disapprove of how I portrayed them. As this sank in, I could feel the block dissolving. I went back to my typewriter and my fingers flew across the keys late into the night as I finished the chapter.

I handed *Fighting Two Colonialisms* to the publisher in 1978. The vivid dreams began: I am walking down the street stark naked. I desperately try to cover my breasts with my arms, but I know it's no use. People stare and I can't hide. It needed no Freud to interpret the meaning. I woke up with relief, but still apprehensive. I was now exposed to my critics, to anyone who chose to read the book. When I held the first copy in my hands, it felt good, very good. I had finally actually completed something.

Soon after, with a book as part of my résumé, I was offered a consultancy at the second UN Decade on Women conference, to be held in Copenhagen in July 1980. I was hired to write papers on the effects of apartheid on women in southern Africa, On April 18, 1980, Zimbabwe became independent. The negotiations between the liberation movements and the Ian Smith regime, which had declared unilateral independence from Britain in 1965, had ended in victory for the people of Zimbabwe. Two Kenyan colleagues brought a bottle of champagne into the office, and we toasted the victory as if it were ours. Rhodesia was now Zimbabwe. South Africa next!

Jennifer took over as editor and we benefited from her political acuity. The downside for *Southern Africa* was that it became harder to raise funds now that events in South Africa were being covered by the major media. When the magazine first published, we covered six countries—Angola, Mozambique, Guinea-Bissau, Namibia, Rhodesia, and South Africa. By mid-1980 only two countries, Namibia and South Africa, were still fighting for majority rule. The magazine had lost its core purpose, and now with the regular coverage of South Africa in the mass media, it lasted for another three years, until 1983, when we closed up shop. What was lost was an insightful political and economic analysis, thanks mainly to Jennifer, that was seldom found in the mainstream media.

When the UN consultancy ended, I had more time to think about my future. My longing for my continent resurfaced—it had been four years since I was last there. I was longing for a child. At thirty-six that dastardly biological clock ticked away furiously as if fused to my heartbeat. But first, before years of child-rearing brought an end to my travels, I wanted one more trip back to Africa. But how? The answer came with a phone call from John Saul in Toronto. John, the political scientist who had worked in Africa, written widely on southern Africa, and was highly regarded for his knowledge, his analysis, and his writing—*that* John Saul. I had known him for years because of our anti-apartheid activism. The last time I saw him was in Toronto when I was on a speaking tour shortly before my book was published. I sat next to him as he drove me to his university for a talk. He turned to look at me and said: "I have much admiration for you." I was flabbergasted. *Me?*

"I wish I could write the way you write," he continued. "If your book is as good as your articles, you will have a lot to contribute." I was rendered silent by his praise. Now, on the phone, he got quickly to the point. He was editing a collection of articles written from the direct experience of European and North American *cooperantes,* international volunteers who were working in Mozambique to contribute to national reconstruction. The book would cover topics such as agriculture, health, economics, education. There was one issue missing: women. Would I be interested in going to Mozambique to do research and write that chapter? *Would I!*

I applied to the Ford Foundation and was interviewed by the head of the Africa Division. "So, how did you feel walking through the door of Ford to apply for a grant?" he asked. "Have you changed?" I knew he was teasing and testing. He was right, though. In the past I had regarded Ford as a supporter of liberalish causes that held back revolution. I shot back. "It's not me who has changed. It's Ford." He liked that. My grant was approved. It was a generous one and would cover my expenses for travel to and in Mozambique, as well as time to write up my research when I returned to the United States.

I had it all planned out: I would be there six months, tops. Then get pregnant with our first child, wait two years, and have our second.

I departed for Mozambique in September 1980.

Part Four

24 — Across the Border from Home-Home

As I descend the metal stairway onto the Maputo airport tarmac I feel the summer heat rise up to envelop me. I slow my step and inhale my first full breath of African air after a four-year hiatus. Earthy, loamy, leafy, with a tinge of smoke, a tinge of sea air, a tinge of diesel fuel—the familiar fused scent that confounds words. I am buffeted by a swirl of joy and sentimentality that settles in a knot in my throat. I shoulder my heavy bag as I walk toward the low airport terminal. Ahead of me a long banner straddles its outside wall, swaying slightly in the humid breeze: *bemvindo a uma zona libertada da humanidade*. Welcome to the Liberated Zone of Humanity. The words sing. They hold the promise I am hoping for: a country that will benefit all the people. Buoyed by the message, I enter the small terminal, with its peeling paint and cracked floor. But I am not at all depressed by this shabby interior—this is a country struggling to wrest itself from its recent past, *não é*? It has more pressing tasks at hand than catering to the first impressions of visitors. Like building a free Mozambique, ending poverty, building socialism.

I wait in the slow-moving line for my turn with the immigration official. I wait in another slow line for the obligatory monetary exchange into Mozambican *meticais* bearing the portrait of the slain first president of Frelimo, Eduardo Mondlane. And I wait for my two large suitcases to arrive on a creaky baggage carousel.

Then I walk into the liberated zone of humanity.

In the crowd is my friend Judith Marshall with a broad smile on her face. Judith, a Canadian, had arrived in 1978 to work in the Ministry of Education and had invited me to stay with her. She was one of the dedicated volunteers whom Mozambicans referred to as *cooperantes*—people from the solidarity world who came to Mozambique after independence to contribute to the reconstruction of the country and help build a new society based on equality.

"Have you been waiting long?" I ask after we hug hullo.

The plane was late and I can't imagine a system in this underdeveloped country that provides updates on arrival times. I assume many hours of waiting for delayed arrivals. But Judith smiles the smile of an old hand.

"Oh no, not at all," she says. "We just listen for the plane flying over before it lands. Then we head for the airport. I just got here."

As she drives into the city I take in the Lisbon-style buildings and broad boulevards lined with acacia trees. Traces of my first time entering Guinea-Bissau cling to me as I oscillate between two states: high expectation and nagging apprehension. Unlike Judith, I am not here as a member of a solidarity organization. Rather, I have come on a quest, similar to the one that took me to Guinea-Bissau—a quest to find the story behind words. In this case, they were the words of Samora Machel, president of Frelimo and the first president of Mozambique: "The liberation of women is a fundamental necessity for the revolution, a guarantee of its continuity, and a precondition for victory." If this declaration has legs, then I will have many positive stories to relate.

So why the apprehension? Once I completed *Fighting Two Colonialisms*, I had sublimated the hard times that had plagued me: the painful doubts about my competence, those intermittent stabs that told me I wasn't intellectually or analytically up to the task. I brushed these aside with a "Now, *that* wasn't so bad, was it?" Instead of resting on my achievements, I raised the bar. This time I was writing alongside John Saul and other serious, experienced contributors to the book. I once again have demons to fight: What had I been thinking? How could I possibly live up to John Saul's expectations?

While I try to reconcile these two reactions, a third pushes its way to the surface, outmaneuvering them both: I am close to home. Southern Mozambique shares a long border with South Africa. Mozambique's history is grafted to its neighbor's, and the future of

Mozambique could well provide a glimpse into what revolutionary change might mean for my country. Not only as a journalist and a conscientious observer, but as a South African, I will be listening, taking notes, asking questions, and writing about the successes of a revolution just across the border from home-home.

Soon after arriving I write to my John:

> I can see why people, particularly South Africans, are drawn to working in Mozambique, despite the frustrations and difficulties at so many levels. Mozambique is so integral to the South African outcome. It is a country that is trying so hard to achieve its goals, the obstacles are gargantuan, but it starts to grip you and being South African, it is possible to feel part of a process of liberating and developing the whole region.

JUDITH'S APARTMENT STOOD HIGH on the edge of a cliff on Avenida Patrice Lumumba, renamed, like many of Maputo's streets and boulevards, after African heroes and other venerated political figures: Avenida Amilcar Cabral, Avenida Eduardo Mondlane, Avenida Julius Nyerere; Avenida Mao Tse Tung, which was near Avenida Karl Marx, which intersected with Avenida Vladimir Lenin; Avenida Friedrich Engels ran along an escarpment overlooking the sea below. We walked up the chipped stairs of her building, with gaps where tiles had once sat fast, past the walls in need of painting. Vasco, her *empregado*, meaning "worker" in Portuguese—carried my suitcase. Judith explained that the elevator was prone to breaking. In addition, the water pressure was so low that it regularly did not make it to the upper floors, in other words, her apartment.

The sense of dilapidation vanished the moment I entered Judith's home. The spacious living room was bathed in light from floor to ceiling. French doors leading onto the balcony overlooked the Maputo River, the sea, the city, the docks. Wonderful. She showed me my room. My home for the next six months.

On my second day, I set out for a run before breakfast. Dressed in my usual running outfit—athletic shorts and T-shirt and sporting my new sneakers—I exited Judith's building and turned right, running at a steady pace up Avenida Patrice Lumumba through an unkempt park overlooking the water below. The morning air that filled my lungs was fresh and gentle. A young guard in military uniform standing in front of an impressive government mansion called out his approval, and I waved back. Enjoying a sense of freedom I never felt running in New York, I picked up my pace, checking eagle-eyed for stones or uneven paving that could send me flying. I sprinted left into a wide street and stopped dead in my tracks. It looked like the city's entire workforce was being disgorged from dozens of minibuses. It was 6:00 a.m.— rush hour for the workers from the city's *bairros*. I remembered the young woman on the bus in Tanzania who thought I was dressed inappropriately, and I was. I should have known better by now. I quickly turned around and walked purposefully back to Judith's, feeling like an ignorant *mzungu*—a stupid white person—exposing myself to the women dressed in *capulanas* or neat office attire and the men in long pants and shirts, respectable and appropriate. It was my last attempt at a run. Instead, I jumped rope on Judith's balcony, on the edge of a cliff. Just me and the expansive view below while I followed the small figures below walking up the path to the top of the cliff.

I soon became part of the polyglot circle of supporters who came in response to Frelimo's call to help rebuild Mozambique. Many had come right after independence in 1975, after spending years in solidarity work in their home countries in Europe and the Americas. Doctors, nurses, engineers, teachers, literacy specialists, researchers, academics—they helped fill the gaping hole left in the economy when almost all of the 250,000 settlers fled the country after the Portuguese coup, leaving behind an African population that was 99 percent illiterate; only 20,000 Portuguese Mozambicans remained to throw their lot in with the new government. Those who fled destroyed what they couldn't take with them: medical supplies, vehicles, agricultural equipment. The sometimes idealistic, occasionally arrogant Western volunteers were not always welcomed, but Samora Machel was quick to staunch any grumbling. They were militants who shared a common cause, he said.

On the weekends, at dinner parties, house parties, group trips to the beach, we would discuss and dissect to the point of obsession the state of the revolution as it had emerged in the previous week, to be praised or stripped apart for its failure to live up to our views of the socialist experiment. The conversations were often heated, always passionate. I would listen and sometimes join in, but mostly I felt like an outsider because I wasn't working there. One friend said she envied me. *Cooperantes* were so involved in and confined to their particular work site that they often succumbed to tunnel vision, she said. In contrast, I had a chance to travel around the country and see so many different facets of national reconstruction. For my part, I envied their deeper immersion and understanding.

Among my friends were South African exiles. As such they did not consider themselves *cooperantes*. They had not come on time-bound contracts; Mozambique was their interim home. For Mozambicans, to be South African was to be a comrade, a fellow revolutionary. South Africans came to Mozambique either to use Mozambique as a safe base and training ground for armed struggle or to work in Mozambique as a way of contributing to national reconstruction. They tended to be more skeptical than most of the *cooperantes*.

"For me, coming to work in Mozambique wasn't about believing in Mozambican socialism," explained Dan O'Meara, a white South African and ANC member who was a researcher at the university. "Our initial contacts after we arrived were ANC comrades who were far less starry-eyed about Mozambique than many of the *cooperantes*. It was definitely no socialist nirvana. For me, coming to work in Mozambique was really, *really* important because the liberation and reconstruction of Mozambique was a major step forward in the anti-apartheid struggle."

Ruth First and Joe Slovo, both high on apartheid's enemies list, had been forced into exile in the early 1960s and were among the first exiles to relocate to Maputo after independence. She was appointed director of the newly formed Institute of African Studies where Dan worked, while Joe continued as chief of staff of Umkhonto we Sizwe—MK, Spear of the Nation, the military wing of the ANC. Soon after I arrived, Judith invited Ruth for dinner and we formed a bond over my writing. She passed along to me information on women in Mozambique that I might not have been able to access otherwise. She offered to comment on my chapter when I was ready. I accepted nervously. While I would value her exacting opinion, she was known to level crushing criticism of anything she didn't consider up to her high standards.

For South Africans the transition was not as smooth as for the *cooperantes,* some of whom were supported by their governments as part of their development aid to Mozambique. It took months for the still small, overstretched bureaucracy to register South Africans as Maputo residents, which would entitle them to a ration card for monthly staples such as rice, oil, and fresh greens. One friend, Linzi Manicom, was breastfeeding when she arrived; she sometimes went to bed hungry and worried that her milk would dry up.

Even though most of the *cooperantes* lived simply, they lived well, particularly compared to their Mozambican colleagues. They employed *empregados* for household tasks, such as standing in line for food supplies; this freed them up to focus on their own work. I asked Judith how she felt about these arrangements. She acknowledged her own discomfort at the "white madam" role and countered it by trying to establish a solid employer-employee relationship, paying Vasco well, with clearly defined work hours, weekends off, paid vacation time, and sick leave. "It would be irresponsible not to employ people," she said. "Mozambicans need work." She was occasionally able to supplement her rations by visits to Swaziland, returning to Maputo with whole-grain flour, cheese, and other items seldom available in Mozambique. Vasco took great pride in preparing lunch, the main meal of the day, when Judith took her mandated two-hour break. I can still recall his sublime *matapa,* made from finely ground peanuts, coconut milk, manioc leaves, chilies, and dried shrimp. We ate like queens in a land of poverty.

These long lunch hours were also a source of discomfort. It was one of the markers of inequality between the *cooperantes* and their Mozambican colleagues. "We *cooperantes* have mobility, we have cars, we live close to our workplaces," Judith told me one evening, as we sat at her dining room table eating leftovers from lunch. "We don't have to get up at four in the morning to fight for transport into work. There is little food in the homes of my colleagues at the

Ministry of Education, and toward the end of the month, none." She knew of many families who had to make do with tea and bread for the last few days of each month until they could line up for their rations. "So they usually come to work without breakfast, facing a two-hour lunch 'hour' but no money to buy lunch." It troubled her, but there was little she or others could do about it. They had to focus on the reality that they were bringing skills to a country that desperately needed them.

Judith had come to Mozambique after three years working in Ghana under the same Frontier Internship program that had sent Gail to South Africa and brought Suzette to New York. What Judith found there appalled her. She encountered droves of British expatriates whose condescension toward the Ghanaians was palpable and the power they vested in themselves unmitigated. In contrast, she heard reports of Frelimo's insistence on a bottom-up approach and the need to place trust in the rural people. "I loved their emphasis on education and health as well as agricultural production," she told me. "I loved Samora's statement that the liberation struggle was Mozambique's university. This statement was so powerful it stayed with me for years."

"I wanted to be part of a socialist moment," she continued, "an anti-imperialist moment on the very doorstep of apartheid. I believed Mozambique would take a different road." This had resonance for me. At the same time, I smiled inwardly. John Saul had recently changed the title of the collection we were working on from *A Different Road* to the more realistic title, *A Difficult Road*.

Judith and I spent one Saturday afternoon in her kitchen, congenially preparing dinner for a few friends. We cut off the rinds of a butternut squash, the only vegetable available in the stores that week, and diced it into one-inch squares. There had been rumors that yogurt was being sold in a few stores and we had used up precious gas to successfully track it down that morning. With chicken stock from Judith's freezer and generous tablespoons of peanut butter that she had brought back from a recent trip to Swaziland—Black Cat, the brand of my childhood and my memories—as well as some pinches of Mozambican hot spices, I was happily preparing one of my favorite, effortless soups. Vasco had baked a loaf of whole-meal bread the day before to go with it.

That evening I heated up the soup while Judith and the guests sat chatting at the dining room table. The door handles in Mozambique were the same as those I grew up with: horizontal levers rather than U.S.-style round knobs. As I walked briskly out of the kitchen carrying the soup, the door handle hooked the wide sleeve of my long dress bringing me to an abrupt halt. The pot of soup merrily continued its momentum and flew out of my hands with such velocity that it landed upside down on the floor, the thick soup intact beneath it, nary a splash evident.

I groaned in horror. "Oh no! There goes our meal!"

"No way!" countered Judith, who rushed into the kitchen, returned with a flat metal baking sheet, carefully pushed it all the way under the pot of thick soup and righted it up. Our dinner was saved. The next day I noticed a dull circle bordered by a few splash marks on the floor where the soup had landed. If the wax and varnish had added flavor to the soup, we hadn't noticed.

AFTER YEARS OF CIVIL WAR next door in Rhodesia, the white-minority government was finally forced to surrender, clearing the way for Zimbabwe's independence in April 1980. Mozambique had supported this struggle both out of solidarity and out of necessity—a war across its borders was undermining its own security. This came with many sacrifices. The Rhodesian military had regularly launched cross-border raids into central and northern Mozambique, forcing Mozambique to pump up its defense budget to the detriment of national reconstruction. With this war over, Mozambicans could return to building their nation. South Africa was now their only hostile neighbor. At the time of my visit, a sense of relief and hope was palpable.

Within the first week the Organization of Mozambican Women (OMM) had set up a program for my visit. I would visit communal villages whose aim was to centralize educational and social services while enabling communal production that would both feed the village and bring in revenue by selling its surplus. I would visit state farms whose aim was to feed the nation as well as generate foreign exchange by exporting a surplus. I would visit factories and women's organizations in shantytowns on the outskirts of towns and interview village tribunal judges and local and national leaders. I would cover much of Mozambique from Maputo and Gaza provinces in the south to Niassa and Cabo Delgado provinces in the north. When not on the road, I planned to be based in Maputo, where I could write my chapter for John's book and allow myself to absorb daily life in this new country as it tested the waters of post-independence reconstruction.

25 — "Now We Have Hope"

The old blue Portuguese-hand-me-down jeep rattled in protest as the driver floored the accelerator and maneuvered it through Maputo's haphazard morning rush hour traffic, sharing the road with trucks, jeeps of all vintages, brand-new buses filled with workers heading to the factories that skirted Maputo, overcrowded mini-buses, and the ubiquitous newest model SUVs belonging to embassies, the UN, and government ministries. He slowed down when he was caught behind jalopies that chug-chugged along and then circumvented the large traffic circle at the edge of the city, finally picking up speed as the buildings and houses and shops gave way to open veld.

This was my first trip outside of Maputo. I had been picked up in front of Judith's apartment at six that morning for the drive to a communal village in Gaza Province a hundred miles from Maputo, where I would spend three nights with Anastácia Guimarães, the OMM staff member who would act as my interpreter. From the front passenger seat, I stared through the cracked windscreen at a southern African landscape of cashew and fever trees and brown dry earth dotted with patches of green and clusters of thatch-roofed, mud-walled houses, where cows with protruding ribs grazed nearby. We passed the occasional man on a bicycle, the occasional woman with a bag of goods balanced on her head, a baby tied to her back. It was as if a film had been lifted from my eyes, allowing me to see to the far horizon where the earth meets the perpetually high African sky. The scene was in total contrast to Cape Town, but it reminded me of my long bus rides in East Africa and my childhood visits to rural South Africa. As we sped along, the Portuguese word that I had recently picked up slipped into my thoughts: *saudade*, which defies precise translation but captures for me a state of intense longing and melancholy that came with knowing I was close to home. My shoulders relaxed and my breath flowed more evenly as any worries about how my trip would turn out receded.

Two hours later the jeep turned off the main road just before Xai-Xai, the provincial capital, and entered the village of Três de Fevereiro, with its wide unpaved road and well-kept houses surrounded by large fields. Like many villages, it was named after a significant event in Mozambican history; February 3, 1969, was the day that Frelimo's founding president, Eduardo Mondlane, was assassinated.

A group of women sang and danced their welcome in front of the newly built administrative center. We stepped down from the jeep and were introduced to Mama Leia, the head of the village's OMM. Over the next three days the women would share their stories of the past and the present, the difficulties of living under the Portuguese and the changes in their lives now that they had won their independence.

As often as I could, I sat with Mama Leia and a group of women under a magnificent tree near the administrative center, a faded Mozambique flag waving slowing in the breeze from a rough pole. For the women, this was an unanticipated rest. They teased me that my "work" was sitting with them in the afternoon while theirs was laboring in the fields. I told Mama Leia that my grandmother's name was the same as hers, spelled Leah, but pronounced the same way: *Lay*-ah. "Then you are my granddaughter," she said and insisted I call her *gogo*, the African term for grandmother I knew from childhood. I would soon come to respect this strong, independent woman I saw bossing around men, square jaw jutting out, showing no sign of deference.

"How did you feel about moving to the village and leaving your family home?" I asked Mama Leia the first time we settled down to talk. Most extended families in the rural areas of the south lived in isolated homesteads. By concentrating people in communal villages, the government could provide schools, literacy classes, and health clinics; the people could elect their own local governments and justice tribunals. I was skeptical. *Machambas*, family plots cultivated by the women, were the basis of the economic and cultural life on the homesteads. How could they be persuaded to move so quickly? I hadn't taken the weather into account.

"The water washed away our crops and our houses. We *wanted* to move," my *gogo* responded. I knew about the floods, the worst in decades, that had deluged southern Mozambique in 1977, smoothing away the banks of the Limpopo River. At least a hundred people had died. Homes were destroyed. Crops and livestock—cows, pigs, goats, chickens—were lost. The agricultural infrastructure collapsed. If it had not been for quick action by Frelimo and international donors, hundreds more lives would have been lost. "The Portuguese would never have done anything to help us. Frelimo saved us." Then she chuckled. "We were turning into fish, we had lived in water for such a long time!"

"The water mobilized us, not Frelimo!" another woman joined in. "The water never stopped to ask us if we wanted to leave. We just had to *run!*" It was one reason why Gaza Province had a higher percentage of communal villages than the north, even in the provinces liberated during the armed struggle.

People don't simply up and move without serious cause, particularly from land that had belonged to their families for many generations. It could mean leaving behind rich alluvial soil near the river to reestablish family plots on higher ground—away from the vagaries of the weather perhaps, but the land was less arable. But the land was where mango trees and cashew trees grew, where chickens scratched and cattle grazed. Most importantly, it was where ancestors were buried: abandoning their villages meant abandoning their ancestors, and with it the loss of ancestral protection. It was home.

"Did you need to ask anyone for permission to move?" I asked Mama Leia. I was curious about whether the move was perceived as a threat to men's authority and control. In the south, the social structure was patrilineal: when a woman married, she moved from her father's home to her husband's. "I am a widow," she replied, "so I didn't have to get a man's permission to move."

I was beginning to understand why more women than men lived in Três de Fevereiro. Many were single, either widowed or without men because their husbands worked in the mines in South Africa or at jobs in Maputo. Polygamous marriages provided a rather ingenious opportunity to stall. Men would set up one wife and her children in a communal village, while the other wives would continue to cultivate the *machamba* and attend the homestead. In the northern provinces, in contrast, where matrilineality and matrilocality were the norm, it was often the man who jumped at the chance to relocate, hoping to weaken the strong ties between his wife and her family.

It was easy to spot the houses belonging to migrant workers in South Africa. These were constructed from brick or mortar, rather than the traditional mud and wattle—building materials not easily available or much more expensive in Mozambique. For close to a century, the gold and diamond mines had been a major source of income for Mozambican men. Even though exploitative, they were still more than most Mozambican men could earn at home. And the remittances they sent back went a lot further than they did in apartheid South Africa.

"We had a lot of angry men returning from South Africa!" Mama Leia said, and the women sitting with her burst out laughing. "They saved their money for *lobolo* for a second or third wife, only to find, when they returned, that *lobolo* is no longer allowed." Mama Leia was referring to the customary bride price paid by the bridegroom to the family of the bride-to-be.

Frelimo had come down heavily on traditional practices they viewed as anathema to the new Mozambique: polygamy was oppressive to women and unacceptable; *lobolo* was akin to buying a wife, who then had to do the bidding of her husband; arranged marriages denied freedom of choice and were likely to be unhappy; consulting *curandeiros*—traditional healers—was considered retrograde. Religion in general was frowned upon. These customs, the women assured me, were no longer practiced. They had gone the way of colonialism. Well, maybe not quite so. Instead of *lobolo*, I soon learned, there were the "gratification gifts," supposedly voluntary gifts given by the bridegroom's family to the bride's, simply to say thank-you for raising such a perfect daughter. These "gifts" had the same value as *lobolo*: same number of cows; same set of *capulanas*, the lengths of cloth that women wrapped around their waists or used to tie their babies on their backs; same amount of cash.

One night there was a ruckus when a young woman, Maria, was arrested for hitting her mother-in-law. The next morning, a "court" was hastily convened, including members of the village justice tribunal, OMM representatives, and other village officials. In attendance was Maria, her mother-in-law, and the witnesses. Sitting solemnly on chairs in a semicircle, they deliberated for most of the day. According to Mama Leia, Maria said little, other than to agree that she had acted badly and would mend her ways. She was sentenced to two hours of work in the communal fields daily for a number of weeks. Anastácia was curious to know more about what had happened and joined Maria early the following morning when she worked alone in the field. Maria soon opened up to her. Her husband, she said, had saved money from his earnings in South Africa and asked his mother to arrange a second wife and negotiate the *lobolo*. Before their fight, her mother-in-law had told her that her husband was planning to build a house in Três de Fevereiro for his new wife, who came from a neighboring village. She was upset and humiliated. For Maria, the slogan called out at OMM meetings—*Abaixo a poligamia!* Down with polygamy!—could have given her hope. Except she never spoke up during her hearing. And neither did the tribunal delve deeper. I could only assume they didn't want to uncover what they didn't want to admit was continuing. And so the status quo remained.

One of the mornings we set off at 5:00 a.m. for a brisk walk to the collective fields on the edge of the village where open tracts of land were allocated for cultivation. The co-operative fields were worked almost exclusively by women, working one day a week while continuing to farm their *machambas*, the real source of food for their families. In principle, the members shared the proceeds after the tractor rental and seeds were paid for. In fact, there was not much to share, and the coop was failing, as they were throughout Mozambique. Women preferred to focus closer to home on their *machambas*, which guaranteed food for their family's table and made it easier to handle the other daily tasks: child care, fetching water, collecting firewood, pounding grains, cooking, cleaning. At one point when I was talking with the women under the tree, four others carrying an assortment of containers scurried by heading for the water pump. One woman turned and waved to us.

"There's never a moment's rest," Anastácia called out to them. "We only rest in the grave!"

"Ai," came the quick reply, "but how do we know? No one has ever come back to tell us!"

Women's work and responsibilities did not seem to have changed much. Yes, there were now some women leaders. And they no longer had to worry about forced labor and the harsh reprisals by the colonial administration. But what more? Mama Leia was quick to answer. Much had changed, she assured me. There was a health clinic and a school for both girls and boys. For the first time in her life she had been able to vote for village councils, regional councils, and the national assembly, which included women. They had new wells and water pumps, which replaced long treks to water sources or scooping water from polluted rivers.

"Our lives have completely changed. I have a say in my life, how I live it," Mama Leia told me. Her voice was determined. "Before we just worked, worked, worked. We had no hope. Now we have hope. We have hope for the youth and for the children born now."

BY THE END OF MY TRAVELS OUTSIDE of Maputo, my notebooks were filled with observations and personal reflections. I had watched women proudly driving tractors on a state farm, where a quarter of the mechanics were women. I had visited a cashew factory where women from the rural areas were earning enough money to pay back the *lobolo* their family had received so they could divorce their abusive husbands. I had been to a biscuit factory where men and women earned the same salary. I saw women in literacy classes, eager to read but hampered by a shortage of teachers, poor eyesight and no glasses, husbands trying to prevent them from attending, and the all-consuming domestic labor. I had attended a hearing in Maputo where the judge was a highly capable woman; two of the five members of the tribunal were women, a ratio repeated in many provincial districts. I had visited communal villages that boasted a woman on all of their councils and committees, only to discover at some of them it was the same woman in every position. Scratch the surface and layers of obstacles surfaced. Sometimes I felt like I was on a roller coaster. Other times I felt inspired. The obstacles were real, but so was the determination to build a new country.

MY LAST TRIP OUT OF MAPUTO was to the northern province of Niassa. While traveling I noticed a blood-streaked discharge from my left breast. I dismissed dark thoughts. After all, I could feel no lump. After all, I was only thirty-seven. The many hours on pitted roads in a bumpy jeep must be to blame. Back in Maputo I mentioned it to a *cooperante* friend, Julie Cliff, an Australian doctor. She advised me to have a biopsy. *What?!* Two days later, on January 15, 1981, Judith drove me to the airport for my flight to New York. "I'll be back in two weeks," I assured her as we hugged good-bye. Her face was more worried than mine.

A biopsy revealed I had breast cancer, ductal carcinoma in situ. In laymen's language, this meant that the cancer was caught early and was unlikely to have spread beyond the ducts. For the next few weeks John and I read everything we could find on treatment, while fending off a sense of desperation and doom. I was assured my cancer wasn't fatal and I began to feel less anxious. After consulting a number of doctors, I opted for a fairly new treatment: lumpectomy and radiation. Chemotherapy was not necessary. And I wasn't going to die. I sublimated another anxiety: Would cancer mean I couldn't have children? I put it aside. I had to focus on recovery.

I was advised to be treated in Boston and moved to a friend's house for five weeks, John driving up each weekend. Five mornings a week I drove to the cancer institute for a few minutes of zapping. When I returned to the house, I would settle down to work on my chapter for the Saul book. I reached the last zap in a state of total exhaustion and returned to New York. Slowly my energy returned over the next few months. I completed a draft and began itching to complete my truncated visit to Mozambique.

My mother (left) with her
brother Sam and sister Sophie.

My parents on their wedding day.

Moses and Leah with Sam (standing) and baby Sophie; stepsons behind.

With Jennifer Davis (right) at New York City Women's March, 1976.

Southern Africa, 1973: my first published article.

Women's group circa 1982: Suzette, myself, Gail, Marilyn, Janet, Jennifer, and Marti.

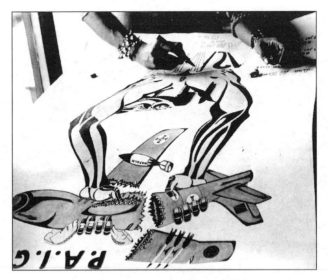

Tonio drawing poster for OAU exhibition.

Listening to the news from Portugal after the coup.

In the eastern front with militants; Mario Ribeira (left).

Fina Crato in the eastern front (center).

Lina (right) talking with women in Tete Province who fled Renamo.

On a visit with Judith to interview women in a bairro of Maputo.

Mozambique 1983.

Mama Leia (my gogo) at Três de
Fevereiro communal village.

Khayelitsha.

Kate outside the community center in Khayelitsha.

Amandla! Kendra and John at the docks to welcome last prisoners off Robben Island, 1991.

Westerford High School auditorium.

View of Table Mountain while writing on my cousin Gill's balcony, 2011.

26 — "I Will Give My Own Life If Necessary"

On January 30, 1981, just days after my return to the United States, South Africa launched its first major raid on Mozambique. Truckloads of South African commandos pushed seventy miles beyond the border, into Matola, a suburb of Maputo. They attacked three ANC safe houses, killing thirteen South Africans and a Portuguese national whom they mistook for Joe Slovo.

The attack was part of South Africa's "total strategy," aimed at destabilizing the whole southern African region. Botha was convinced, with reason, that the newly elected U.S. president, Ronald Reagan, and Britain's prime minister, Maggie Thatcher, would provide political cover for South Africa on the global stage. Samora Machel's response was a show of bravado and a demonstration of solidarity: "*Que venham!* Let them come!" he declared in a public speech a few days later. "Let all the racists come here, and then the great majority, the twenty-three million South Africans, can take power there! Let them come, and let the end of apartheid draw ever close! Let them come! And we'll bring war to an end once and for all, for everyone!"

In October 1981, nine months after my precipitous departure, I arrived back to find a more vulnerable Mozambique. My treatment and recovery had overshadowed what was happening there, but I now felt the meaning of the attack with full force. In a strange way, the anger that consumed me made me feel closer to home.

During this visit, Lina Magaia blew into my life like a refreshing wind. Journalist, economist, determined activist, she became a trusted interpreter and informant, a friend who guided me through the changing political and economic climate. Lina was a few years younger than me, about my height at five-foot-eight or -nine inches, and a powerhouse of a woman, with an easy chuckle and a deep voice. Our friendship would continue for decades, both in Maputo and on her occasional visits to the United States. To her, I was African, a comrade from the continent. She provided a lens for viewing Mozambique and the workings of the revolution, and the destruction that South Africa wreaked on her country. My writing began to reflect this angle, focusing less on the role of women and more on the impact on women and children.

Lina was born in Maputo in 1945. Her father was a teacher; her mother was uneducated, from a rural family. Her father was determined that his children would get a good education. When Lina was ten years old, he was deemed sufficiently "civilized" to be granted the status and privileges of an *assimilado*. Lina transferred from a segregated mission school to one that catered to the children of settlers. As the only African in her class she was exposed to constant discrimination and denigration. In response, she challenged her teachers at every turn. "It was good training," she said, chortling in a way that lit up her full round face. "It taught me to stand up for injustice, not only for myself. For the rights of my people."

In 1961, when Lina was sixteen, Eduardo Mondlane visited Maputo. He was working for the UN in New York at the time, a post that enabled him to visit Africa. Unbeknown to the Portuguese administration, he was already involved in the formation of Frelimo. She absorbed all he had to say—his analysis of colonial oppression in Mozambique, his reference to the wave of independence sweeping through Africa. She began writing articles for publication, her first foray into journalism and into exposing injustice. It didn't take her long to join a clandestine Frelimo cell, and in 1965 she decided to join the armed struggle based in Tanzania. As a precaution, she asked a friend to sew a hidden pocket into her handbag where she could hide the Frelimo documents she needed to enter Tanzania. But the secret police found out, and as she and her friend were saying their emotional good-byes they burst into her house and arrested her. With a nonchalant "Ciao!" her friend swung Lina's bag over her shoulder and walked out the door. Without proof of her intent to join Frelimo, she got a relatively light three-month prison sentence. She was released with a warning: if she took part in politics, whether inside the country or out, her father would be arrested. She had little choice but to stay put.

A few years later Lina was granted a scholarship to study economics in Portugal. In Lisbon, she was exposed to new ways of thinking about revolution and politics and was soon throwing herself into the underground anticolonial activism. Her studies suffered and she came close to losing her scholarship. Admonished by her father, she settled back into her studies, only to face a new challenge: she was pregnant. Abandoned by her Mozambican boyfriend, she dropped out of university to support her baby boy while continuing to direct her energies into the struggle.

Then came the coup in Portugal.

In April 1974, while I was listening to the newscasts in Guinea-Bissau, Lina was witnessing the events as they unfolded around her. After right-wing Portuguese fired into the house she shared with other Mozambicans, the movement sent her and her two-year-old son to Tanzania. There she enlisted in the Frelimo army and placed her son in the party's child-care center several hours away from where she was based. But the toddler missed his mother, refused to eat, and was weakened by dysentery. He died in her arms.

"It was the Portuguese who killed my little boy," she told me, still aching for her lost child six years later. "If it had not been for colonialism, for the need for the war, he would have survived." She made a promise that she would never stop fighting for the children of Mozambique so they could have the life she could not give to her son.

"I will give my own life if necessary," she said.

Meanwhile negotiations between the new Portuguese government produced a cease-fire and handed over complete power to Frelimo in September 1974, and on June 25, 1975, the day Samora Machel was inaugurated as president of Mozambique, Lina marched into Maputo with the triumphant Frelimo army. She was home. There she met Carlos Laisse, her future husband and father of their four children.

Lina was invaluable to me. She provided economic, political, and social context. Lina did not simply translate language; she translated culture. Soon after we started working together, we visited a small women's agricultural cooperative, one of many that had been established in the *zonas verdes,* the green zones on the outskirts of Maputo, to encourage urban agriculture and generate a cash income. We were shown around by the co-op president. We saw poorly cultivated fields dependent on rains that had not come. We saw cages of undernourished rabbits, some showing signs of mange; a few perky ducklings wagging their tails as they waddled about; some skinny chickens scratching in the stony ground. After the tour, the twenty coop members gathered around us in a clearing. They sat in a semicircle on the ground, straight-legged and straight-backed, while Lina and I sat on squat wooden stools brought out for us. Some held babies on their laps, while a few young children played on the outskirts of our gathering. At the edge of the group sat two local officials, also on stools, a man from the district Frelimo office and a woman from the local OMM chapter. The man held a notebook and a pen on his lap.

The women were quick to respond to Lina's jokey manner with their own banter, providing an energy that was absent from the co-op itself. Needing no urging, they took turns to tell us about their lives under colonialism and how much better they fared after independence. As they talked they expressed pride in their co-op, just two years old, where they each put in three days a week of work and then cultivated their own *machambas* on the remaining four days. They seemed undaunted by the poor harvests, which provided very little for them to divide up among themselves, let alone to sell. As I listened, one question kept coming into my head: What motivated these women to work with such commitment without tangible benefit? Lina turned to me, ready to translate my questions. I explained that I was stumped by this particular one, finding it hard to phrase in a way that would elicit more than pat answers. She grasped my problem instantly. "Tell me," she said, looking around the circle and taking in each woman in turn, "if a man comes here tomorrow and says to you: 'I will buy your cooperative and pay you a regular salary each week to continue working here,' will you sell?"

There was a murmur of "no's" and "nevers," accompanied by vigorous shaking of heads. This is *our* cooperative, they responded. "Every day we see progress even if it is slow. You have just seen our new little ducklings. They will grow and bring us an income." The united front was broken by one young co-op member. "I would definitely sell," she said. "Why?" Lina asked. The woman stood up and looked directly at Lina, speaking in a strong voice.

"You're pregnant," she said. Lina's newest pregnancy was just beginning to show. "You *believe* that the baby inside you will grow up healthy and look after you in your old age just as we hope our ducklings will. You don't know, though, do you? As for me, I must feed my children. I must feed them now."

The reaction from the two officials was immediate. The OMM cadre looked sternly at her. The Frelimo cadre, pencil poised, asked officiously, "What is your name?" The woman's confidence crumpled. There was silence. All the women stared down into their laps, visibly perturbed. Lina was up in a flash. Clapping her hands and swinging her large, supple body she began to dance as she stretched out her hands and pulled one woman after another to her feet and led them in a rousing Frelimo dance and song. When the song ended, the women were laughing. The tension was released and the official had put his notebook away.

Toward the end of our visit, I randomly asked some of the women to tell me their names and offer details about their backgrounds. I avoided the "dissenter," not wanting to embarrass her. Lina nudged me. "Ask her," she said. "It is important that she and others understand that she can give her name without repercussions." I did. This time no notebook was whipped out, I suspect because of Lina's seniority, and when the women danced and smiled their good-byes as we started to leave, they were joined by the two officials, broadly smiling. Quintessential Lina.

For the rest of my visit, which lasted until the end of January 1982, Lina was my regular companion, and by the end of my trip I had a lot of material. I returned to New York to write my chapter and other articles. Perhaps now I could finally get pregnant.

MY ROUTINE CHECKUP WAS DUE in the summer. It wasn't routine—my cancer had returned. I called Mervyn Susser, a South

African doctor friend, for advice. He and his wife, Zena Stein, also a medical doctor, had been forced out of South Africa in the early 1960s after opening a clinic in Alexandria, the African township outside of Johannesburg. They were now prominent and well-respected heads of departments at Columbia University Medical School. Not long into the conversation, I heard an anguished shout in the background from Zena. Mervyn put the phone aside to find out what had caused her reaction. I waited anxiously.

"Have you seen the *Times* this morning?" he asked when he returned to me.

"No," I responded.

He drew in a deep breath. "Ruth First has been killed by a parcel bomb," he said. He paused, the pained silence between us more tangible than a shout. Then he continued, his voice croaking: "In her office at the university."

On August 17, Ruth had been opening her mail as her staff assembled for a meeting. A large envelope with a UN return address looked innocuous. She opened it. It exploded, killing her instantly and injuring several of her colleagues. She was fifty-seven. The signature of the apartheid regime was stamped all over the assassination; letter bombs were increasingly being used against exiled activists, both black and white.

My last memory of Ruth was at Belém in Mozambique, at one time a gem of a resort frequented by Portuguese settlers and white South African pleasure seekers, now faded, where I spent a weekend with South Africans working in Mozambique. I had been touched by Ruth's solicitude for my cancer, so out of character with her reputation for lacking sentimentality.

During the day, we took in the beauty of the blue-green bay and the ocean, dancing with shimmering light, and felt fortunate to be there. We spread our towels on the sand, and lay in the sun, a pastime sublimely relaxing to those of us conditioned in our youth to white South African beach culture. At that moment, what more could we desire? Joe alone was fidgeting, unable to surrender to the warmth of the sun. He got up to get something from their room, a book perhaps. Joe was known for his humor, his brilliance, his general good nature with friends, all evident most of that weekend. But at that moment he seemed more like a bumbling spouse.

"Which is our room, Ruth?" Joe asked. Without looking up Ruth motioned to a low building with rooms looking over the bay. Joe ambled off. A few minutes later he was back.

"I can't find it."

Ruth sighed and raised herself on her elbow, pointing more precisely toward their room. "That one."

Joe ambled off once more. Once more he returned empty-handed, a slight petulant note in his voice. "I still can't find it."

Ruth became exasperated. Everyone who knew them was aware that their marriage accommodated fierce arguments, which centered mostly around their divergent political beliefs. "The *only* thing you can do," she spat out with the acerbic tongue for which she was renowned, "is run a revolution. And *that* still has to be proved."

We laughed. Joe shrugged it off, laughing with us. By the time "*that*" was proved, Ruth had been gone eight years. Joe would return to South Africa to a hero's welcome and join the government. He died of cancer in 1995. At least one of them had savored democracy.

I GRASPED AT THE REASSURANCES my doctors offered. My cancer was "indolent," slow-moving and still very small. However, a mastectomy was now unavoidable, although further treatment would not be needed. While I found comfort with this diagnosis, I couldn't rid myself of darker thoughts: What did this mean for John's and my plans to start a family? "What about pregnancy?" I asked each doctor I saw. I got wildly differing opinions, ranging from: "You're cured, get pregnant tomorrow" (my radiologist) to "You're a sensible young woman. You wouldn't play Russian roulette with your life" (an oncological gynecologist). John and I obsessed about the pros and cons and found it impossible to make our own decision. My oncologist promoted calm.

"The problem is we don't know what we are talking about," he said, his honesty reassuring to us. "There is a belief that the hormonal changes that come with pregnancy will trigger recurrences." He did not subscribe to this view. "There is simply not enough data, and the little there is suggests otherwise." I was part of a new group of cancer survivors wanting to have children. As feminists we had delayed childbirth until our late thirties, believing we had plenty of time. Most women in my situation were advised not to have children. Hence the paucity of reliable data.

"You need to live your life as if you're cured," he said. "I do advise, though, that you wait two years just to be sure."

When Janet, now an oncology nurse, gave me the same advice after consulting an oncologist she respected, my fears subsided. I was close to thirty-nine. I forced myself to refrain from counting the days and months and plunged back into my Africa work instead.

I BEGAN PLANNING A RETURN VISIT to Mozambique for mid-1983. I had a new assignment: to write a monograph on rural transformation and peasant women for the International Labor Organization. While my previous visits to communal villages would form the basis of the report, I needed to update my material. And to update myself on the impact of the war. Yes, war. In just over a year since my previous visit, Renamo—Resistência Nacional Moçambicana—had, aided and abetted by the South African regime, instigated a growing internal conflict. This Mozambican rebel group was the creation of the Rhodesian regime as part of their strategy to undermine the Zimbabwean armed struggle. With independence, Renamo now fitted perfectly into South Africa's schemes.

The apartheid regime was nervous. For decades, it had been sheltered from the continent's changing political landscape by a virtual wall of colonialism and racism, as impenetrable and inviolable as any made of iron and stone: Angola to the west; Mozambique with a long border to the east and north; and white-ruled Rhodesia to the north. This buffer zone was no more. The support Mozambique offered the ANC posed an ominous threat against apartheid's very survival. By fomenting conflict, South Africa hoped to obliterate this threat. As a result, Mozambique was now in an escalating state of war.

27 — The Ripple Effect of the War

On this third visit, I already know the ropes. I walk briskly toward the airport building to be near the head of the inevitably slow line to change my dollars into *meticais*. Once again, I feel revitalized just being back. But I am immediately aware that something is missing. I look around, puzzled. Then I get it: the banner is gone. I am no longer being welcomed to the zone of liberated humanity.

Was the absence of the banner a signal that Mozambique, under growing pressure, wanted to be more accommodating, both to South Africa and to donors who might be scared off by the government's socialist ideology? Was it aimed at the hope that the United States and Britain would rein in apartheid's onslaught? Were they moving away from their socialist ideals? Probably a bit of each.

Not long after I deposit my bags at Judith's apartment, I take a walk down the long, sloping hill to the *baixa*, the area near the docks, to make my habitual visit to the main Maputo market. I had discovered the energy of African marketplaces during my trip through Egypt and East Africa, and I have been drawn to them ever since. South Africa had no equivalent; segregation and control of movement of the African population had assured that. I like to breathe in the earthy smells of fruits and vegetables sold by women and look at the household goods and electronics sold by the men nearby. I stroll among the bustle of people as they fill their baskets and chat, catching up on local news and gossip, to the background noise of chickens and the general clattering sounds of a marketplace. I am not prepared for what I see. There is nothing there. Women sitting behind a cement platform that serves as their "store," with nothing more than two bunches of parsley or a bunch of mint on display in front of them. Not even the greens that are a staple here. There is an inevitable *bicha*—a line—and I join it for eggplant, which costs about the same as it would in New York. The next day a friend happens on carrots, which run out quickly. There are rumors of lettuce and cabbage later this week but the *bichas* will be long.

What I see in the market is the ripple effect of the war. There is a severe shortage of fuel throughout the country. At the same time, drought has laid waste to much of the land. The South African onslaught makes it more difficult to ride out the disaster. The textile factories are producing 10 percent less than usual due to both the failure of the cotton harvest and the lack of transport. Cashew production, a critical export, has taken a beating, affecting foreign exchange. Stores are empty. Markets are bare. Peasant farmers who are able to cultivate are producing just enough to feed their own families: there's no fuel to transport surplus crops to the cities. Villagers affected by drought and conflict desperately flee to the cities in the hope of finding food and shelter. They arrive at the doorsteps of relatives, who are expected, by custom stretching back through time, to provide for family in need.

Emma worked as an *empregada* (domestic worker) for my British friend, Teresa Smart. Emma's ration card was hardly enough for three people, but now she had to stretch it to feed eight. "What can I do?" she asked Teresa, desperation in her voice. "There is a war going on. We can't send them away!"

The answer for Emma was *Operação Produção*—Operation Production—launched in February 1983, a few months before my third visit to the country. The intent of the program was to relocate unemployed, nonproductive Maputo residents to the fertile north in order to alleviate the pressure on the city while at the same time helping to solve the farm labor shortage in Niassa, Tete, and Cabo Delgado. House-to-house checks began. Men and women who could not show that they were employed or failed to produce a Maputo resident's card were deemed "nonproductive" and taken to processing centers. Women, many working at home in the informal sector, were particularly vulnerable to the often arbitrary decisions of officials. Within days they were flown north. At first the overburdened Maputo residents were relieved. Then doubt set in. An appeal process was instituted, but too late for those already relocated.

The stories of women scooped up in these raids were particularly poignant: women who worked in the home were being forcibly removed from their families; young women were accused of being prostitutes. Sometimes neighbors or family reported them just to settle a personal score. The parallels with the South African expulsions to the Bantustans were not lost on me.

I wanted to see for myself. Within a week of arriving in Maputo, I boarded a plane for Niassa with Teresa. The centers set up for the so-called *inproductivos* were out of bounds for us, but we were allowed to visit women who, we were told, were playing an active part in agricultural production on state farms and in communal villages. Teresa argued that we would be gathering such mundane, boring information that there was no need for anyone to accompany us. And so, with only a driver and a car we were sent tetherless to visit three sites, all within an hour's drive of Lichinga, the capital of Niassa. Lussanhanda communal village was home to 276 families with well-tended vegetable gardens, a new school building, a health post and health worker, and a viable 250-member agricultural coop. Unango, a larger village the size of a small town, was a former Frelimo reeducation camp for people who had collaborated with the Portuguese. Matama was a state farm whose 2,000-strong workforce now included 600 *inproductivos*. The women we met told similar stories about being rounded up and arrested, taken to a detention center, and flown north within three or four days.

At Unango we interviewed four young women who were accused of being prostitutes. Two, Maria and Presilhina, aged twenty-two and nineteen, told us, their tone breezy, their smiles bright, that they did not want to return to Maputo. They had recently married local men. Ana, wiping away tears from time to time, told us how much she missed her *companeiro*, her common-law husband, who was in the army. We never learned the name of the fourth young woman who sat staring down at her lap, looking traumatized and never saying a word.

At Lussanhanda, we met a forty-four-year-old widow, Gloria, whose story echoed what I had been told in Maputo about personal vendettas. She lived with her son, a policeman, and her habitually unemployed nephew, whom she had raised from infancy. When the brigade came to get him, he wasn't home so they took his wife. When Gloria took food to the young woman, she too was detained. "Until we find your nephew," she was told. They found him. She wasn't released. Gloria shifted uncomfortably as she told her story. Then she looked down and finally said, in a soft voice, that the problem was the chief of her neighborhood block. He made it clear that he wanted to sleep with her. She refused. He became a predator. She continued to deny his advances. Now that he had some power, he had happily abused it. It was he who sent her away.

Our final visit was to Matama. We interviewed eight of the thirty women settled there. They had arrived with nothing more than the clothes on their backs, they told us, and no money. When they washed their clothes—without soap because they had none—they hid while they dried or pulled on in their wet clothes. They slept in a shed with a leaking roof, covering themselves with discarded wheat sacks. But far worse, said their spokeswoman, Regina, was the authorities' insistence that they marry male workers, who pestered them mercilessly and sometimes tried to use force. Some women had given in, but not this group of eight. Regina's cheeks flushed as she sat in her faded, threadbare clothes, looking at us with pleading eyes, an expression mirrored in the eyes of the other women who sat with her.

"I keep the letters from my husband as proof that I am already married," Regina told us. "It's a long, long way back home. This is not a life."

Back in Maputo we asked for a meeting with one of the government leaders who was in charge of *Operação Produção*. He was delighted with the program. "Already in this short space of time," he said in fluent English, "culture and customs are being exchanged between the north and the south. Everyone is benefiting." Perhaps noting the look of skepticism on my face, he continued: "With such a big relocation, of course, comes friction. Nonetheless, its negative impact is very small. It's of little consequence." Any mistakes, any missteps, had been corrected, he told us, estimating that maybe 2 percent of the *inproductivos* should not have been there. "We returned those," he assured us. I glanced at Teresa. She was as flushed as I was.

"I wonder whether we shouldn't regard women's work as productive even if it is unpaid," I suggested. He responded in a voice that brooked no patience with my naïveté. "I say to you, and I insist on this point, that it is more important to earn the meat to put in the pot than to just stand waiting for the meat to *come* to the pot. You take from the pot what you put into the pot."

Meat? The average Maputo family seldom had the means to buy meat. Women worked hard, performing all manner of domestic labor to put food of any kind "into the pot." I took a breath to calm my agitation. "It doesn't take much to appreciate," I ventured, "what can happen when thirty new women arrive among nineteen hundred men." He agreed that this was indeed a serious problem. "It is easy for a group of these kinds of women to slip into prostitution under such circumstances," he said. Teresa and I stared at each other aghast, for a moment completely speechless. One of us blurted out that some of the women we spoke to had common-law and even legal husbands. "Ah, they didn't leave *one* husband," he was quick to respond with a sneer in his voice. "They didn't leave *one* boyfriend. They left several husbands and several boyfriends." He drew out "several" for emphasis. "They are prostitutes."

A WEEK AFTER OUR VISIT to Lichinga, Teresa and I drove to Gaza Province in the south to attend some of the several thousand meetings being convened throughout the country in preparation for the OMM Extraordinary Conference, to be held at the end of 1984. This proposed event had spawned something of a people's social movement in the spirit of Frelimo's mobilization in the liberated zones. People gathered in towns, villages, and *bairros,* in cooperatives, state farms, and factories; they held spontaneous discussions at bus stops, in shops, in marketplaces to debate the agenda, which included polygamy, *lobolo,* early marriage, adultery, initiation rites, divorce, prostitution, relations within the family, women in production, single motherhood. OMM wanted to know how both women and men regarded these practices, how they could be reformed. Reports from these meetings were analyzed and compiled into a document to be presented at the conference.

Teresa and I sat for hours listening to heated discussions. This was Mozambique and OMM at their best. Polygamy and *lobolo* aroused so much interest that additional meetings had to be convened for the other issues. Although women led the meetings, women in the audience had to be urged to contribute when the men monopolized the meetings. They expressed their feelings in other ways. At one village, an angry muttering buzzed whenever the men defended polygamy. "It is better to have more than one wife," said one man. "When one of my wives goes to visit her family, then I can stay with the other wife. When one is ill, the other can cook for me. Without a second wife, I would suffer too much." When the women's murmurs crescendoed into jeering, local male leaders rushed around, gesticulating, shouting at the women to behave themselves. The protestations only quieted down when an older woman stood up. "I am the only wife of my husband. If I am sick, he cooks." Loud prolonged applause. Occasionally a man denounced polygamy. "We no longer want more than one wife," said a monogamous villager. "We must end this or a woman is nothing more than a *capulana*. You buy one today, another tomorrow. It cannot be like this any longer."

We left Gaza, inspired by what we had heard, and by the process itself, once again feeling the promise of a new Mozambique. The conference held in November 1984 was something else. I would hear from *cooperante* friends that along with the positive energy it generated came disdain for women like those we had encountered on our visit to Lichinga. President Machel attended the full proceedings, constantly interjecting and dominating the discussions. Signe Arnfred, who worked with the OMM during this period and has written about gender in Mozambique, was appalled when Samora Machel jumped to his feet, cutting through the OMM general secretary's report and pronouncing: "To be an unmarried mother is a disgrace! The concept, the very phenomenon, must be abolished." This was too much for OMM, which normally followed the party line. The final conference document emphasized that unmarried mothers should be supported, not castigated.

What about the liberation of women as a "fundamental necessity for the revolution and a precondition for its victory"? Machel seems to have come a long way from that proclamation.

Having heard so many disturbing stories, particularly the ones connected to *Operação Produção*, I needed to work out what to do with them. I had first arrived in Mozambique to write about its progress through human-interest stories, through the stories of women. But now cracks had begun to appear in the beautiful façade that independence had constructed, and disappointment was seeping through them. A question insinuated itself: Was it worth it? For this?

One thing was clear: in Mozambique, where I watched the beginning of the country's unraveling, it was South Africa that was pulling at the threads.

28 — "Define Your Terms, Comrade!"

Soon after my visit to Niassa, I am sitting in one of Maputo's few cafés with Dan O'Meara, a South African friend. The café is showing its wear. The metal table rocks as we lower a cup, lean on an elbow, take a sip of water from a clouded glass. We are chatting about, obsessing about, fantasizing about South Africa. We do this well—and often. Our nostalgia for South Africa weaves itself through our conversations, which range from the personal to the political and back again, often with little distinction between the two. But it is getting late. Time to head back to Judith's apartment.

"I need to be getting home," I say, as a waiter comes over to clear our coffee cups. We watch as he nestles one cup inside the other, stacks them on a dented metal tray, and walks off. Dan turns to me with a teasing expression.

"Define your terms, comrade," he says. I grin back at him.

Home—what exactly did that mean? That night and the days that followed, thoughts of home traveled through the pathways of my brain, resurrecting old connections as they hopped from one trigger word to the next: Longing for home. Proximity to home. South Africa. Struggle for freedom. Resistance against apartheid. Liberation of Mozambique foreshadowing the liberation of South Africa. Neighbor. Revolution. Home-home. Home for me could be a hotel room after a day of sightseeing. It could be Judith's apartment where I stayed a few months at a time in a country that wasn't mine. It was certainly my apartment in Manhattan. But these were the places I lived in— the places of my exile and emigration. Home-home was South Africa,

Cape Town, the mountains and the sea out of which they rose: the land of my birth and my heart.

Mozambique satisfies my longing for home. The same languages in tone and inflection, even the occasional words in the south. The same terrain and light and bird song. The air that conjures memories of smoky fires and pungent brush and the vast veld. I long to be back in my own country; I long to immerse myself physically once again. All I have is the coverage on TV, the press reports, the discussions with comrades in Mozambique, with South Africa–based activists visiting New York. They reinforce my place as an onlooker. I want to break that barrier. I want to hear and see the resistance firsthand.

South Africa is calling me.

When I left South Africa in my early twenties, I was ambivalent and somewhat naïve. I became an activist. I needed to both protest it and explain it, so I became a journalist. I became a feminist because I wanted to change the power relations that hold women in place. I became a writer of books about women and Africa so I could meld my two passions. It was as if the many hats I had donned were hanging on the same peg. I had written about Guinea-Bissau. I had written about Mozambique. Why was I not writing about South Africa?

But breaking my self-exile was not so simple. As a U.S. citizen, I needed a visa. But the consulate in New York was certainly not going to give a visa to a known anti-apartheid activist. Michael, my friend from Cape Town who was still living in Montreal, had the solution: "Don't apply in New York." It turned out that the consul in Montreal was more willing than most to issue visas. So I "lost" my passport. Michael handed my blank new one in to the consulate on my behalf, saying that I was living in Vermont for a short while and Montreal was the nearest consulate. I got my visa.

On March 16, 1984, Mozambique and South Africa signed the Nkomati Accord, a nonaggression treaty whereby South Africa would stop supporting Renamo and Mozambique would expel members of the ANC. Machel was pushed to the negotiating table by the escalating crisis. Renamo was gaining momentum. Reports of forced recruitment of child soldiers were frequent. Attacks on villages were on the rise; health workers and teachers, symbols of a new Mozambique, were being specially targeted. People were being displaced. People were being killed. It was becoming unsafe to travel outside of Maputo. A climate of fear was beginning to pervade Mozambique that just a few years earlier had been celebrating the end of the war in Zimbabwe. Nonetheless, signing the treaty was a risky calculation. The ANC was reduced to a skeleton diplomatic mission of ten people. Umkhonto we Sizwe (MK) would no longer be able to conduct military operations across the border into South Africa. Within days, South Africans, including Joe Slovo, were flown out of Maputo.

I was disturbed by the photos in the media of a smiling President Machel and his wife, Graça Machel, shaking hands with a smiling P. W. Botha and his wife. I did not for one minute believe this would stop the South African regime. As Jennifer commented caustically: "When you sup with the devil, you need to be sure you have a very long spoon." Could there be a spoon long enough? There wasn't. To the South Africans in Mozambique, the announcement of the Nkomati Accord came as a shock. Dan wrote:

> There was the anger about the way it was presented. We were told not to talk about it. The message was that they had tamed these horrible Boers and that they had succeeded in getting a promise that they would stop doing all the horrible things they're doing. Well, if you believe that, you're bloody stupid. Say it was a strategic necessity, yes. Say comrades, we have to do this, fine. Just don't claim a victory.

I was angry that Mozambique had abandoned the ANC but I understood that they had little choice. And I was certain that the South African regime would continue to wreak havoc on Mozambique. I needed now to focus on writing about South Africa.

29 — "I Am a Visitor to My Past"

As the plane flies low over the white suburbs of Johannesburg in May 1984, an American friend's amazed comment floats into my head: "Every single house has a swimming pool," he had said. "Every single house!" To keep my mind off the knot in my stomach I play a game: spot the house without a swimming pool. There are few. Then the plane lands and I am in the queue for foreign passports. Despite my visa, I feel apprehensive. Will the immigration officials have lists of prohibited visitors?

My hand shakes a little as I fill out the blue immigration forms with a new pen I have bought for my trip. I list "family visit" as my reason for entering. The line is slow but steady; no one is being held up for special questioning. Then it's my turn. The official is charming. Welcomes me with a big smile and then, looking at my pen, says: "First, I must try that!" He takes it from me, turns it over, and tests it out on a blank form, telling me he has a passion for pens. "I just *have* to try out every new one I see. This is a good one." While he chatters he checks through a book in front of him. I hold my breath. Then he looks at my form. "Only three weeks?" I smile back at him. "Ag man, but you were bawn yere!" He pronounces the "ag" as if he was clearing his throat in the Afrikaans way. "You can stay as long as you like. You'll have no problems."

Elated, I walk into the baggage area to reunite with my suitcase filled with tapes and batteries and film, and to reclaim my status as a journalist.

Back in South Africa after seventeen years, sensations that I had firmly suppressed begin to demand attention. I worry that my innate shyness and the insecurities that had been imprinted on my youthful self would resurface in the familiar physical and emotional territory. At the same time, I grapple with a new question: Who am I? A South African coming home after so many years? An American journalist coming after a story? Had I forfeited my South African heritage to those—the activists, the fighters—who are risking their freedom and their lives while I, as part of the international anti-apartheid movement, am perfectly safe. How will South Africans respond?

Georgina Jaffee is at the airport to meet me, her brown hair wild around her face, just as I remember it. She is grinning and I grin back. I feel a surge of fondness: I am in safe hands. We first met two years earlier at an anti-apartheid conference in Montreal. She had been living in Canada for a number of years and was about to return home. She is now living in Joburg and is politically active.

Georgina makes it her mission to ensure I have a successful visit. She introduces me to activists—most are members of the United Democratic Front. UDF, a broad-based anti-apartheid movement with a membership of over 3 million, was formed the year before my visit. It is a nonracial coalition of some four hundred civic, faith-based, student, worker, community, and other organizations. It has both energized and helped shape the growing resistance movement. It is eight years since the Soweto uprisings, and defiance is everywhere. All this against a backdrop of increased repression, fear, and brutality. I feel small in comparison: people are risking their lives; I am looking in through a three-week window. Would I have left if this new wave of resistance had existed when I was younger? I don't know. But I did leave. And now there is no place for me.

I have a chance to meet one of my heroes. At a political gathering one evening, Georgina introduces me to Helen Joseph, one of my heroes. I am familiar with her story from her memoir, which was smuggled out of South Africa, was one of the many banned books I devoured when I left. I have seen photos of her younger self when she was one of the leaders of the women's march on Pretoria in 1956. Now I see a tall, sweet-faced woman, her soft skin and fine gray hair giving the impression of a kindly aunt, and I remind myself how much this woman threatened the apartheid regime. Soon after arriving in South

Africa from England where she was born, she married a dentist, but it wasn't long before she was appalled by the racism and oppression she found in South Africa. When her short-lived marriage ended, she threw her energies into fighting for justice in South Africa and never remarried. She was charged with treason, jailed, banned, held under house arrest. She was mercilessly harassed by the police, who tossed bricks through her windows, fired shots into her house, and even rigged a bomb to her gate. She had been unbanned only recently and could now attend meetings.

Helen is interested in talking further, so a few days later we meet for tea at a local café. There she plies me with questions about Guinea-Bissau and Mozambique but is reticent to talk about herself. She is close to eighty. Despite the rising resistance, apartheid is still deeply entrenched. It seems unlikely that it will end within her lifetime. Georgina is working with an organization that is helping laid-off miners to gain other skills. She takes me to an African township outside of Johannesburg where she has a meeting in a church. I wait outside. Then two of the trade union organizers sit in the back of her car and take us on a tour. They point out the shacks, the living conditions, the general and very obvious poverty while telling me about the program they are running for unemployed workers.

"Would it be okay if I take some photos?" I ask. They agree and Georgina stops the car. I jump out and start clicking away. Suddenly a police car comes out of nowhere and two policemen jump out. They ask for our IDs. I show them my American passport. Georgina shows her ID card. The Africans show their passes. We are told to follow them to the police station. We do. The car is silent. When we get there, they put Georgina and me in separate rooms. One policeman says to another in Afrikaans (they didn't notice that my passport stated I was "bawn" in South Africa): "Let's see if they tell the same stories." Georgina and I had taken the precaution of agreeing on our story beforehand: I am a tourist. I am with her because she is taking me sightseeing in Joburg afterward. I wait alone in the small bare room while they interrogate Georgina. Shit, I think. How stupid could I be! I've lost the early-warning sense that I once had when I lived in South Africa. If I had just taken photos out of the window, they might not have noticed. On the other hand, they would have been suspicious of a car with two white women and two Africans driving slowly through the township. I worry most about the trade unionists who risked so much to take us on a tour. After about a half hour two policemen come into the room and stand while they ask me questions. They buy my story but charge Georgina with being in a township without permission. I am relieved to find that they have released the Africans. A few months later Georgina has to appear in court. Her partner represents her. He makes a good case and the charges are withdrawn.

In Joburg I am the journalist, the gatherer of information. It is not a city I am familiar with; I visited only twice during my childhood. I have to get to Cape Town for the other parts of me to come into focus. My senses are now raw as I take in the familiar surroundings. I walk up Adderley Street, which cuts through the center of the city from the foreshore toward the mountain whose towering presence is visible from every angle. Table Mountain—as recognizable as the face of a close friend but grander than I ever remember. I have dreamt this view so often—how do I know this is real? But there it is. More than anything else, the high, flat-topped, deeply creviced, rock-faced mountain tells me I am back. But am I home?

In the first few days I am an onlooker of a familiar but dreamlike scene. Through the window of my rented car, the scenery unfolds and unfolds. I am engulfed in waves of recognition and gasps of astonished pleasure at Cape Town's beauty. But I remain a visitor to my past, which sends out no tentacles, no lifelines to draw me closer. For years South Africa has been the substance of my dreams and my fantasies, the generating force for my politics, the source of my commitment. And here I am, back at last, but it stands by, coldly, aloofly, not allowing me to assimilate. Who am I—a New Yorker, an American—or South African? I feel stranded, adrift, somewhere in the middle of the Atlantic Ocean. I belong nowhere. I have no home.

When I am not in the company of activists, I am appalled at the complacency of whites. Even the best intentioned can't break out of their cocoons. Their lives are so comfortable, so stagnant and oblivious. One friend from my parents' generation laughs when I offer to make coffee. He says, "We have a black coffee machine." He means their domestic worker. A black machine to do the work. Whites accept their privileges as the norm, theirs by right. I find the tone of the women's voices jarring. It has the drawl of a spoilt child, a slight lilt, and an upward pitch at the end of the sentence, the suggestion of a question even though it's a statement. It is the fusion of underlying timidity in a male world and the assertiveness of people used to getting what they want from their "inferiors." In contrast, the African women I meet are anything but diffident, anything but maimed by guilt. They are strong, activist, resisters.

My cousin Gill Mudie, five years older than me to the day, daughter of my mother's brother Sam, sees in me a new, stronger woman. She uses the word "congruence." "It is something that my friends and I often observe in South African women visiting from England or the United States who have made a definite niche, a career for themselves. Their strength is evident." She thinks a moment. "But mostly what is evident is the lack of guilt. White women here, however together or successful in their work and personal lives, are marked, maimed even, by their guilt."

Then slowly, like a numbed arm regaining its flow of blood, I find I am being reabsorbed. My accent begins to change. I say "weatha" with that flat South African intonation; I say "bettah," not "bedder." I recognize more than the scenery. It's the walk of the people, whatever their background; it's their friendliness and smiles as eyes meet on the street. It's the humor that I had almost forgotten, the sounds around me that hold the different languages, mingled with the sea and the ferocious Cape Town wind. It is beginning to feel familiar again, and with that familiarity comes the sharp pain of what this country is, what this government does. Coming at me like waves I see the poverty, the inhumanity, the racism, the gross oppression set against the privilege and the whiteness that is my lot. I push aside my ruminations of home. I am ready to hear the stories; I am ready to record.

In 1984, the Group Areas Act and forced removals are in full swing. Hundreds of thousands of Africans are being uprooted and relocated: the government has decreed that the lands they have lived on for generations are "black spots" in areas that have since been decreed "white." Photos and footage of homes being bulldozed and people being herded onto trucks and driven away to bleak, under resourced areas has caught the world's attention, so the government is now sending the bulldozers in at night. By the time of my visit close to 20 percent of the people of South Africa have been uprooted from their homes, their communities destroyed. I can't write about everything given the short time I am in South Africa. I will write about the removals.

ONE OF MY VISITS WAS to Driefontein, 230 miles from Johannesburg, where, in 1981, a community of ten thousand people had received removal orders. I accompanied Pete Harris, an energetic and determined young member of a human rights law firm that was challenging the removals. We spent the night illegally in the home of Beauty Mkhize. Her husband, Sam Mkhize, was the leader of the protest against the removals. He was killed, unprovoked, by a white policeman who was acquitted of all charges.

"We are like dead meat now," one resident told me. "We can be shot at any time. We are like birds in the sky to be aimed at. If we shot a wild animal on one of the white farms, we would go to jail for a long time. The whites can kill a human being and be congratulated."

Beauty had stepped into her husband's shoes as leader. She worked out of their home, the hand-cut stone house that was built by her husband's grandfather on land he had bought before 1913. On the day of our visit, a nonstop stream of people—old men, old women, young men, young women—brought their stories of widespread local harassment to her house: pensions not processed; new passes deliberately delayed so that it was impossible to find work; job listings withheld. One elderly woman, who had waited almost two hours for her turn, looked aghast when Pete promised to get back to her as soon as he could. She got to her feet with deliberate slowness and began to walk away. Before she reached the door, she turned around and glared at him.

"I can't believe that you are doing nothing!" she said. "You know I have no food. You know I have no one to support me. How can you let me go away with my hunger?" She continued out the door, heavily placing one flat, bare foot in front of the other. It was a hard moment.

But there was no answer other than an end to the wretched system.

The people of Driefontein never did move. The national and international outcry finally got to the government. It lifted the removals policy soon after I returned to the United States.

The people of Mogopa were not as fortunate. Like Driefontein, Mogopa was a "black spot." Their richly resourced land, one hundred miles from Johannesburg, had been legally theirs for over two centuries. They lived well off it, supplemented by income from work on nearby farms and in the mines. They had established their own schools, built churches, sunk boreholes for water, and erected windmills. Their cattle were well tended and so were the fields, which provided a surplus to sell in the nearby town. They refused to move. In February 1984, armed police descended on Mogopa, working with dogs, forcibly loaded people and belongings onto buses and trucks. Not permitted to take their cattle, they hastily sold them to local white farmers for less than a quarter of their worth.

They arrived at their barren resettlement area to find a place without water, unsuitable for cultivation, without schools, work, transport, far from shops. Facing starvation, they asked their paramount chief to provide an alternative that was within his jurisdiction. Conditions were not much better in their new place, but they felt safer, less vulnerable to police intervention. It was here that I visited them.

An old woman came up to greet me. Perhaps because I was white, she thought that I would have answers to her questions. She looked at me out of her deep, pained eyes. "Do you know when we are moving from here?" she asked. "We can't live here. We have no water. We have lost everything. I used to have a six-room house..." Her voice trailed off and I followed the line of her arm, which she directed toward her new "home," a small tin shanty, unprotected from heat and rain, broken furniture that had once filled her house in Mogopa leaning against the outside of the wall. "When will we go back home?"

I could offer her no solace, no hope. Her universal longing for home was far more than for a physical place. It encompassed a desire for dignity, to be treated as a human being; to no longer be made to feel worthless, discarded, disregarded, "like dead meat." It was an open wound that could not be healed. My quest for home paled. I had not been forcibly uprooted. I had voluntarily got on a plane and left South Africa. I was among a very few South Africans who had the option. Even my leaving smacked of privilege. I could not escape it. I had to think again about what "home" meant, not just to me. Talking to the elderly woman and seeing her pain, I felt ashamed.

Eventually in the new democratic South Africa, the people of Mogopa were among the first to have their land returned. I don't know how many of the 3.5 million people forcibly relocated by the South African government have been able to go home. Certainly not the majority.

Despite the horrors I witnessed, I took away hope when I left South Africa. People like those in Driefontein were fighting back. UDF was rapidly growing in strength even as the government came down ever more heavily on the protestors. What was clear to me was that the story was no longer only one of a downtrodden people. Resistance, people taking back their history, confrontation, revolution had now become the story.

30 — A Serious, Full-Time Job
in the Movement

When I returned to New York I became glued to the nightly news as scenes of protest and police violence in South Africa entered my living room, and those of millions of Americans, via CBS, NBC, and ABC.

As I watched, it was the police whips—the sjamboks—rather than the guns that really got to me. When the police, mostly but not exclusively white, aimed guns at the protestors it seemed to me to be just an extension of the government's military power: procure arms and ammunition; equip the police; train them to shoot accurately; send them into the townships. Then, like so many automatons, the police would raise guns as taught, place target in crosshair, shoot. A mechanical, almost impersonal final step in the long process of repression. Anonymous.

However, the whips were something else. The thrust of the long leather sjamboks seemed personal, infused with hatred. The stretching way back of the right arm. The sjambok, trembling a moment at its apex before descending in an arc, cutting through the air with as much force as the arm could exert to provide as much pain, as much destruction as possible. Filled with the lust of its own power, the motion was repeated again. And again. Until the victim was on the ground, in fetal position, arms over the head in an impotent attempt to protect, and then lying still, while the sjambok continued to descend. I could hear in my mind the sharp swish and the thud against a body, a live body. The perpetrators, in dark blue pants and light blue shirts—caught in Technicolor on our living room television—their bodies pivoting to the rhythm of the sjamboks. Here was the essence of racism on display: the protection of privilege, culture, everything they believed they had a right to, and the victim on the ground did not.

Then there were the dogs. In other circumstances, man's best friend, man's protector. Beautiful, faithful, friendly dogs. German shepherds, particularly smart: the breed trained to find people trapped in earthquakes, victims of natural disaster. Brave, proud working dogs. Here they were working dogs, too, excited by the mayhem around them, trained to tear at clothes and flesh. Transformed from friend to an extension of the oppressor. Another weapon in the arsenal of apartheid. The next night I watched again.

IN AMERICA, APARTHEID HAD BECOME a household word. As each year passed since the Soweto uprisings in 1976, protests were heating up. Now in the mid-1980s, it became evident that South Africa was caught between the growing resistance and the escalating international condemnation marked by boycotts, divestment, and calls for sanctions on the one hand and its growing inability to maintain its economy, its way of life, its very power, on the other.

It was no longer only activists protesting the evils of the South African regime; ordinary Americans were outraged and inspired to take action. The more the media captured the horrors of apartheid, the more it became apparent that the totalitarian state would fall. The only question was when.

The combination of seeing the oppression in South Africa firsthand and watching the violence playing out on the nightly news—and the fearless resistance of the people—left me grappling for my next step. *Southern Africa* was no longer being published. My consultancy at the United Nations had ended. My Guinea-Bissau book was now five years old. I needed a more reliable income than the occasional speaking engagement or writing assignment. And I needed to get more directly involved with the fight to end apartheid.

Then Jennifer Davis came to the rescue. She was now executive director of both the American Committee on Africa and its educational wing, the Africa Fund. Gail Hovey had just resigned as research director and she offered me the job. My life was coming full circle. ACOA had supported Defence and Aid before it was banned. It was my first contact with the anti-apartheid movement when I arrived in New York in 1968. Now I would actually get *paid* for doing work I was already committed to.

U.S. corporations had been propping up apartheid for decades with loans, investment, and critical technical support. When South Africa experienced capital flight after the Sharpeville massacre in 1960, U.S. banks, led by Chase Manhattan, stepped in with $40 million in loans. By 1982, U.S. financial engagement—not including trade—topped $14 billion. Aided by documentation provided by ACOA and the Africa Fund, the public became aware that unions, pension funds, universities and colleges, state and local legislatures, and many faith-based organizations had financial connections to corporations doing business with South Africa. This research was essential to the rapidly growing U.S. anti-apartheid movement. Now it was not just a handful of activists who disrupted shareholder meetings; irate shareholders were doing it themselves—and getting results. The data that ACOA was uncovering was helped by the ability in the U.S. to access information that corporations were legally bound to make public. This was not the case in Europe and Britain, where the anti-apartheid movements focused on a sanctions campaign and on the import of consumer goods, including fruit and vegetables, which the U.S. did not import. It was only in the U.S. that the divestment movement could take flight.

And now I was part of it.

AT THE BEGINNING OF NOVEMBER 1984 I opened the door to the office on Broadway in lower Manhattan and walked into my new job. I peeked around the door to Jennifer's small office—as executive director, she had it all to herself. The other work spaces, equally small, that lined the passage were crammed with the handful of staff members and a rotating number of dedicated interns. Jen sat behind her desk, surrounded by piles of files and newspaper clippings. "Welcome to the fray," she said, indicating the only chair that was not encumbered with papers.

I already had some idea of what my role would be; we had talked about it when she offered me the job. I would be compiling and updating information that related to the divestment and sanctions movement, the latter not only in the United States but in Africa and Europe, as well as producing fact sheets, reports, and other documents about apartheid and its social, economic, political, and legal implications.

We were known for providing the now extensive anti-apartheid movement with reliable information that cut through hyperbole. Inaccuracies would play into the hands of detractors. Apartheid was egregious enough; there was no need to inflate the horror. Our job was to ensure that no one could pick holes in our arguments for divestment, that there were no fuzzy areas to be exploited by right-wing detractors. Jen could spot the slightest overstatement, and I soon learned to be far more rigorous than I usually was.

"The divestment movement is moving fast. We need to update our question-and-answer fact sheet," she said. Our fact sheets helped anti-apartheid activists have arguments at their fingertips.

"When do you need it by?"

"Yesterday," she answered. We laughed. I had a lot to learn.

Then we turned to the subject of salary: $14,000 a year—about $32,000 in today's currency. I assured Jen I could manage as I had articles pending on my trip to South Africa. Nonetheless I knew it would be tight. John and I had very little savings—not good for starting a family, which we hoped to do soon; it was almost two years since my cancer treatment had ended. Luckily John had recently landed a job with an NGO, which paid somewhat better than union organizing. We still calculated that I would only be able to take two months of maternity leave.

I left Jen and walked down the passage to my desk at the back of the office pondering my assignments. I passed Dumisani Kumalo's open door. "Hey sister!" he called out and laughed his signature laugh, deep and infectious. "Welcome aboard!" His "sister" reminded me that I was working with two other South Africans in an organization that proclaimed itself American.

In 1981 George Houser retired as executive director. George had founded ACOA in 1955 to support independence movements against colonial rule in Africa. This lifetime commitment—he died at the age of ninety-nine in 2015—grew out of his work as a leading civil rights organizer. He was one of the founders of CORE—the Congress for Racial Equality and an organizer of the Freedom Rides. "The struggle in Africa was to us, as Americans, an extension of the battle on the home front," he said in 2003. Although his work in the civil rights movement was based on the concept of nonviolence, he respected the right of the liberation movements to adopt armed struggle, understanding that they knew their own contexts and would therefore need to make their own decisions about direction and tactics. And so ACOA as an organization supported the right of liberation movements to adopt armed struggle in their quest for independence.

Her sharp political strategizing and emphasis on grassroots organizing were critical to the success of the divestment campaign. I once heard Canon Fred Williams, a prominent Harlem religious leader, toast her: "Here was this Jewish woman who made it possible for ACOA's Religious Action Network to do its work—this coalition of primarily black, male clergy and their churches." Referring to Jennifer's tendency to be reserved and self-effacing, he continued: "The public Jennifer is so reliable—the one to look more deeply, to insist on principle, to keep focused even in the face of terrible opposition."

One of my favorite photos, taken in 1980 when she gave one of her many testimonies to the UN, captures her spirit. Cigarette burning in her right hand, severe black turtleneck sweater with a silver pendant that catches the light, eyebrows arched, eyes intent, expression severe, she presents her research to the organization.

Jen had grown up in a liberal Johannesburg family; her father was a well-respected pediatrician, and her mother was a trained pharmacist who had fled Germany when Hitler was on the rise. She was already politically active in high school in the late 1940s. At university she joined the Unity Movement, one of the South African liberation organizations, and refused, whenever possible, to participate in the privileges afforded whites in South Africa, such as all-white cinemas and other public events. (Looking back now, it puzzles me that it never even crossed my mind to avoid segregated cinemas.) She began to contemplate leaving when her five-year-old daughter, Sandy, came home from school and asked her if Andrew, a close African friend, was a bad person.

"Not at all," Jen assured her. "Why do you ask, darling?"

"The teacher told us today to be careful of black people because they are all bad people." Jen knew then that it would be impossible to protect Sandy or four-year-old Mark from the influences of apartheid and the bigoted thinking that came with it.

Life became increasingly dangerous for activists after Sharpeville. In 1966 she and her husband decided to leave.

I could only agree with the assessment of Canon Williams, that Jennifer "looks ever so more deeply" and "Is ever so more principled." I knew I would learn a lot working with Jen. The first time I asked her to comment on something I had written, I did so with trepidation. We sat in one of the bedrooms of the country house we once shared in the Catskills, she on the bed, me on the floor, while I waited for her verdict on the three-page outline I had drafted for my Guinea-Bissau book.. I watched her as she read it through, then flipped back to the first page to reread sentences, and finally put it down on her lap. And sat thoughtfully for a moment longer.

"This is very good," she said. I breathed out. "It is well written. It captures the intent of the book succinctly." She made a few small editing suggestions. I couldn't have felt more relieved if I had passed a grueling exam.

Jen and DK, as we called Dumisani, were a formidable team. She often told me that she felt amazingly lucky to have worked with him. He had no ego and cared deeply about the same issues. In that respect, they were the perfect match. At the same time, they were polar opposites. Where Jen was self-effacing, he was outgoing and charismatic. He always seemed to be enjoying himself. "Ebullient" was a word I always associated with him. Nothing fazed him. Nothing was impossible. He held audiences in his thrall—whether local, state, or national legislators, religious groups of all faiths, organizations of all political persuasions, campus groups. How many voters, how many students, trade union workers, members of faith based communities he galvanized in the divestment campaign we can never know. But his influence made a serious impact. He appealed to all because he treated all equally, with the same humor, understanding, and firmness. He was passionate about his work and it was infectious. But it did have its challenges. He often returned from one or other of his whirlwind trips, exhausted by the effort to build coalitions that surmounted the racism he found in America. He had come to speak—in a church, at a city council meeting, on a campus—about the importance of the divestment movement. But first he had to deal with real-life America. He would meet whites who were eager to push for divestment; he would meet blacks who were eager to push for divestment. He would insist on joint meetings. When he worked with city councils and state assemblies, he would strongly advise that in order for a divestment bill to have a shot at becoming legislation, it should be sponsored by at least one white member and one black member, one Democrat and one Republican, and represent generations young and old.

There are few public photos of DK during this time. He always stood back while allowing someone else the limelight. "It was a joint effort," Jen says, referring back to the grass roots, the groundswell that made the difference. Neither she nor DK would take credit for the work they did. But without their passion, without the careful research and the sound data that ACOA and the Africa Fund produced, I believe it would have been a different story. And in the new South Africa, President Thabo Mbeki, who succeeded Nelson Mandela, would present her with a medal of honor in recognition of her contribution.

BY THE TIME I JOINED ACOA at the end of 1984, forty U.S. companies had withdrawn their investments from South Africa; another fifty would do so the following year. By the beginning of 1985 Citibank had refused to make any new loans, and Chase Manhattan refused to roll over its short-term loans, creating a major financial crisis. Barclays would take a similar stance to Citibank a year later. Through all this, President Reagan continued to argue for "constructive engagement." He would say in any forum that provided the opportunity that divestment and sanctions would only hurt black people in South Africa. Change could only happen through dialogue. Those youth in South Africa trying to storm South Africa's bastille had given up "dialogue" a long time ago. Dialogue presupposes that two parties are willing to negotiate. The whites were certainly not. They were not ready to make significant compromises or to even acknowledge their position of privilege. The response was to increase violence and repression.

Reagan worked hand in cozy glove with his friend and ally, Margaret Thatcher, who reflected both their views in a CBS interview in July 1985. There she said, in her unctuous voice: "I think a policy of sanctions would harm the very people in South Africa you are trying to help. . . . I agree with a policy of trying to influence South Africa by other means. The present Government is moving forward in the direction we wish them to go, faster than any other. . . . Sanctions will harm, not help." I didn't know whether to laugh or scream.

Archbishop Desmond Tutu repeatedly pointed out the fallacy of this argument: "Those who invest in South Africa should not think they are doing us a favor; they are here for what they get out of our cheap and abundant labor, and they should know that they are buttressing one of the most vicious systems." His voice rose where other South African voices were silenced, many already imprisoned for their outspoken political positions. The message that I heard again and again from South African visitors to our office was that the people were already suffering beyond endurance. Divestment could hasten an end to that suffering.

President Reagan had his comeuppance a year later, in 1986, when Congress overrode his veto of the Comprehensive Anti-Apartheid Act. The CAAA banned all new U.S. trade and investment in apartheid and barred all federal departments and agencies, including the police and the military, from providing funds and assistance to South Africa. It was one of the several straws that eventually broke the apartheid camel's back. It added its weight to the divestment and sanctions bills already passed by local and state legislatures and spurred the sanctions movement in Europe as well. From 1982 to 1985, the divestment campaign drove over $4 billion of U.S. capital investment out of South Africa.

ACOA and the Africa Fund tracked it all. Working there at the time, I could clearly see a pincer movement: the grass roots pressuring from below while the twenty-member Congressional Black Caucus strategized with TransAfrica from above. At the same time, members of Congress were lobbied in Washington and besieged by voters locally. Senator Richard Lugar, a Republican and the chair of the Senate Committee on Foreign Relations, complained that he couldn't even watch his kids play baseball in his home town in Indiana without being accosted by constituents demanding to know what he was doing about apartheid. It was this kind of pressure that led him to cosponsor and pass the CAAA. "We are against tyranny," Lugar pronounced on the floor, "and tyranny is in South Africa!" One young senator spoke movingly of how his conscience dictated that he break from his president for the first time. His name? Mitch McConnell (later Senate majority leader). He, like many in his party, joined with Democrats to guarantee the override. Voting their conscience? Perhaps. But it was more likely about their fear of losing in the upcoming elections. The divestment campaign had insinuated itself into every aspect of political and economic life in the United States, driven by people of all ages, creeds, colors, ethnicities, and political persuasions, who demanded that their elected officials "do something" about apartheid.

IN TRYING TO JOG MY MEMORY about my time with ACOA and the Africa Fund, I looked online for the video *I Ain't Gonna to Play Sun City*, which was a high point of anti-apartheid education in 1985. The project was launched by Artists United Against Apartheid, which was founded by activist and performer Steven Van Zandt (Little Steven), who first gained fame as a guitarist for Bruce Springsteen's band. Sun City, a sprawling, Las Vegas–style casino built by a South African magnate in one of apartheid's barren Bantustans, Bophuthatswana, was apartheid's innovative attempt to sidestep the international cultural boycott called by the United Nations. South Africa managed to convince several high-profile entertainers, among them Frank Sinatra, Linda Ronstadt, Queen, Ray Charles, and Rod Stewart, that they would not actually be performing *in* South Africa but in an "independent homeland." This fiction allowed performers to ignore uncomfortable facts and go for the big bucks.

I sit in my living room and bring up *Sun City* on YouTube. The camera hones in on the vast lavish complex, blue U-shaped swimming pool in the foreground, surrounded by lush green veld, a brief scene of dancers swaying to music under a huge electronic Sun City banner. A mellow, white South African woman's voice intones: "Sun City is the showcase of Bophuthatswana, one of the so-called independent homelands where South African blacks have been relocated." *Wait a minute!* I sit up straight and listen more carefully. That voice is mine! I recognize the accent and timbre. "Your accent is *so* South African!" my daughter Kendra exclaims when she listens to it later. Yes, it is, or was thirty years ago, but what startles me is that I don't remember recording this. It must have been in the studio where the video was produced. I assume that the producers wanted a white South African woman's accent to emphasize both authenticity and white privilege—as well as the ability, perhaps, to pronounce "Bophuthatswana" effortlessly.

My voice goes on: "It's a lavish resort where you can relax and enjoy some of the world's headline entertainers. It's part of the reality of apartheid." The luxurious scene jumps to gunshots and scenes of violence as police attack youthful protestors and the "reality of apartheid" is brought home. Miles Davis in profile sets the tone with his signature trumpet introducing the beat of the catchy song, "Ain't Gonna Play Sun City." Scenes of slender white women sunbathing and chips being handled at gambling tables contrast with scenes of resistance and many prominent entertainers declaring that they weren't going to play Sun City.

Little Steven produced the video with Danny Schechter, "the news dissector"—a well-known radio, TV, and print journalist who had been involved in South African protests since before I arrived in the United States. He was politically savvy and quick to find opportunities to expose the evils of apartheid. They wanted to show that South Africa was not a land of victims but of people who were fighting back.

It took me a little longer to appreciate Danny. I first got to know Danny soon after I arrived in the United States. When I returned from Guinea-Bissau in 1974 he interviewed me for his Boston radio program. I was nervous: it was one of my first interviews, and he made no effort to make me comfortable. He shot questions at me in a way I thought pompous, but I was too intimidated to assert myself. "Well," he said dismissively as he switched off his mic, "that was the worst interview I have ever done." He didn't air it. It took me some time to get over my humiliation and to fully appreciate his contribution to the struggle, but I eventually came to regard him as a friend.

Little Steven hoped to get five or six artists interested in joining the *Sun City* project: over fifty responded—jazz musicians, rock musicians, rap artists, folk singers, among them Bob Dylan, Bono, Lou Reed, Miles Davis, Peter Gabriel, Bonnie Raitt, Keith Richards, Ringo Starr, Run-D.M.C., Bruce Springsteen, U2. It became a mammoth undertaking. Big names meant big egos, which Jennifer, providing background information for them, had to often navigate around. The result was a vibrant seven-and-a-half-minute video plus an LP with additional numbers on it. My role—apart from the voice-over—was to produce the two-page notes that were inserted in every copy of the album. Even if I didn't remember being part of the video, the style of the insert was obviously mine, prompting one ACOA colleague to pronounce: "This was your most popular publication *EV-VERRR!*"

The profits were close to $1 million, funds that the Africa Fund was able to channel to ANC's education and cultural projects and to the anti-apartheid movements in the United States and Europe.

By the time "I Ain't Gonna Play Sun City" aired, I was pregnant. My plan was to work until my baby was due in February 1986, take off two months, figure out child care, and return to my research job. I couldn't afford not to.

31 — "How Much Does She Weigh?"

I stand in a glass alcove dense with foliage. A temporary addition to the greenery is a tall Christmas tree bedecked with angels and other ornaments that glint in the bright morning sunlight of the house in Cambridge, Massachusetts. John holds up our camera and centers me in the viewfinder. I stand sideways in a pair of black velvet pants and a black turtleneck sweater covered by a cream-colored woven African shirt that had once belonged to Amilcar Cabral, a present from Gil in Cairo. Underneath that shirt my belly rounds out in front of me. My face, grown chubbier with pregnancy, glows with contentment. Our baby is due in seven weeks. A girl.

We are once again spending Christmas with South African friends and their families, as well as their American spouses and children, Jews and non-Jews, hosted as in most years by Margie. Anthony Lewis, her husband of three years, has welcomed our community into his home as warmly as she has. As the day progresses I fantasize about next Christmas: our daughter will be ten and a half months, the first baby in some years. Will she be crawling all over or an early walker getting into toddler mischief? Will she have blue eyes like her father and Leonie? Green eyes like mine? Chubby like my baby photos?

Disquieting moments break through these thoughts as I become increasingly conscious of a lack of movement. An occasional half-hearted kick, a fluttery feel, but not the earnest kicking I would expect. Two nights later, back home in Washington Heights, I sleep fitfully, waiting for signs of action. Almost none. I call my obstetrician early the next morning, and Dr. Wolf's comforting voice banishes my fears. I do as I am told: I shoulder my maroon messenger bag filled with work and set off to the hospital for a stress test, confident that I will be continuing downtown to ACOA right afterward. At Columbia Presbyterian I am hooked up to a fetal monitor. The baby's heartbeat is strong. "Looking good," the nurse says to me, patting my arm in encouragement. "But we have to wait for her to move. However long it takes." More than an hour later a furious beeping breaks through my now drowsy state. In an instant, the nurse and technician are in my room, followed by my doctor. My baby's heart rate has dropped from the normal 150 to 60. "You need an ultra sound to see what's going on," he tells me. What is "going on" is that she has very little amniotic fluid and each time she kicks, the umbilical cord tightens around her neck, limiting her oxygen intake and slowing her heart rate.

"Well," Dr. Wolf said, smiling from above his white coat after he has explained these menacing details, "You are going to be a mom today." He leaves the room to telephone my husband. About forty-five minutes later John walks in. Always light-skinned, his face is now pale, almost translucent and waxy. His blue eyes are bugging out and his usually wispy blond hair is an oily matt from perspiring in his rush to get to me. He says nothing but takes my hand. I cry for the first time. We barely have time to hug before I am wheeled into the operating room and put under a general anesthetic.

When I surface from the caesarian, I was still under the bright lights with John at my side. "All's well," he says. A rush of relief.

"How much does she weigh?" He hesitates. "Two pounds." His voice is barely audible. Then, in a stronger voice: "But really, *really*, she's going to be fine." I turn away. All I feel is dread.

"Can I bring your baby to you?" The voice is kind. I look up, still woozy, to a hand extending from a nurse's white sleeves as she places my newborn next to me. I try to take in this "baby" lying across my shoulder. Her head, smaller than a tennis ball, is turned away so that my first glimpse is of her straight dark brown hair. She is the length of a twelve-inch ruler, her wrinkled skin a reddish hue. The emotional pain is as sharp as any physical pain. How can a baby so impossibly small survive? Then the same white-sleeved arms take her away and she is whisked off to intensive care.

I would later learn that a fibroid had grown under the placenta, robbing it of nourishment, but nature ensured that the little that made it through focused on her lungs, heart, and brain, all of which were healthy. Now all she has to do was grow, medical folk with smiles too bright are quick to tell me. It takes me much longer to accept, and to let go of some of the consuming anxiety that stays with me while she spends two months in an incubator. When we finally take Kendra home she weighs four and a half pounds.

ONE THING WAS CLEAR. Leaving Kendra in child care after just two months of maternity leave was unthinkable. I resigned my job, maintaining a link by joining the board of directors of the Africa Fund. I had to figure out some occupation other than mother of a preemie. My three visits to Mozambique had produced a large trove of interviews, notebooks, photographs, tapes to transcribe—more than enough for a book. Problem was, my material was fast becoming dated; it had been four years since I had been back. I submitted another proposal to Ford and received a second grant to cover a year of writing and a trip back to Mozambique. When Kendra was eighteen months, still small but showing welcome signs that she would yet be in sync with her age, I booked a flight and left for a four-week trip to Mozambique in June 1987.

After John dropped me off at JFK airport I felt on edge. I counted my bags: suitcase, computer bag, handbag—one, two, three. I count again. One, two, three. Right number. I check my passport. Again. I check my ticket. Again. Something is missing. I am unnerved. Something *must* be missing. Then it hits me and I laugh to myself, almost out loud. What is missing is Kendra's diaper bag, which has been my constant companion when I travel, whether on the A train from Washington Heights or farther afield to London to visit my mother and Leonie, or to Toronto to visit John's mother and sister. I feel like someone who has had a limb severed and still thinks it's there.

I am already missing that little squirt of a thing. John will be amply helped by Janis, a friend who has acted as Kendra's second mother; Bridget, the eighteen-year-old minder from her day care who will bring her home every day and stay until John gets back from work.

But I won't be there. I ache already and I'm not yet airborne. At the same time I am eager to get back to Africa. I have to admit that looking after a toddler can feel claustrophobic. I long to take off, just like that, the way I used to: to fantasize, then plan, then do. This is no longer possible. I am tethered; my wings have been clipped. Now I have this one opportunity to snip the cord, reattach the feathers, and take off for four weeks. It brings a quiver of excitement. I am about to be on my own again. Back to being a journalist, back in Mozambique. When boarding is announced, I pick up my hand luggage—one, two—and enter the plane.

I arrive in a war-torn country. I thought I was prepared for changes that have taken place since 1984. I wasn't.

32 — "What About the People?"

It is the small hours of the morning of May 29, 1987, in Maputo. Four simultaneous attacks are launched by South African commandos. One attack is on a warehouse used by the ANC. Three people are there at a time. Two are South Africans who manage to escape, one by hiding in a barrel. The young Mozambican guard is killed.

The other target was a mistake. A young Mozambican couple are asleep in their beds. With them is their two-year-old daughter. In a second room sleeps their seven-year-old son. Their domestic worker shares his room. It's two in the morning when the attackers break down the door. Some are black. They speak Portuguese. Some are white and speak a language which sounds like Afrikaans to the domestic worker. They tie the hands of the young mother and father behind their backs. Their son runs into the room in terror. He tries to go to his parents. The invaders force him back into his bedroom. The little girl tries again and again to reach her mother. She is pushed aside. With their hands still tied, the couple dash to the balcony and scream for help. 'We're Mozambicans!' they cry out. 'Help us! Help us!' The attackers take aim and let loose a volley of bullets. The guns have silencers.

As they leave, the soldiers toss the toddler onto her mother's body, as if discarding a bag of garbage. When the Mozambican police enter the apartment, the little girl is still clinging to her mother. Every time the phone rings she rushes eagerly to be the first one to pick it up. 'Mama?' she asks, her baby voice rising in hopeful expectation, 'Mama?'

A week after the event, on my first day in Maputo, I listen to Becky Reiss relate this story when we talk late into the night to catch up with news. I am staying with her this time. Judith has recently returned to Toronto. Becky is one of my more fearless, practical friends, who even as she relates this and other current information about Mozambique, remains undaunted by all that was happening in her newly adopted country where she arrived one year earlier to work with the Ministry of Health. We have been friends since 1979 when, in her early twenties, she walked through the door of the Southern Africa Committee office and simply announced that she was there to work with us. She had recently arrived from California and she was enrolled in a master's program in public health at Hunter College.

Later in bed I revisualize the scene in the apartment. The little girl is not much older than Kendra, who is safe and sound in New York. It is my first realization that this trip is going to be harder to deal with emotionally, not only because of the stepped-up conflict but because now that I have my own daughter my anguish burrows deeper than I could have anticipated.

The attacks were the first direct instances of South African aggression since the signing of the Nkomati Accord three years earlier. Mozambique was paying the price for its solidarity with the South Africa struggle, not only through Renamo but now directly from South Africa. I had so easily, so glibly, described the "solidarity" movement in the United States. I had felt pleasure when Cabral, in Jennifer's living room over a decade earlier, spoke of the importance of our solidarity with his revolution and the strength he and his colleagues took from it. It gave gravitas to the work we were engaged in. Now I felt humbled, sobered, even embarrassed. For me, solidarity had meant publishing a magazine, joining protests, talking on campuses to women's groups, to faith-based organizations, to anyone who wanted to listen, to writing articles and books, learning firsthand about Mozambique and passing on what I found to others so they too could express their solidarity. For Mozambicans, on the other hand, solidarity meant sacrifice. And sacrifice meant conflict and death. The word I had so easily used now stalled on my tongue. It had orphaned a two-year-old girl. And uncountable more.

Who among all of us strong supporters of the Mozambican armed struggle and Frelimo's vision of a socialist society would have dared imagine what is happening now? South Africa has won this round with its invasive destabilization policies, which is harming the economy. The sense of war is everywhere. Maputo is akin to an island, the roads that fan out in all directions are too dangerous to use on a regular basis. The hospital is full of wounded civilians.

The same evening Becky describes the South African attack I ask her about *Operação Produção*. Since my visit to Niassa I had continued to wonder about the unhappy women involuntarily relocated there. Such a hot topic of conversation and debate four years earlier, it was now shrugged off as one of those unfortunate failures. Ah well, bad move. However, it has come back to bite its architects. The fertile and underpopulated province of Niassa is now a major area of Renamo operations, aided by many of those disgruntled transplants from the south.

SOON AFTER ARRIVING I GOT together with Lina Magaia. She was the one I was looking forward to the most to fill me in about events in Mozambique. In the past few years she had continued to track the way South Africa's "total strategy" has been destroying the day-to-day lives of the people of Mozambique.

Lina was now living in Manhiça, fifty-five miles from Maputo, working as the director of the economic department for the state-owned sugar factory, Maragra. At first her children traveled back and forth with her between Manhiça and Maputo. It did not take long for the road to become too perilous, so she and her husband, Carlos, agreed that the children should live full-time in Maputo and go to school there. Lina herself kept driving the highway, back and forth, refusing to join a convoy. Instead she drove seriously fast, she assured me. Alone? I asked her. She laughed: "No, not alone. I have my bottle of whiskey and always an automatic pistol."

But she did have second thoughts. Was she doing the right thing? Was she, as gossipers would have it, neglecting her children? She had left her first son for the struggle, and she had lost him. Worried that she was making them pay for a decision that was not theirs, she consulted her father. "Lina," he told her, "you have to stay in Manhiça. What you're doing there is good for the people, good for Mozambique.

Don't come back before your work is completed just because you are being pressured. Think about the people."

"I am lucky because I have another place to live," she told me when she related the story. "Where can the people from Manhiça go? I was given the unique opportunity to get an education. I must use it. And always, always, I ask myself: What about the people?"

Thrown together as we had been, our friendship had grown with long drives over bumpy roads when it was still safe to travel far and long into-the-night conversations in the variety of places we could find a bed. I can still hear Lina's voice as she called me "Stefan," a husky, gravelly voice, full of satisfying and infectious laughter or vociferous outrage or sheer enjoyment. "Stefan, let me tell you about . . . " and she would launch into another story. She took on the role of a fellow journalist, a partner—a comrade. At the same time she could judge me. She reproached me with full-throated irritation when I mentioned that I and my *cooperante* friends did not like to shop at Loja Franca, the foreign exchange store, because it catered only to those privileged enough to have foreign exchange—U.S. dollars, British pounds, South African rands. "Don't be *ridiculous*," she said to me and by extension all the idealistic *cooperantes*. "We need the foreign exchange. We *rely* on you to shop at the store!"

Manhiça was her family's home—a prominent southern Mozambique family—where she had spent much of her time as a child and teenager. In the early post-independence days it had been relatively prosperous. Peasants cultivated enough food for their families; they had oxen and ploughs and could sell their surplus; they could purchase consumer goods—clothes, shoes, radios, bicycles. That was then. Now no more. She listened as villagers told her about merciless killing sprees, boys kidnapped and forced into the army and never seen again, women and girls raped. There was a local saying, *dumba nengue,* which translated as "trust your feet." Those who trusted their feet were the ones who fled, abandoning their homes in order to survive.

As a journalist, she wanted to tell the world so that the terror would stop. Within a year of my visit she published a book, *Dumba Nengue, Run for Your Life: Peasant Tales of Tragedy in Mozambique.* Among the many horrors it related was one I found especially shattering: A group of women and young children had been forced to march a very long distance. At the end of the journey the "bandits," as Renamo soldiers were often called, pointed to those who could return home and those who had to stay. The latter were mostly boys between ten and fourteen who would be forced to become soldiers themselves. Some very young girls were also kept to become sex slaves. As Lina wrote in *Dumba Nengue*, "To demonstrate the fate of the girls to those who were going back, the chief of the group picked one, a small girl who was less than eight. In front of everyone, he tried to rape her. The child's vagina was small and he could not penetrate. On a whim, he took a whetted pocketknife and opened her with a violent stroke. Then he took her in blood. The child died."

My research and interviews began shifting, almost imperceptibly at first, from women's role after independence to the impact of the South African government's role in destroying efforts at national reconstruction. Every story I heard, every village and town I saw, every report I read, was tainted by the dense ominous shadow cast by Mozambique's neighbor to its south and west.

33 — "Night Is Turning into Day"

I sit in the passenger seat as Becky maneuvers her blue Land Rover through the hectic drive-where-you-can early-morning Maputo traffic. I turn back to look at the city. The buildings, tall and white, beam in the morning sun like corroded obelisks rising off the banks of the Maputo River and the protective curve of the bay. Our destination is the Eduardo Mondlane communal village in the district of Boane, near the Swaziland border, about twenty miles away, an area that has been under attack. I am struck by a certain irony. On previous visits the most challenging part of setting up my program was sorting out transport. This time transport is not an issue. I can use Becky's Land Rover any time; it's old but not as old as the OMM one that has since been scrapped. Except now it is unsafe to drive more than twenty miles out of Maputo before entering active zones of conflict.

I asked to visit a village that has been subjected to raids to interview women there. Eduardo Mondlane is under siege, I was told, but only at night. It is safe during the day. Safe enough for Becky and me to visit. On our way, we pass by a town to pick up the district secretary of defense, elegant in his new, freshly ironed pants with brown and green camouflage splotches, topped by a jacket of uneven green and brown stripes. The revolver in a leather holster strapped to his belt looks, to my admittedly inexperienced eye, new and unfired. Small comfort if we are to encounter rebels. He looks to be in his early twenties, a child when Mozambique won its independence. I feel an immediate empathy for his many responsibilities. His district, not far from the South African border, is under constant attack and I can only imagine he has many a sleepless night.

When we reach the village, someone is sent to find the secretary general of the village branch of OMM. He returns accompanied by a slight, older woman, adjusting her *capulana* around her thin waist as she approaches. It is new and I suspect she keeps it for special occasions, such as when unexpected visitors arrive. Her cream sweater covers a blouse frayed around the edges; she has on one blue cotton terrycloth sock and one black nylon sock, slipped into canvas shoes with the backs folded under because they're not her size. She introduces herself as Mavis Gideon. I comment on her English, not expecting anyone in the village to speak it. She replies, haltingly, that she is from South Africa. She married a Mozambican miner, but that was many years ago and now her English is poor. We set off with her for a tour of her village. We walk along a sandy and stony thoroughfare that separates rows of small houses and the small plots that surround each one. Washing is stretched across lines alongside mud-and-reed houses that are well-kept but in need of repair. Unlike Três de Fevereiro I see no sign of remittances from men working in the South African mines. The countryside is brown as far as the eye can see, stretching across open, never-ending veld. It is not the brown of rich earth or of the dry season when you know the rains will come again. It is more the absence of color, every last trace of moisture extracted, sucked into the hot air, never to be replaced. Skinny children who come to stare show the signs of severe poverty. Their clothes are ragged. Some have large *kwashiorkor* bellies, the telltale mark of malnutrition. Mavis points out the remains of houses that were recently attacked, some burnt to the ground. Others look as if they need rethatching. I ask whether they too have been attacked. "No," she explains, "the river has run out of reeds." I assume it is because of the drought.

"How can a river run out of reeds?" asks the more knowledgeable Becky. Despite the drought, the Umbeluzi is still flowing.

"There's only one place where we can gather reeds and not be attacked," Mavis says, pointing in the direction of the river and shaking her head. So, she says, everyone from the district goes there now. It's stripped bare. Aha, the river *has* run out of reeds.

"Night is turning into day," comments a skeletal elderly peasant whom we pass on our walk. His voice is low and raspy. "What does he mean?" I ask. The bandits used to come only at night, Mavis explains. Over time, sixteen villagers have been killed, mostly militia members. At least three rebels were killed. So for months most of the residents have slept away from the village, wherever they can find some secure place; with relatives in nearby villages, on the verandas of buildings in the town, hidden in the bush. They return in the morning to cultivate their crops and continue their lives. But now the bandits have started to raid in daylight. So much for this village being safe during the day, I think.

As we continue I ponder how women's work and responsibilities are entangled with the war, undermining to toxic effect any gains they might have made since independence: The danger of collecting firewood. The worry about their children's health and safety. The months without ready access to water. The depletion of stores from previous harvests. The inability to cultivate food for their families because the rains have not come and the normally twice-yearly harvests have failed. The inability to forage for food. Some food supplies come from the state, some from the district, but it isn't enough, Mavis explains. Widows and women without husbands to help them have nothing. The neighbors have no surplus but try to share. They are trying to hold onto their seeds until the rains finally come. Meanwhile when their children are hungry, what can they do? Some families have no choice but to eat their seeds.

"When was the last attack?" I ask.

"A few days ago," Mavis answers with no change of expression. She tells me that a number of boys were abducted when bringing their cattle back to the village. They were ten years old. We stop to talk to the grandfather of one of the abducted boys. Just then we hear a commotion down the road. People come running into the village, shouting, gesticulating, Mavis's son-in-law among them. Catching his breath, he explains that he had gone to chop wood about a kilometer outside of the village. Some bandits shot at him. He fled, calling to others as he ran back to the village. More come running into the village. The villagers gather, their faces creased with anxiety. Becky and I exchange apprehensive looks. I think of the long unprotected road we must travel back to the town and the one solitary control post manned by a few soldiers. Becky has another concern: once before she had been asked to leave an area because her Land Rover's presence could act as a beacon, singling out the village as special, jeopardizing not only her own safety but that of the villagers. The secretary of defense is unconcerned. *"Não problema,"* he says. We will be returning to the town in the opposite direction of the bandits. We are polite women. And trusting. We continue our visit. We comment on the well-stocked clinic and talk to the health worker who grew up in the village. He no longer sleeps there. His work puts him in danger.

I become aware of Mavis's increasing uneasiness and am less able to ignore my own. As long as we are there, we are keeping her from her family and any arrangements she might want to make. "Let's go," I say firmly. No more *não problema's* can shift my resolve. Becky agrees. We head for the car, followed by a group of villagers, and say our good-byes. As Becky revs the engine I comment: "Sure glad that we have four-wheel drive." I am thinking that we might need to take a shortcut across the veld. "Oh, *that!*" she says unperturbed. "Hasn't worked since before I got this car."

Becky drives fast. I look toward the distant hills and wonder which bush, which tree, which hill provides cover to the Renamo rebels. I am all too aware that we can simply drive away, heading for Maputo and the safety it provides, leaving behind a village full of vulnerable people. As we slow down at the control post, the defense secretary merely nods to the guards, says nothing about the bandits, and we are waved on. Perhaps I had been worrying unduly. Wimp, I think as we soon enter the hubbub and safety of Maputo. The next day I learn from a Canadian water engineer who had arrived in the village soon after we left that his NGO has instructed him not to visit the village again. Okay, not a wimp. I also learn that the soldiers at the control post were alerted by men from the village. They went as fast as they could but were too late. I am puzzled by the behavior of the local secretary of defense. Was he playing down the danger because we were there? If so, he could have jeopardized the lives of the villagers, who are now even more isolated.

How often had I heard the words *não problema*? No problem—even when there clearly was. Of course, people have to go on living each day. The line between what is accepted as normal and what is considered dangerous shifts as the war escalates. It is only a problem when you are actually caught in an ambush, actually attacked, actually kidnapped. Julie told me she had been at a medical conference in Maputo where many health workers had risked travel by road to get there. "Weren't you worried?" she asked one. "No, there was no problem," he assured her. Then he added, as if an afterthought, "The car behind me was attacked. But I had no problem."

But there *is* a problem. A huge, ominous, horrible problem. South Africa is just across the border. Home-home is just across the border. Although the border with Mozambique is a relatively short one, South Africa casts a dark dominating shadow all the way to Mozambique's northern border, crushing everything in its wake by means of Renamo, by means of its incursions across the border, its assassinations of exiled citizens, all in the name of anticommunism, antiterrorism. All in the name of preserving apartheid.

My anger rips me apart and I feel impotent. I will document, document, document. That is all I can do. The pen is mightier than the sword. Really? Indeed, the sword won out against colonialism. Now the sword is trying to smite a fragile country and its people.

BUT THERE WERE OTHER MOMENTS when Kendra is at the center of my thoughts. I took myself on long walks around the city, one of my favorite pastimes. I stared, probably rudely, at a young woman and her baby who walked past. She was holding her baby, perhaps six months, by the waist, arms straight out in front of her, their faces at the same level. She talked to the baby animatedly, nodding her head, smiling a loving mother-smile while the baby laughed back. The sharp dart of missing was so strong I had to take deep breaths to recover. Another time, I watched a young man carefully balancing his baby on his back, holding it with one arm stretched behind him as he bent forward and with a practiced hand pulled a *capulana* around the child and then tied the ends of the cloth against his chest. It was a maneuver I had seen often—but never by men. An image of John carrying Kendra in a snuggly on his chest is clear in my mind's eye, a scene no longer unusual in the United States. I curse myself for not having a camera as I both smile and get teary.

What were John and Kendra doing now? Afternoon here is early morning in New York. Was he getting her ready for school, chatting and laughing with her as he often did? Or was he groggy from too little sleep, too much child care, and just going through the motions? Whatever the case, they were at home together in our apartment, in New York. The emotion I felt about leaving Kendra behind had a voice of its own. I have actively resisted calling New York home. I have placed a shield between me and the country I emigrated to twenty years ago. That shield served to protect my emotions, to say, "I am different. You see, this is really not my home. I still speak with a South African accent. I still cling to words like 'arse,' not 'ass,' 'tom-ah-to,' not 'tomado.'" But, that voice teases: "Ah, but that accent is overlaid by an American one. You have an American child, and you are missing her more than you have ever missed anyone before. Hey, what does this mean?" Who am I missing? Not South Africa. Not so much. I am missing Kendra. I am missing John. I am missing the life I have in New York. Home?

I have visited Mozambique four times now. My Portuguese has remained pathetic, but I slip back in with ease, like donning an old comfortable and comforting coat. Part of this is geography, I know; it is the proximity of South Africa and Cape Town. But geography isn't all. Mozambique itself, with its hope and its horror, has got to me too. The more I visit Mozambique, the more I get to know the country and its troubles, the more attached I have become. I envied people like Julie and Becky who have chosen to live there. Could it possibly be a third home, albeit a transient one, a place I missed when I was not there, a place I wrote about day in and day out as I worked on my book? By writing about this country, about its women, about the conflict, I was constantly close to it even when I was not physically in it. It was a presence in my mind all day. I dreamed about it during the night. And unlike South Africa, when I found the longing too intense, I could plan another trip back. At the same time it was in New York, in the United States that I was writing, living with John, getting pregnant, having a child. These were anchors more solid than Mozambique. I could temporarily pull up anchor and head back. If so, could New York still be only second place to South Africa now that I had a family there? In the last days of my visit, I toggled back and forth with these thoughts. It all felt muddled and unresolved. Home versus home-home. New York versus Mozambique versus South Africa. What I did know was that South Africa had not lost its sway; deep inside I continued to feel a powerful allegiance to it as a country. At the same time, I was aware that I had to be cautious about the nostalgia and yearning I was wrestling with. Nostalgia, by definition, is for things past. My South African past is filled with anger at the conditions under which the majority of South Africans live. Yearning though is for a future, a yearning for freedom that is yet to come.

With these thoughts I returned to New York.

I had been forewarned, and I steeled myself for it: Kendra would be angry with me when she saw me again. Expect to be ignored, I was told, punished for deserting her. I would need to woo her back. I mentally prepared to do so. Tired from the long flight, I opened the front door of our apartment. Kendra was standing at the end of the passage that led to the living room. She looked up and saw me. "Mummy!" she screeched and ran as fast as her little legs would carry her, throwing her arms around my knees and hanging on for dear life. A wide grin lit up her face, as it did mine. I picked her up and hugged her and danced around the living room, utter bliss flowing over me from the warmth of my child. Tears flowed simply out of the pure and complete love I felt for her. For the next week Kendra made sure not to let me out of her sight. Like a puppy, she followed me into the kitchen, into the bedroom, into the bathroom. She wasn't taking any chances. Last time I had gone out the door I had not come back for a long time. But other than that, she showed no lasting signs of being abandoned. And I quickly resettled back into my writing routine.

I WAS BACK IN NEW YORK two weeks when Becky called me from Maputo to tell me that she was coming to New York unexpectedly and

asked whether she could stay with us. Of course, I said, delighted that
I would see her again so soon. Within a few days she was sitting on
our couch, John and I in chairs opposite. My delight turned to dismay
when she explained the reason for her return: she had been diagnosed
as HIV-positive. At first we were rooted to our seats in shock, then we
both jumped up, pulled her up, and hugged her. We all knew it was
a death sentence. There was no treatment. How long, was the question. One year? Five? She told us that she had been concerned by how
tired she had been feeling lately. I had certainly noticed, but I put it
down to hard work and insufficient sleep. "Just go to Zimbabwe and
get tested," Julie, the doctor who had urged me to get a biopsy, had
advised. "This is something that we medical practitioners all worry
about. It's likely to be negative." The absence of testing facilities in
Mozambique meant that Zimbabwe was the closest option. As part
of her job on a research project on sexually transmitted disease for
New York City in 1982, she took blood samples from sex workers. She
remembered many needle sticks, blood splattering when one jerked
her arm. Transmission through body fluids was still to be discovered.
Nobody used gloves then. Ironically, Becky ran an AIDS hotline for
the city when she herself was harboring the virus and when HIV was
still labeled a gay man's disease. She had little patience with ignorance
born out of prejudice. When a panicked policeman called to say he
had just arrested a gay man and wanted to know whether he was at
risk for AIDS, she responded: "Did you fuck'm? If you didn't fuck'm,
you're fine." A man who panicked when he used a public telephone
booth after a gay man got the same response.

After a few weeks, she decided to return to Mozambique. "As long
as I am healthy enough, I am going to continue to work there." She
was not going to sit around and wait for death, she said.

Becky continued to work in Maputo for two years until she was too
ill to continue. She then returned to live with her mother and sisters
in California. She died two days short of her thirty-fourth birthday,
on March 9, 1991.

MY BOOK *AND STILL THEY DANCE: Women, War and the
Struggle for Change in Mozambique* was published in early 1989. At

the book launch at Hunter College, Albie Sachs was there to introduce it. It almost felt like a miracle that he was. I knew Albie from my Defence and Aid days in Cape Town. He was a lawyer who had been banned and served time in ninety-day detention; later he had gone into exile in London, and then Mozambique. A legal adviser for the ANC, he was also a professor in the law department at Eduardo Mondlane University. He took an interest in my work and organized my visits to local justice tribunals, one of the Frelimo initiatives he extolled. On National Women's Day in Mozambique, April 7, 1988, a public holiday, Albie was looking forward to a run on the beach and then a swim. He put the key in the door of his car, which was parked on a wide boulevard outside of his apartment building, and began to turn it. Our friend Sam Barnes drove by on the other side of the road, her three-year-old daughter, Maya, in the backseat of her car. He turned away from the door to wave to her. The car exploded. Sam's wave probably saved his life. Albie lost his left arm and his left eye. Like the bomb that killed Ruth First, there was no doubt about where it came from. In the year since the attack, Albie had fought his way back to health and was now spending a few months in New York. Before he introduced the book, I introduced him. I remember the day very clearly, I said, when someone called me to say that Albie had been assassinated. I called John at work, crying so hard he couldn't understand who I was talking about, and in his own fear he thought something had happened to Kendra. A few hours later the news was revised. "Albie was like Lazarus and rose from the dead," I said.

Part Five

34 — "Are You Planning to Return?"

Make South African ungovernable!" This call by the ANC in April 1985 had been picked up with fervor by the United Democratic Front, the trade unions, and community activists. They forced apartheid's local and township authorities out of one community after another and replaced them with their own structures and committees, so by the end of the 1980s, these communities had effectively become quasi-liberated zones. By 1989 the resistance in South Africa had reached fever pitch.

Demonstrations and protests were part of the fabric of the country in revolt, as well as action by Umkhonto we Sizwe, MK, the military wing of the ANC. But so was the refusal of the apartheid government to let up. Even though we knew that the behemoth was standing on ever more shaky ground, the sheer force it leveled against the people of South Africa still seemed impossible to shake. The deaths and arrests continued. Repression heightened. Viewed from the distance of New York, apartheid appeared to remain rock solid despite its distinct fissures. Behind the scenes, we would later learn, negotiations had been going on between Nelson Mandela and the government, which believed that it could tame Mandela, get him to renounce violence, and turn him away from the ANC. Perhaps they thought that twenty-seven years in prison had weakened this man. The change of government from totally intransigent (P. W. Botha) to somewhat less intransigent (F. W. de Klerk) provided a wedge to pry apartheid open. When de Klerk came to power in August 1989 he could see the writing on the wall, a script that was drawn from revolution within its borders and ANC/MK military incursions from without; from international economic isolation of which the U.S. divestment campaign was a major force; from a South African economy that was breaking apart at the seams; from the corporate class, including the Afrikaner business community, which had been happy to reap the benefits of cheap labor but were now not so sure that apartheid was working in its favor.

De Klerk was not blind. An unknown quantity when he took office, he stunned the world on February 2, 1990, by announcing he would release Nelson Mandela, terrorist and number-one enemy of the state, and unban the ANC and other political parties. Still, it would take three more years of negotiations in which Mandela and his fellow ANC leaders stood fast, for de Klerk to come to terms with the fact that majority rule was the only solution.

And so, there I was, on February 11, 1990, in my mother's small London house, watching one of the most momentous events of the twentieth century: Nelson Mandela's walk to freedom. And just over a year later, I once again stepped onto South African soil. Soil that was finally free. Soil that felt firm under my feet. There I was met by a beaming Pippa at the Cape Town airport, in the city of my birth.

MY VISIT CAME AS A NEW ERA was unfolding and my senses were constantly ignited by images new and old. A new South Africa was just around the corner but the old South Africa of white privilege would not go lightly away. I tried to focus on the high points. We joined hundreds of others at the Cape Town harbor to greet the last of the political prisoners leaving Robben Island. These were members of MK who were against negotiations and initially refused to leave the prison until victory on the battlefield was assured. Only after Mandela went to the island to persuade them that the negotiations were necessary did they agree to accept the government's offer of amnesty. As I write this, I look at a photo on my desk that brings back that moment: John standing, looking toward the sea, Kendra on his shoulders, a backdrop of fists raised high in the air. When I look at it I can hear the strong shouts of *Amandla!* Power! Yes, we believed, real freedom was coming.

There were times during that trip when I became impatient with John. I wanted to reencounter Cape Town, to reconnect with the source of my years of nostalgia to absorb the South Africa and the Cape Town I knew and the one I didn't know that was unfolding before me. To do this, I needed to create a buffer of solitude around me. But John needed explanations, contexts, history. This was his first visit to Africa, and he was becoming attached to my first home. His manner drew people to him and I found myself benefiting from his insights.

As planned, we visited Durban, the capital of KwaZulu-Natal, up the east coast, where we stayed with our friend Pat, whose brother, Michael, had been killed in a carjacking. I remembered my visits to this city in my childhood; closer to the equator, it was a winter resort for Capetonians who wanted a release from the damp cold. Durban's end-of-summer humidity reminded me of Maputo, not that far north. Like many cities in East Africa it had a large Indian population. Indians were first brought to South Africa in 1684 as slaves. In the second half of the nineteenth century they were brought as indentured workers for the sugar plantations in Natal Province, and shortly after they came independently as traders. It was where Mahatma Gandhi began his political career after arriving in 1893 as a lawyer, staying on to lead the movement for Indian rights until 1915, when he returned to India to push for independence from Britain, and win.

As we walked through the central market one afternoon we were accosted by the pungent aromas that infused the air. We passed high pyramid-shaped piles of curry powders in all hues from red to orange to yellow, contrasting with the browns and blacks of cumin, cloves, coriander, and other spices, each with a tag indicating its type. One caught John's eye, his guffaws drawing me toward the object of his laughter: mother-in-law exterminator. I began to lag behind him, holding Kendra's hand as she slowed to examine this or that. I came up to him in conversation with an Indian merchant who was trying to persuade him to buy a carved African ceremonial chair. John, a polite Canadian, was explaining that it was too big and too heavy to take with us, even though it was very attractive. I had once carried a similar one back to New York in my luggage after a UN trip to West Africa: it failed to survive the trip, splitting down the middle. I stood for a moment wondering whether we could take this one in our luggage until common sense won its place. Meanwhile John and the merchant had moved on in their conversation. When he discovered that John was from Canada, he veered from trying to sell John some of his goods to asking his opinion about the future for South Africa. I sensed he was hoping for the unfreighted opinion of an outsider, someone with a broader perspective than he himself felt able to latch on to.

"What do you think will happen if the ANC takes political power," he asked. "We just don't know what they will do economically."

John thought for a moment in his measured way. "I think that the ANC is very principled and they are unlikely to oppress others because their own oppression is too fresh in their minds."

The merchant looked at him skeptically, slowly shaking his head, not so much in disagreement as in thought. "Yes, well, although we were also classified as nonwhite and had limits, we were able to do better than the Africans. We—and the coloureds, for that matter— were granted privileges within the system that gave us advantages economically. So we have something to lose." There was apprehension in his voice.

"I can't really talk for South Africa, but I would think that small businesses are less likely to be affected in the national economy," John responded.

"But we are worried that the climate for business, even small businesses, would be ruined by an ANC government. That is our fear. We don't know what their economic policy will be."

As I listened in on the conversation, I wondered if the merchant was thinking of what had happened in Uganda in the 1970s, when Idi Amin drove out the Asians from his country, regarding them as leeches on the economy, not sufficiently "Ugandan." Again John thought a moment before answering, drawing on his own analysis of economics. "I should think they will be constrained by the wants of international capital, and they will have to take this into account. No new government can risk a rapid flight of capital."

The merchant stood mulling over John's response. "I hope you are right," he said.

I TOOK KENDRA TO MY CHILDHOOD haunts: the expansive saltwater swimming pool on the edge of the ocean in Sea Point and Kirstenbosch Botanical Garden, with its rolling lawns and fabulous flora, the mountain towering above us. We walked up Government Avenue past the Parliament building, the destination of the thirty thousand marchers back in 1960, to have tea at The Company's Garden open-air café, now serving both blacks and whites, and feed the demanding squirrels and doves. We went to Muizenberg Beach at low tide to skip and hop in the waves that rippled out far from the beach in shallow rows. There were some dramatic changes since my childhood: Black children now frolicked on the sand. Black children Kendra's age played on the swings and slides. Black mothers were there in bathing suits with their own children and in their uniforms as nannies for white children. The South Africa Kendra was seeing was not mine. Watching her, I found myself surreptitiously wiping away tears of relief. Finally, *finally*.

While we were in South Africa informal negotiations between the ANC and the National Party were underway. What kind of South Africa would emerge? It was not yet clear. Negotiations had been continuing from time to time for the previous nine months. I heard the issue debated from one friend to another, from Cape Town to Durban to Johannesburg. What troubled everyone was the level of violence— violence encouraged by the government, which was in no hurry to begin the negotiations or allow them to succeed on ANC terms. The rulers hoped that the elation at Mandela's release would die down and Mandela could then be relegated to a washed-out old man who had emerged from prison after twenty-seven years, out of touch with the situation on the ground. They were wonderfully wrong.

What was more sinister, though, was the support that de Klerk and his police were giving to those who were fearful of losing their own power once the ANC came to power. The most egregious was Gatsha Buthelezi, chief of the Zulu people and head of the Inkatha Freedom Party, one of apartheid's most prominent collaborators. He had benefited both politically and financially. The South African government stood aside while Inkatha staged massacres of ANC supporters. It was known that the government was attempting to launch a third force, and Buthelezi suited their needs. Although this did not deter the ANC and its followers, it did mean that by the time of elections in April 1994 many thousands of people had been killed: ANC members and supporters; Inkatha members and supporters; others caught up in the attacks. All this fueled more tensions in the townships, where explosions of anger were directed against those suspected of collaborating with apartheid.

OUR VISIT WAS NEARLY OVER. We were in a taxi driving to Helen Joseph's modest house in the Johannesburg suburb of Norwood. Since I first met her in 1984 we had corresponded occasionally, and when I called to let her know we were in South Africa, she invited us for tea. As the taxi neared her house, I explained to Kendra that Helen was a brave woman who fought for a better life for those who have suffered from poverty, and had been treated badly by the old government simply because they were black. "Just like Martin Luther King!" she piped up in her high voice. Before leaving for South Africa she had learned about the civil rights leader as part of Black History Month in school. "Yes, very similar to him," I replied. I looked up and caught the African taxi driver's eyes twinkling back at mine through the rear-view mirror. Had she been a South African child she might have responded, "Just like Nelson Mandela." Well, as a white child, perhaps not quite yet.

Helen greeted us warmly and ushered us into her cozy living room where tea was waiting for us. She was as self-effacing and gracious as I remembered her. She showed us an album with photos from her eighty-fifth birthday party, which she had celebrated a year earlier, just two months after Mandela's release—photos of ANC leaders and other prominent friends who had been kept from her for decades due to bannings, house arrest, prison, or exile. "I never thought I'd live to see them again," she said. She put the album aside to pour out the tea and hand around the biscuits.

As she held her tea cup and saucer in her hands ready to take the first sip, she leaned toward me and asked, "Tell me, Stephanie, why did you leave South Africa?"

I was stymied. Helen, as a British citizen, could have left South Africa any day of the week. In her second memoir she wrote that she was often asked why she didn't leave South Africa:

> Part of the answer lies in my utter hatred of the security and apartheid laws and practices of South Africa. It is my belief that by staying in South Africa, having suffered some of the persecution inflicted by the government, by being prepared to accept whatever lies in the future, I can make my stand clear.

What answer could I possibly offer? I had no story of flight into exile, no story of jail or threatened jail, of banning or personal harassment. I had left because of my hatred of apartheid, not because it hounded me. I did not have her courage. I decided to be straightforward. To be chronological.

"I left in 1967," I began.

"Oh," she intercepted, her voice conveying complete understanding, "That makes sense." She knew well the political hiatus after Sharpeville and the crushing of resistance in the period when Eric and I made our decision to leave.

"And now?" she asked. "Are you planning to return?"

I couldn't answer. Not yet. Helen's question unsettled me. My ambivalence about home had returned in full bloom. Could I call a place home when I was not living there, had no intention of living there? Yet the moment I returned to South Africa, the moment I stepped off the plane in Cape Town, I felt disoriented. Helen's simple question made me feel unmoored. Where did I actually fit in this world?

35 — No Longer the "Skunk of the World"

J ennifer and Gail went to South Africa as part of the international monitoring team for the first democratic elections on April 27, 1994. Jen stayed on to represent ACOA at the inauguration on May 11. I decided to stay in New York, fearing that I might lose my job at the UN if I took time off—a decision that I have never ceased to regret. Instead I watched on television: aerial views of lines snaking across the South African veld, of people waiting patiently for hours to cast their first liberating vote. I read what those voting for the first time were saying: "Now I can die with happiness in my heart," one eighty-year-old man said, "Now I can walk like a real man." Another said, "Thank God that before I died I tasted voting."

From Jen and Gail I could catch that there was talk of violence in KwaZulu, where Jen and Gail were to be observers. Some of the monitors in their group were nervous and relieved when they were given bulletproof vests. Jen tried hers on and it went down to her knees, impossibly heavy. She refused to wear it. "If the voters have the courage to vote," she insisted, "they deserve to have observers." No one had the gumption to express hesitancy again. The ANC won by a landslide. In the crowded stadium where Nelson Mandela was inaugurated as the first black president of South Africa, the atmosphere was electric. Jen listened as he spoke:

> We have triumphed in the effort to implant hope in the breasts of the millions of our people. We enter into a covenant that we shall build the society in which all South Africans, both black and white, will be able to walk tall without any fear in their hearts, assured of

their inalienable right to human dignity—a rainbow nation at peace with itself and the world. . . .

Never, never and never again shall it be that this beautiful land will again experience the oppression of one by another and suffer the indignity of being the skunk of the world.

Let freedom reign.

The sun shall never set on so glorious a human achievement.

The next day, Jen wrote to the women's group about Mandela's acceptance speech party:

I have been at my first ever Presidential acceptance speech party— and what a party! As we waited the mood was wonderful—lots of our old friends—who hugged and kissed me and kept saying over and over: "Thank you" [and] "We couldn't have done it without you." [I was] introduced [by one] as the pillar of the U.S. anti-apartheid movement. The mood kept building and the room filling.

When Mandela spoke, he was strong-voiced but very unstrident. He reached out to everybody. Started, in his charming way, by apologizing for his voice. He had a bad cold: "When I saw my doctor early this morning he told me not to use my voice for today and tomorrow and so in two days my cold will be better! So I ask you please don't disclose to my doctor that I am talking to you here."

He said he received calls from many leaders in the last few hours [including] de Klerk. "In former days we often quarreled, had heated exchanges, but at the end we were able to shake hands and drink coffee." To the people of the world he said: "This is a joyous night for the human spirit—for you too." He talked about the courage of the people. "South Africa's heroes are legendary across the generations: but it is you the people who have won this victory." [He] called on all South Africans to celebrate the birth of a new nation—but celebrating must be peaceful, respectful and disciplined. That is democracy. Time to heal.

Then it was party time. "We did it! We did it!" Hundreds of people hugging, kissing, waving little SA flags, dancing. It was beautiful.

MY MOTHER LIVED TO ENJOY this moment. We spoke regularly over the phone and shared our joy at the election. Then nine months later, in early 1995, Leonie called from London. I knew from her taut voice that the news was bad. Rose had suffered a burst of mini-strokes, she informed me, and was in hospital.

Just a few days earlier she had been cheerfully telling me how much she was enjoying her new flat in the small senior citizens complex that she had recently moved into; how she had won hands down at Scrabble when playing in the communal room with her new friends; how relieved she was to no longer climb the stairs in her house. Would this be our last coherent conversation?

I left immediately for London. For four days I remained at her side, and then too soon I had to leave. Back in New York I began to mourn my loss. For years we had spoken regularly on the phone and exchanged letters. I had kept her up to date on the doings of Kendra, whom she adored. After her strokes we still spoke over the phone, when her caregiver dialed my number or I initiated the call, but they were words, not conversations. Her essence had gone, but every now and then the old Rose came through like a brief lightning flash. On what turned out to be my last visit, she sat beside me on the couch. Her back had acquired a prominent curve; her head was permanently down so that her view of the world was her lap. The BBC nightly news was covering a labor action, the newscaster having to shout against the background of chanting strikers who held their placards high. Up jerked Rose's head in one sudden move as she focused momentarily on the scene. "Give all the money to the workers!" she shouted at the TV, finding fleeting strength in her voice. Then her head flopped back to her chest and she resumed her vacant pose. I left the next day. A few days later, on September 19, 1995, she died in her sleep.

Leonie outlived Rose by five and a half years. She died of a massive stroke the day after her sixty-second birthday, on March 21, 2001. I read the obituaries that extolled her achievements. Only then did I realize the strong influence she had made on ballet and modern dance in London, how highly regarded she was.

36 — "Apartheid Is Over but the Struggle Is Not"

I am back in South Africa, this time for three months, this time alone. It is a dream come true. I have visited regularly during the twenty years of majority rule, mostly for a maximum of two weeks at a time, often less, for UN work or on holiday with John and sometimes Kendra. This time, from March 2011, I have another grant from the Ford Foundation, with no specific agenda than to absorb post-apartheid Cape Town, follow whatever each day brings, and work on my book. My first stop is Pretoria, to spend a few days with Pippa.

I am still reacclimatizing myself to driving on the left side of the road when I stop to fill Pippa's Ford Focus at a gas station just around the corner from her house. I look under the dashboard for the lever to pop open the gas cap. I can't find it. I must look pretty desperate to the attendant, who is standing next to the car door patiently holding his hand out for the key. Oh yes, South Africa, gas caps are locked with keys. "Oh, I'm so sorry. I'm not used to this car," I say as I roll down the window and pass him the key.

"Are you Australian?" he asks. "No, I was born here." I thicken my South African accent, which sounds fake because I cannot remember what my South African accent was. He nods and his smile is now brighter. He fills it up, and I am about to drive off when I realize I am still holding the tip in my hand—something else I have to get used to—as he continues to wait, a grin now on his face. God, what a ditz I must seem! As I drive off, I find myself nonsensically pleased that he didn't think I was American. Australia, also an ex-colony, feels culturally closer. I am trying to blend in, but I find it's not possible. I am constantly asked where I was born, and I constantly elicit surprise when I reply, "South Africa."

I enter the Pick n Pay supermarket. I walk through the aisles, the shelves displaying foods from my childhood. I add biltong to my cart. And a package of Provita. And Cape-style multigrain bread. At the checkout, I grab a Lunch Bar as a greedy afterthought. I am barely out of the store before I rip open the plastic package of biltong and savor the sliced, dried game meat. The flavor is warm and fills my mouth. I have to chew hard, but that only increases the flavor. Then I gobble up the Lunch Bar and close my eyes to the mingling of chocolate and nuts and caramel. I sigh. Later that evening I add Rajah Hot Curry Powder to the onions I am sautéing. Whoosh! Its pungent aroma blasts out of the pan and travels deep into my nostrils, startling the memory part of my brain. I breathe it in again and again.

Slowly familiarity seeps in. How wonderful it all is. Until…

I take an evening walk with Pippa and her three dogs, two German shepherds and a golden retriever. We walk down the road, houses with large gardens next to houses with equally large gardens, all surrounded by high fences, walls topped by electrified wire. Signs declare armed response with the security company logo. As we near each house a cacophony of sound erupts, and dogs of all sizes, but mostly large and fierce-looking, rush to the high electronic gate in a whirl of frenzied barking. They continue to bark as we go by, passing us on relay style to the dogs ahead who pick up the action. It is a rolling howling burglar alarm.

A friend complains that she is having trouble sleeping. "Have you tried sleeping pills?" I offer helpfully, thinking I can give her some of the ones I brought to help with jet lag. "No, I can't. I need to be able to wake up alert in the middle of the nights if . . ." She trails off, her sentence incomplete but her meaning clear. Everyone who lives the life of privilege has a story of violence to tell. A friend tied up in a bathroom with her stepson while thieves raid the house; a few months later, the same thieves return, knowing that the goods will have been replaced—and this time the stepson is alone. Sally's friend killed when she returns home to a burglary in process. The father of a friend killed when he is packing up house to move in with his daughter. Some people tell me these stories to show what a terrible violent society South Africa has become; others are fatalistic—we all know that not enough has been done to alleviate poverty in a society where hopes and expectations were once high.

The following week I am in Cape Town. My mountain stretches wide and high above me from the patio of my cousin Gill's house where I am staying. I walk down to the city, along Government Avenue through The Company's Garden, where I had introduced Kendra to the joys of feeding the pigeons and squirrels. My nostrils breathe in the satisfying blend of greenery and flowers on this clear, warm day. At the bottom of the avenue I turn left toward St. George's Cathedral, where Archbishop Tutu still gives an occasional sermon. I walk into the vaulted crypt, now the Crypt Memory and Witness Centre. The current exhibition is "Glimpsing Hope, Marching for Peace." A photo hangs from the ceiling all the way to the floor: a peace march in September 1989 calling for an end to the violence in Cape Town. I read the description: It was sparked by the killing of twenty-three people in Cape Town townships in the aftermath of the tricameral parliamentary elections, a government ruse to claim democracy: three Houses of Parliament, one for whites, one for coloured, one for Indians. None for Africans. Thirty thousand people marched. This number triggers a memory from my past. It is the size of the anti-pass march on Cape Town soon after the Sharpeville massacre in March 1960. The 1989 march is led by Archbishop Tutu in his maroon robes alongside other religious and political leaders: blacks, whites, men, women, young, old, in business suits with ties, in shirt sleeves and T-shirts, serious faces, smiling faces, somber faces, glowing faces. The faces of a people who know they are winning. Five months later almost to the day Nelson Mandela made his walk to freedom.

The 1960 march contributed to my leaving South Africa. This one in 1989 contributed to my ability to return.

A few days later I am driving my rental car to Khayelitsha, a mainly African township, the largest and poorest in Cape Town. Sitting next to me is Kate Ncisana, who was part of a group of fifty-seven women and men, accompanied by fourteen children, who squatted in the cathedral in 1982 for twenty-three days to protest the pass laws, which prevented them from joining their husbands in the city. She has invited me to meet with some of the women. Kate and I chat about our families. I tell her I have one child. She tells me she has two, seventeen years apart. She worked as a live-in domestic for a white family. "I didn't want more than one child when I could not live with them and when I didn't have my own place."

We reach Khayelitsha and drive up to a small community center. Six women join us—Sindiswa, Dorothy, Cynthia, Angelina, Evelyn, Ethel—and two men—Jack and Six. They sit in a semicircle in the small room. I am in familiar territory: the journalist, the conscientious observer, sitting poised with a pen and paper, a white among Africans. But I, like them, am a South African. Who am I really at this moment? A Capetonian wanting a sense of the complexity and diversity of my city? Whose diversity? The recorder of stories that are not mine? That's obviously the point, but I feel somewhat voyeuristic. I am reassured when the women are eager to tell me about their involvement in the anti-pass campaign and about their lives in democratic South Africa. What am I going to do with their stories? But then I think: These may not be my stories. But they are the stories of South Africa. We are all part of the crazy patchwork that makes up the tale of South Africa. As I get into their vivid telling, I feel welcomed, and my discomfort vanishes.

They tell me how they came, with their children, to live illegally in Cape Town in the early 1980s. It was both a form of protest and a quest for survival: they were refusing to be parted from their men any longer, refusing to be subjected to laws that meant they had no means of income in the rural areas of the Transkei and the Ciskei, both Xhosa-speaking "homelands." They lived in the shadows, dodging the police because their passbooks did not have the proper stamps. They went in a large group to the local township administration to demand permits to stay. When the authorities told them to come to a meeting to discuss the situation, they saw it as a victory. Leaving their children behind, they headed in good faith to the meeting place. They were arrested, forced onto buses, and driven back to the Transkei, over seven hundred miles away. For three months they lodged appeals with the local Transkei authorities to allow them to go back and fetch their children. They were provided with twenty buses, but were warned: you only have permission to go to Cape Town and return directly with your children. Sindiswa Nyny laughed; "It was duck and dive, hide and seek!" They once more vanished into the dense morass of plastic sheeting, corrugated iron, and wood-scrap shacks, into the narrow pathways of Nyanga, where thousands of Africans were living both legally and illegally.

In March 1982, fifty-seven women and men, accompanied by fourteen children, donned their Sunday best and headed for the city to attend the service at St. George's Cathedral in the center of Cape Town. When the service was over, they refused to leave. For twenty-three days, with the support of the cathedral, they fasted, not giving up when some had to be taken to hospital and one woman miscarried. When they were assured that they would not be arrested, they left the cathedral. Their actions, covered by the national and international media, gave impetus to the anti-pass campaign. Four years later, in July 1986, the government rescinded the pass laws. Although it made a huge difference to these women, it was a pyrrhic victory for the African population in general. The government continued to draw on its arsenal of laws—the Land Act, the Group Areas Act, the Homelands Act, among others—to prevent Africans from exercising their newly given right.

When President Nelson Mandela was inaugurated, Kate and the Nyanga squatters rejoiced. The streets of Khayelitsha were alive with dancing and partying to herald the dawning of a new South Africa. They could now hope for a better life for their children and grandchildren.

They are still waiting. They wait for basic services. Even though some, like Kate, have moved into the small cement houses that are being built as part of an ambitious government housing program, 70 percent still live in shacks; 77 percent do not have piped water. They wait for job opportunities, particularly for the youth, who face 53 percent unemployment. "The young people are told they have no experience," said one woman. "How can they get experience if they can't get jobs?" They are waiting, too, for education to improve. The statistics are grim: 18 percent of the schools have no access to electricity; 20 percent have no water supply (hence no flush toilets); over 92 percent have no real library. In many places, particularly in rural areas, money budgeted for schools, books, and equipment never gets past the pockets of those in charge.

For three hours the women talk and I listen. At the end, Kate sums up the mood of the group: "Apartheid is over but our struggle is not."

THE NEXT WEEK I ATTEND the annual celebration of Founder's Day at Westerford High School, my alma mater. Sitting in the auditorium with other alumni I scan the nine hundred students aged twelve to seventeen. Like all public schools in South Africa, Westerford has its own uniform, in the familiar maroon, gold, and gray school colors. The students wear them with casualness: shirts half out, maroon blazers worn by some, not others; ties off, ties on, some loose around the neck; the girls wear dresses in the colors I remember, though shorter than we were allowed to. This level of comfort would have been frowned upon in my day, as would the joking around and noisy exuberance as they enter the hall, turning to talk to the girl or boy behind them as they file in. We would have entered in silence, backs straight, blazers and ties neat, or faced detention.

This student body is a microcosm of the new South Africa. The students are not only Christian and Jewish; they are Muslim and Hindu. Under 50 percent are white. The remainder are coloured and Indian; few are African. The catchment area for the school effectively excludes most potential African applicants. The majority continue to live in far-out townships such as Khayelitsha and therefore attend school in their own district. Fees are charged to enable Westerford to keep up its academic standards in a country where the public allocation for education must now be divided among all schools. There are scholarships.

I am sitting next to two classmates, Lois and Stan. Lois turns to me. "Isn't it wonderful how mixed Westerford is now?" she says. I nod in agreement but I feel a heavy mood descending when I think of how much more is needed before equal access will become a reality for all of South Africa's children. Before the ceremony, I took a walk around the grounds, strolling past the vast playing fields, the new sports center, the large swimming pool and then back into the building where art work, some showing serious talent, is pinned to the walls of the airy corridors and science labs and classrooms are bathed in sunlight. A question dogs me: What about the overcrowded Khayelitsha schools—with no water, or electricity, or even books?

As the ceremony draws to a close, the Westerford orchestra strikes up the national anthem. We all rise to our feet. The three-part anthem begins with the rousing, previously banned anthem from the struggle. My voice cracks with emotion as I sing the Xhosa words *Nkosi sikelel' iAfrika* ("God bless Africa"), which segue into *Die Stem* (The Call) and my voice gets louder, the Afrikaans words carved into my being since childhood: *Uit die blou van onse hemel* ("Out of the blue from our heavens"). Then the English, translated from the original Afrikaans anthem:

> Sounds the call to come together,
> And united we shall stand,
> Let us live and strive for freedom
> In South Africa, our land.

The anthem of the new South Africa incorporates the anthem of the old South Africa, symbolizing what we believed would be possible and what we are still striving for, "freedom in South Africa, our land." I try to ignore the tear on my cheek because I don't want to bring attention to my sentimentality. As I sing, the thought occurs to me: I have never felt the tiniest bit emotional over the anthem of the United States. It does not connect me with my adopted country.

37 — "A Deception"

A month later I fly to Maputo for a few days to visit friends, most particularly Lina. I am startled by how dramatically she has aged since I last saw her in 2008, looking much older than her sixty-six years. Her face is flat and grayish. Gone are the wonderful round cheeks and glow. She now limps unevenly, dragging her leg forward. She shows me a dark black mark up the side of her calf and tells me that she has been treated for melanoma. That she has had a stroke. That she has a heart condition. I slow down my pace to match hers as we walk to the edge of the sidewalk to hail the three-wheeled scooter taxi. The price shoots up because of me. Uncharacteristically, she ignores it, having little energy to remonstrate. The driver weaves and swerves between cars and revs his engine to dart ahead. I am relieved when we arrive at the outdoor café on Avenida Frederick Engels. We walk slowly to a table on the patio with a view of the broad river. Music blares from loudspeakers. I have to struggle to hear her speak in a voice so much softer than before.

I ask Lina what she is thinking about her country. "Stefan," she says, shaking her head, not at me but at her inner thoughts, "Mozambique for me is . . . " she pauses, searching for the word she wants in English, "a deception." Her voice is hoarser than ever.

"What do you mean?"

"It is about politics. You know, when I was young, in my thirties, I learned a new Mozambique where there would be equality. I could dream about a very special Mozambique. When I listen now to recordings of Samora Machel speaking, I say to myself: this is not the Mozambique of today. It has changed. How is it possible for some people to become so rich in a country that is so poor? If the Mozambican economy is growing at seven and eight percent per year over recent years, why does that not help the majority?"

She feels personally let down.

"I worked for the good of my country. From 2000, when Ivan died, I felt tired, discouraged." She stops, looking distraught for a moment as she remembers her son Ivan who, in his twenties, committed suicide by hanging himself in their house. "I was empty, yeah, empty. I was nearly like a vegetable." Then her voice picks up and the energy of the Lina I used to know returns for a moment. "Then Saqina had her first baby, Zakane. He helped me to get over my depression. I wanted to make a better future for my grandson."

The next day we continue our conversation in the living room of her house in Bairro Triomfo, which is close to the road that runs along Maputo's long, palm tree–lined beach. The shades keep out the heat of the day.

"One feeling I have at this stage of my life is that I did not achieve the things I believed in. I could not realize my dreams. I wanted to make a good system of education for Mozambican children. I failed. I wanted to make *great* green zones where farming cooperatives could flourish. I failed. I worked internationally, I went to meetings, to conferences, and even there I did not succeed. I ask myself now, did I fail because I dreamed more than was realistic for me to accomplish? Or is there something wrong in my mind so that I wished for impossible things?"

Didn't we all wish for impossible things? Those first, almost magical years of promise after independence made us feel, and particularly the Mozambicans, that the new era that could bring equality and happiness was around the corner. Didn't we all believe in a better life for the future children, whether in Mozambique or Guinea-Bissau or South Africa? But so much is out of our hands, something we can only learn with hindsight. Lina is one of those who tried hardest, whose dreams and visions were among the biggest, so her disappointments are greater. We talk a bit about this, and she nods thoughtfully, trying it on for size. But the size doesn't quite fit.

"My father wanted me to get a doctorate in economics. It was his great dream for me. If he was alive today, what kind of Lina would he have liked to see? What would my mother and my father think of the Lina I now am?"

The force of her emotion fills the space around us. We sit in silence for a while. This does not feel right to me, that Lina should feel so defeated after her immense contribution to her country. There are few people I have met in my life who I respect as much. I am at a loss for words. I try to respond.

"But, Lina, I believe that history overcame us. You sacrificed because you wanted to see an end to Portuguese colonialism. That was the first vision, your first mission. And so you, like many others, sacrificed everything else to make this happen. And you succeeded. It was very, very positive. Without your commitment and your work, who knows what would have happened. You won! You have not let yourself down. Your leaders have let you down."

"But *why*?" The why came out through a sigh expelled with exasperation and disappointment.

"Perhaps it became too easy to find a quick way to make money and corruption set in. It is almost impossible to work against the powerful forces that enable this. How could you have prevented this from happening? I really don't think you can blame yourself. I think you can be very, *very*," I slow down to emphasize each syllable, "proud of what you did, what you achieved and sacrificed to make Mozambique free." My answer sounds trite to me as I make an effort to find the words that would provide some consolation. I am trying to console myself at the same time. "I believe you can look back and say, 'I did what I needed to do then. And the world is a better place because of it.'"

Lina interjects, low-key: "Yeah, yeah." "If you became an economist and you forgot your people," I ask, "what would you feel now?" Lina nods in agreement. "I think your father and your mother would say that you did the right thing at the time. They would be proud of your sacrifices and what you achieved trying to make Mozambique a better place. You could have stayed in Portugal and had an easy life, but you didn't. They would know that ultimately the forces against you were too big."

"Thank you," Lina says, emphasizing each word. Her voice is rough with emotion, is almost inaudible. She looks down, thinking. Then her spirit picks up, and I glimpse the old Lina, pushing through her tired face.

"I will always fight for what I believe in." Her face takes on that determined look I am used to. "My daughter has asked me to write my memoir. She is right. I want to. I said yes to her request. I have much still to do in my life. I can't give up."

She never did write her memoir. On June 27, 2011, two and a half months after this conversation, Judith called me in the United States to tell me that Lina had died of a heart attack. She was given a state funeral and heralded in the press. The honors were appropriate for this woman soldier of the revolution, this Mozambique icon. I felt a deep sadness. I still do.

38 — Finding Home

I am sitting in the backseat of a taxi on the way to Johannesburg's O. R. Tambo Airport. The three months that had stretched ahead so invitingly when I arrived have flown by. I look out the window at the open veld: wavy brown grass, scrubby trees, horizon far in the distance, so familiar to me from my sojourns in southern Africa. Next to me is John, who joined me for the last two weeks of my stay. I find myself edging away, turning my shoulders so that my back is toward him, my green-carded Canadian partner, who represents the future that we are heading toward, one I don't want to face. Not at this moment. I want a last private communion with my country. I gaze and absorb. Words enter my mind, unbidden, pricking like barbs: "I love this country! I *love* this country!"

I have lived in the United States, mostly in and around New York, for almost twice the years I spent growing up in South Africa, and yet I am never moved to say these words about my adopted country. I am not moved by views of the Hudson River, magnificent as it is. I enjoy annual visits to Martha's Vineyard off the coast of Massachusetts and respond with joy and anticipation when I drive to Margie's home down a two-mile dirt road and smell the pure air and the salt of the sea. But I never say, "I love this place." And I could never respond to the taste of a peach the way I did at my cousin Gill's house.

In the two-inch-thick weathered wooden bowl, four peaches rub up against other fruit: bananas, plums, avocadoes, mangoes, pineapples. I casually select a small, perfectly ripe, imperfectly rounded, soft, furry-skinned, bright orange one.

The New Jersey peaches I buy at the farmers' market each summer have a window of a day or two, between underripe and *frot*—before they lose their flavor to their bruises. If you eat them at precisely the right moment, they are pretty delicious. Or so I thought until I bite into my first Cape peach in many years. What I taste is the essence of peach, which enters my mouth, expands there, and flows over my mind, releasing dormant memories.

With this one sensual taste, I am home. I am also reminded of why I had left.

Who picked the peaches of my childhood? Who packed the peaches so that they arrived in stores unbruised? Who could afford to buy them and place them in bowls on tables in scrubbed and shiny kitchens, in such abundance that a child walking by could grab one and eat it as she went about her life of privilege and ease?

It was thoughts such as these that stayed with me throughout my trip, even as Cape Town insinuated itself into me, prodding at buried memories and forgotten senses—smell, taste, sight, sound—that reconnected synapses I had thought were severed forever. There is something about growing up in this tortured, brutal, beautiful country that grabs me and never lets go. I will once more forget the taste of a peach, but I cannot escape the hold.

As I drive to the airport I know that while I don't hanker after the physicality of America, I do hanker after the community I have made there. I have become all too aware that I can no longer claim South Africa as home, even as I continue to grapple, after all this time, with where that home is. And even whether, at this stage of my life, it is necessary to identify it.

It takes the death of Nelson Mandela two years later to fully clinch what home means to me.

THE PHONE IS RINGING AS I walk through the door of our New Jersey home. I rush to pick it up while trying to extricate myself from my long winter coat. It's John.

"Have you been listening to the news?" he asks, the gentleness in his voice setting the tone for bad news. My chest tightens. What now? I immediately conjure up a disaster, natural or manmade, some horrible event flooding the media. Or something terrible and hence newsworthy that has happened to a friend. "Mandela," is all he says. We are both silent for a while. I feel a sharp stab of pain. Finally, the great man is at rest. At rest after a long illness that had already removed him from the world. At rest after a life of punishment and victory. At rest. It is Thursday, December 5, 2013.

I turn on the TV and settle down to watch the nonstop media coverage, switching channels between BBC and CNN and occasionally checking out Al Jazeera and MSNBC. Many networks have suspended all other news for the next twenty-four hours. It is as if the events occupying the rest of the world have simply faded away, overtaken by the death of the first black president of South Africa, an icon to the world. Reporters, newscasters, pundits, obituary writers, photographers provide long and short accounts of his life; the blogosphere and Twitter and Facebook light up; the average man and the average woman find ways to record their respect for Mandela, how he inspired each one of them. I hear references to Madiba, his clan name that suggests endearment and is used interchangeably. I had not expected the extent and the depth of the global response. Is it a cry, in these dark days, for a hero to pay homage to, to remind ourselves that great men can and have existed, that great leaders can make a difference, steer a country and a people this way rather than that, provide hope where hope was dashed?

I can count but a few occasions when, for me personally, time stopped for an instant and history shifted: sitting on the floor in front of Amilcar Cabral and seeing how his face lit up when he spoke about the role of women in the struggle; frozen in place with horror when I heard that he had been assassinated; learning of the coup in Portugal when the news crackled over Teodora's shortwave radio; reading the banner at the Maputo airport welcoming me to the liberated zone of humanity; watching Mandela walk out of prison; watching the footage of the first democratic elections in South Africa. And now, almost twenty years later, moved by how the world mourns Mandela's passing while mourning him myself. I watch the TV coverage into the night, my brain saturated with the remembrances, anecdotes, reflections, accolades, repeated video clips. Trying for original thought, I

find myself repeating the words coming out of the mouths of others—
the clichés as well as the original and poetic. I need a different context.

I get it the following day. By happenstance the quarterly get-togeth-
ers of my women's group had been set for this weekend. Since our first
meeting in 1972 five of us—Gail, Janet, Jennifer, Suzette, myself—
have continued to meet regularly. Now that we no longer live in New
York City, we pick a weekend every two or three months to immerse
ourselves in our friendship. Forty-three years after Suzette and I sat
near Columbia University compiling a list of prospective members,
we continue to meet and have become a unit, a oneness, a holistic
sum of our parts. It is a unique friendship. While one-on-one relationships continue in different configurations, it is as a unit that we
have bonded as we grow older.

Our group provides a microcosm of women in America. We
charted four divorces and four remarriages—one common-law and
one taking place soon after same-sex marriage became legal in New
York State; three cancers, one uterine, two breast—one metastatic,
one bout of radiation, one bout of chemo; two hysterectomies; eight
children, of which six were born after our group started meeting,
including one adoption and my two-pound preemie; nine grandchildren and counting. There are tears behind the last number: one
of Janet's grandchildren died at the age of three months from SIDS.
Besides offspring we celebrated other markers on the trajectory of our
lives: milestone birthdays, from thirtieth to eightieth; book publica-
tions, graduate degrees, and Jen's South African presidential award
recognizing her contribution to ending apartheid.

Jennifer is the one among us who could claim—although she never
would—to have critically shaped the direction of South African history that led to apartheid's collapse through her influence on and
steering of the divestment campaign. She is the only one of us to have
met Madiba. She did so a number of times, both before his life sentence during her own activist years and after his release. With our
collective history of connection to the South African struggle, spending the weekend together was an opportunity to reflect on Mandela's
life, make the space to contemplate, to mourn, to ponder the future.
Our hugs are tight and we take longer than usual to break away. A

sadness hovers over us as we talk about what he meant to us and to South Africa, to the world.

We grimace in unison at the way he is being mythologized in the media. Substantial myths are bound to arise around great leaders. One was that he alone, as the father of the nation, led the South African people's triumph. He himself was always clear: it was a collective leadership, not the achievements of just one man. Once out of prison, in his first address, he reiterated this: "I am a loyal and disciplined member of the African National Congress." He would repeat that the leadership was a collective, that his decisions were made in consultation. Nonetheless many of the myths have merit. He was loved and admired by the vast majority of South Africans, across the many divides that epitomize South Africa—rich and poor, race and ethnicity, the political left, the political right, the various points in between. He stood out, and continues even after his death to stand out, as a leader of virtue, a leader of conscience, a leader who loved and understood his people and made great sacrifices to ensure their freedom.

Mandela was one of the great statesmen of the twentieth century. Like all great leaders, he was human. He brokered an end to apartheid that those with economic interests in this richly resourced nation could accept. It ensured that the rich and white privileged class remained intact, even as it was joined by an ever-expanding black middle and upper class, and in short order the emergence of a controlling and corrupt elite. He was not able to decrease the wide chasm that continues to divide the rich from the abject poor. It is these compromises that South Africa still lives with today. It is his legacy too.

What we want to remember him for this weekend is his role as freedom fighter, his role as revolutionary, one who understood that violence had to be met with violence, something those extolling his virtues were mostly skipping over. The man whom President Reagan labeled a terrorist was given the opportunity, thanks to the resistance of his own people and the support from outside the country, to prove himself to be the leader he was, and emerge as a man of peace. And so, while we mourn his passing, we also mourn the passing of an era when hopes were high, when the election and the inauguration of South Africa's first democratically elected president appeared to herald a promising future; we mourn the demise of our hopes, which turned out to be more ephemeral than we wanted to believe at the time.

THE WEEKEND LEFT ME RELAXED, introspective, and calm over a layer of sadness. After my friends departed, I walked idly around my living room, reliving our time together, picking up papers, dirty coffee cups, and wine glasses, noting the hairbrush forgotten on the mantelpiece. As I headed toward the kitchen a thought tunneled its way into my head, unsettling the calm that resided there: I had no desire to be in South Africa at the moment. Why? Why was I not playing my usual mind games, imagining myself there, in Cape Town or Johannesburg or Pretoria, absorbing the celebrations of his life and the mourning of his death in typical South African style? No, I wanted to be where I was, in the United States. At home. Did Nelson Mandela have to die before I could fully acknowledge this? Or could I simply let go because one of my ties to South Africa was loosened?

This realization stayed with me when, later in the afternoon, I entered the AME Zion Church in Harlem to be with my compatriots at a commemorative service organized by and for South Africans in the New York area. A bustle of South African-ness greeted me as I entered the church. South African music resounded off the stone walls, a little piece of home-home. Outside the church, the temperature was a number of degrees below freezing, the sidewalks dusted with snow. Inside people toyi-toyi-ed and danced in place and belted out freedom songs, countering the lack of heat in the Harlem church. Alongside and in front of me were my compatriots: a rainbow nation—African, coloured, white; men and women. There was a sizable group of born-frees, young South Africans who had known no other South Africa than a democratic one.

In the earlier apartheid days, the church would have been filled with the many familiar faces of exiles and activist South Africans. This time I knew only a few. Exiles had long gone home. The rest of us were no longer exiles. We are immigrants. I am an immigrant, not an emigrant as I once thought, waiting to go back when the time was right. For different reasons, we chose to stay. We were here on a freezing winter day, instead of in hot, sunny South Africa, to mourn and celebrate with our fellow South Africans. Most of us were South African Americans. This is a term I could identify with. "African American" is a label that might be linguistically appropriate, but it is far too charged a term for me to claim: one that does not concede that whites can be African. It is not about where one was born or the continent one identifies with. It is layered with meanings of oppression and power, racism and privilege. By claiming the term in the United States, I would fail to be sensitive to these complexities.

Therefore I am South African American. This blended status is one I can live with here. But in South Africa? Then I am South African, although not always considered that when I meet new acquaintances. "You were born here?" proclaimed one young woman activist I met in 1984. "But you are so American!" Later the same year, when Pippa and Alan arrived in the United States, Alan laughed: "I can't believe you seemed American in South Africa. You are not at all." It's all relative. Here in the church, celebrating and mourning with other South Africans, I was South African. The way the music got to me like no other, the way it resonated with beauty and longing as I listened so that I wanted to get up and dance, made that clear. When I walked out of the church into the cold air, I felt cleansed by an experience of community ritual. A fitting end to the weekend.

Four days later I attended a second memorial, this one at Riverside Church on Manhattan's Upper West Side. Like John and me, hundreds of people had lined up for well over an hour, standing in the wind that blew like icy shards off the Hudson River. A larger-than-life photo of Mandela was propped up at the front of the heavily endowed church, beneath the intricately carved pillars and walls, a cathedral-like ceiling narrowing as it reached high toward the sky. Of the two thousand people who filled the cushioned pews, the majority were American. The speakers were American, black and white, African American interfaith leaders, leaders of New York, many of them well-known. Each spoke about what Nelson Mandela had meant to them as Americans. Feeling part of this spirit, I did not consider myself an outsider.

During one moving eulogy, I reached out to take John's hand. My warm hand fused with his warm hand, energy flowing between us as he squeezed mine and then held the pressure. Suddenly I was on the verge of weeping. This is family, I thought. This is my anchor. It is this person, this memorial in New York, my communities in these United States, that provide me with the ability to walk with positive step, each alternating foot moving forward on steady ground. I belong. It is where I will continue to return, wherever I may yet roam. It is the country that my American daughter calls home as will any future grandchildren. Is this not a place I too can call home?

I begin to play with the idea that my home and my heart do not reside in one geographical space. This feels right. Freeing. It provides a sense of maturity and security. I am no longer seeking something too mercurial to capture. For me, home resides in different places. I feel best where I have a community. And I have several. Some bigger, with deeper roots. Some I visit for briefer moments where I feel "at home" because of the friends that welcome me.

Home is currently Montclair. This is where our house is, where Kendra was raised; it is the United States where I have different configurations of community. Home is South Africa, not just Cape Town, which draws me back by a strong coord and resists letting go when I leave. Home was my parents' semidetached house in London, where they lived for twenty years, a city where my sister had lived from the age of twenty-one. It became less of a home after Joe, then Rose, then Leonie died. I may be an orphan. But I am not a homeless one.

Joseph had asked me: "And now, are you planning to return?" I can finally answer her now.

With Madiba's death, and mourning his passing as a hybrid South African American, I know I have come much closer to resolving the question: For me, home oscillates between two continents. I am at home in both the United States and South Africa. When I am in one, I miss the other. I need both in order to reconcile who I am, to feel comfortable in my skin. At the same time, I cannot pry loose those hooks that were embedded in me the day I was born. Nor do I wish to. Nonetheless, I have lived in the United States since the end of 1967. I have been here far longer than the twenty-three-plus years I lived in South Africa. Hooks have surfaced here too. I have come to love the notion that I have not one home.

In 1981, in northern Mozambique, I walked in the early evening with Anastácia, my interpreter, along a narrow dirt road that led out of the small village we were staying in. The African veld stretched away from us on all sides in the receding light. As we strolled I took in the smell of fires, the sounds of bird calls cutting through the stillness, the voices and activities of homestead life drifting toward us. A young man bicycling along the road dismounted when he reached us and walked alongside for a short time, pushing his bike. He was curious about this white woman in his village, clearly not a common occurrence. Anastácia explained to him in Portuguese who I was. "Aha!" he responded, obviously pleased: *"Uma internationalista!!!"* No, no she insisted, *"Uma jornalista!"* thinking he had misheard. He hadn't.

These many years later, I still like that designation: internationalist. I care about the world—about what happens to the lives of people in this world. The world is my home.

Home. Africa. The World.

And yet, as real as these thoughts and emotions are to me, the words of my father surface out of my childhood: "Never forget how privileged you are." I can deliberate ad infinitum about the complex concept of home, but my land was not stolen from me. I was not subjected to the humiliation of living black under apartheid and the poverty that came with it. I was not deprived of citizenship in the country of my ancestors. I was not forcibly removed from Mogopa, my family home for multiple generations, and then watch as my home, community, my history were literally bulldozed to smithereens. I did not feel the need to ask a visiting young white journalist "When will we go home?" My connections to the place and space I identified for most of my life as home-home come now with a dusting of ash on my tongue. I can only acknowledge that in my quest for home, I have at times failed to heed my father's words.

Outside my Montclair window, as I write these words, it is a bitter cold winter's day. In Cape Town, it is midsummer and hot. I know that Table Mountain glistens in the African light. The sun shines bright in both places. The true richness of my life is that I have many homes.

THE FUTURE FOR SOUTH AFRICA is unknown at this moment, although dark clouds gather. In 1994, with the dawn of the new South Africa, we were carelessly comfortable in predicting the success of our rainbow nation, just as we were confident, twenty years before, that a new society was dawning in Mozambique, one that would forge the way and provide a template for the South African revolution. With Mandela, we felt we could see a path to follow. But imperfections are bound to show up under the light of a halo. In the shadows, apartheid's scaffolding can still be glimpsed. It is not clear when or even if these structures will rust and crumble to dust. What can be commemorated, along with Mandela, is that people were able to confront their oppressors and throw them off. Yet each time victories are charted, a myriad of obstacles surface, and the road ahead may not be any easier. This is what we learned from Mozambique and Guinea-Bissau when they gained independence nineteen years before South Africa.

As I write, I think about what his legacy could mean for the young people all around the world who see him as a model of leadership. And across the years, the words of a speech he gave in Trafalgar Square in 2005 to twenty-two thousand people, return to me:

"Sometimes it falls upon a generation to be great. You can be that great generation," he said. "Let your greatness blossom. Of course, the task will not be easy. But not to do this would be a crime against humanity, against which I ask all humanity now to rise up."

"The Fabric of the Nation Is Splitting at the Seams"

I t is a clear sunny Saturday in Cape Town at the beginning of November 2014. Two days after arriving, I join Gill's walking group on a hike up Silvermine Mountain. I step from protruding rock to protruding rock, up and up. I am breathing out the polluted air of New Jersey and breathing in the sweet, fynbos-scented air of Cape Town mountains. Ahead, Gill is making strides stronger than mine. I am not fit enough to go the distance they will go, but I derive satisfaction from the strenuous hour that I do keep at it. At various points, I pause to take in the view of mountains and sea and sharp cliff faces that stretch around me at 360 degrees. The hikers continue and I walk back down the mountain alone. I am in slow motion. Varieties of fynbos are flowering in vivid yellows and oranges and purple and I examine each one, taking in the mingled scents in the air, the warmth against my T-shirt, the sight of each mountain ridge. My step is light, firm, balanced: the resonance of my inner mood.

I am staying with Pippa, who has moved to Cape Town from Pretoria. I am here on a four-week consultancy. From my desk in her spare room the mountain soars above me in all its moods. I look up at my familiar colossus and I find myself saying, perhaps aloud: "I know happiness." I feel again what held me while hiking: a sense of balance. As a South African, as an American, as a South African American. I am no longer wrestling with the two personages that have incessantly vied for space within me. I need both South Africa and America to sustain me. I recall Gill's word from 1984: congruence. I have reached a state of congruence.

A few days later, on a windy but sunny afternoon, Kate Ncisana and I walk through The Company's Garden. Once again I admire the verdant flower beds and shrubs. We sit on a bench to talk, the squirrels coming to us for peanuts we don't have, the rhythmic cooing of the doves providing music.

"How are you doing, Kate?" I ask. She shakes her head. She is still making beautiful beadwork, has brought me some to buy which I finger like worry beads on my lap. Her daily life is good, she says, and tells me how much she enjoys the early-morning walking group of seniors she initiated for the exercise her doctor has ordered. I am aware that a little bit of light has gone from her gentle, lovely face. She shakes her head ever so slightly at the deeper intent of my question, given the state of South Africa. I recall her words in Khayelitsha in 2011: "Apartheid is over but our struggle is not." Her demeanor and her silence suggest she is querying the struggle part. All she says is, "If I had known what South Africa would become, I would not have fought so hard against apartheid."

We sit in contemplative silence for a while longer, then walk back down the avenue hand in hand, toward St. George's Cathedral, where we first met. We continue into the center of the city and we say goodbye. Kate heads for the bus back to Khayelitsha; I walk up the steep road to Pippa's house in "white" Cape Town, as Kate would say.

These are two of my South Africas. My two sides of the mirror. Since my visit in 2011, the mirror on one side has darkened further, cracked, grayed. I hear from all points of the progressive political spectrum disappointment, anger, sometimes fear. How can we regain our foothold on the path we imagined, going forward to a vital, new rainbow nation? It seems that many of those new to political and economic power saw only the pot of gold at the end of the rainbow, and they grabbed it for themselves. I hear this story over and over: The ANC is losing membership. Its rank and file is disillusioned by the lack of progress and the elite's tight grip on the country's wealth.

There is a growing divide between the wealthy and the average South African. Corruption is becoming the norm, settling in at all levels of leadership, from the lowest to the highest. Poverty is as present as ever. Employment opportunities particularly for the youth remain scarce. A gaseous cloud of disappointment renders deep disillusion.

But twenty plus years on, South Africa can still boast its checks and balances: a free and critical press; a fine constitution, and a constitutional court to protect it; a largely unencumbered judicial system; a public protector—akin to a national ombudsperson—who challenges corruption with impunity. I find room for hope in talking with activists, most far younger than I, who are running or working for organizations that are committed to change, and take heart from the communities protesting the desperate lack of services.

I take these complexities and disappointments back to the United States. They juggle for space in my head with the positive, but it is the positive balls that tend to thud to the ground. When the exceptionally cold American winter finally turned to spring in 2015, South Africa is in the news again. Xenophobia has broken out once more in an explosion of violence: 350 so-called foreigners have been killed since 2008. The frustration at the continued poverty and unemployment, at the lack of promised services, is not aimed against the government—it is directed at foreigners. The large demonstrations of support for the migrants are overshadowed by the violence.

I watch the nightly news and go to the internet for footage of the attacks on Zimbabweans, Mozambicans, Nigerians, Somalis, Ethiopians, many of their small businesses looted and burned. I shudder at the sight of South Africans brandishing machetes, shades of the Rwandan genocide. I can't let go of one particular attack, against a migrant from Mozambique, Ernest Nhamuave. I am haunted by the victim's frightened, pleading eyes, his soft, round, mild face. Four men set upon him with a long knife, a large metal wrench covered in red rust, a shovel with a wooden handle. Their jaws are set, their eyes are hard, they attack with deep hatred. When they finally flee, the photographer and his crew rush him to the hospital. It is too late.

If I was looking for symbols of the death of the revolution, this is it. Nhamuave is a national of a country where one million of its people were killed and two million displaced because his government supported the struggle of the South African people to get rid of apartheid and become a free democracy. The ANC knows this too well—especially President Zuma, who was based in Mozambique before the accords drove him out. So does Archbishop Tutu: "Our rainbow nation that so filled the world with hope is being reduced to a grubby shadow of itself. . . . The fabric of the nation is splitting at the seams; its precious nucleus—our moral core—is being ruptured."

I think back to Guinea-Bissau and the roar from the stadium on the first day of the Soweto uprising when I said, "Today is South Africa's Pidgiguiti." They got it. This was West Africa, too far away to be affected by apartheid but in solidarity with the struggle of their fellow Africans.

Another West African story: Gail happened to be in South Africa when this recent wave of xenophobic violence broke out. She met a Senegalese man who was now living in Cape Town, working in the television industry. She asked him what it felt like to be a foreigner. "Not that good," he replied. Then he told her about the school from his childhood. His class had one hundred pupils and one teacher. Every Thursday they were required to bring in a small donation for the freedom struggle in South Africa. On the wall of their crowded classroom was a banner that said apartheid is a crime against humanity.

Graça Machel, first lady of Mozambique and then of South Africa when she married Nelson Mandela in 1998, gave a eulogy at the memorial service for Nhamuave. "I am South African. I am Mozambican. I am Zambian. I am Zimbabwean," she said. And then: "Migration is in our blood! The borders were created by colonizers. They mean nothing to us because we are one." She emphasized the better economic opportunities that are needed throughout the region. When her eulogy was over, this citizen of southern Africa, of Africa, broke down and cried.

Graça Machel has put her finger on the problem. The root cause of this mindless but brutalizing distinction between "them" and "us" is the economy. South Africa has failed its people, particularly its youth, most of whom don't have jobs and have little chance of getting one. It is not as if the coming of foreigners to South Africa is anything new.

Hundreds of thousands of Mozambicans crossed the border to work alongside South Africans in the grueling conditions in the mines. As did workers from Zimbabwe, Malawi, Zambia, Lesotho. They intermarried, lived together. No violence to speak of. All were black. All were oppressed by South Africa and its laws and practices. Suddenly after independence, the superimposed colonial borders are real in the minds of anti-immigrant South Africans, many of them youth who have no memory or knowledge of what the solidarity and sacrifice of their neighbors meant to their liberation.

I have no crystal ball. What will happen in the future and whether South Africa can break its descent into corruption and bad government, I cannot know or guess. But I have not given up hope. What I do know is that I have seen revolution in my lifetime, in Africa, in my country. I have seen that a determined people—be they from Guinea-Bissau, Mozambique, Zimbabwe, or South Africa—cannot remain crushed forever. When the people rise up, a victory can be theirs.

Resources

BOOKS

Arnfred, Signe. *Sexuality and Gender Politics in Mozambique: Rethinking Gender in Africa.* James Currey, 2014.

Cabral, Amilcar. *Revolutionary Guinea: Selected Texts.* Monthly Review, 1969.

Clark, Nancy L., and William H. Worger. *South Africa: The Rise and Fall of Apartheid.* Pearson, 2011.

Goboda-Madikisela, Pumla. *A Human Being Died That Night: A South African Woman Confronts the Legacy of Apartheid.* Mariner Books, 2004.

LeFanu, Sarah. *S is for Samora.* Columbia University Press, 2012.

Lelyveld, Joseph. *Move Your Shadow, South Africa Black and White.* Penguin, 1986.

Magona, Sindiwe. *To My Children's Children.* Interlink Books, 2006.

Mandela, Nelson. *Long Walk to Freedom.* Back Bay Books, 2013.

Massie, Robert K. *Loosing the Bonds: The United States and South Africa in the Apartheid Years.* Doubleday, 1997.

Minter, William, Gail Hovey, and Charles Cobb Jr., eds. *No Easy Victories: African Liberation and American Activists over a Half Century, 1950–2000.* Africa World Press, 2008.

Msimang, Sisonke. *Always Another Country.* Jonathan Ball, 2017.

Sachs, Albie. *The Soft Vengeance of a Freedom Fighter.* University of California Press, 2014.

Saul, John S. *On Building a Social Movement: The North American Campaign for Southern Africa Liberation Revisited.* Africa World Press, 2017.

————, ed. *The Different Road: Transition to Socialism in Mozambique.* Monthly Review, 1985.

Urdang, Stephanie. *And Still They Dance: Women, War, and the Struggle for Change in Mozambique.* Monthly Review, 1989.

————. *Fighting Two Colonialisms: Women in Guinea-Bissau.* Monthly Review, 1979.

WEBSITES

Africa Is a Country: A site of media criticism, analysis and new writing http://africasacountry.com

African Activist Archive http://africanactivist.msu.edu/

Africa Focus Bulletin www.africafocus.org/

All Africa http://allafrica.com

Daily Maverick www.dailymaverick.co.za

VIDEOS

A Luta Continua, Documentary on the war of liberation in Mozambique, by Robert van Lierop, 1972, https://www.youtube.com/watch?v=BG4IN--oVd8.

Have You Heard from Johannesburg? Seven-part series chronicling the history of the global anti-apartheid movement, 2010, https://www.youtube.com/watch?v=IU48nQUEYtI&list=PLE55A68DAC942EA75.

I Ain't Gonna Play Sun City, 1985, https://www.youtube.com/watch?v=TlMdYpnVOGQ.